SCHOLASTIC

Pocket Dictionary of Synonyms, Antonyms & Homonyms

Scholastic Inc.
New York Toronto London Auckland
Sydney Mexico City New Delhi Hong Kong

Originally published under the title *Webster's Synonyms, Antonyms, and Homonyms* by Ottenheimer Publishers, Inc. Copyright © 1962, 1953 by Ottenheimer Publishers, Inc.

ISBN 978-0-545-42667-1

10 9 8 7 6 5 4 3 2 1 12 13 14 15 16

Printed in the U.S.A. 40
This edition first printing, July 2012
Book design by Kay Petronio

Introduction

If you are like most students, you probably find yourself frustrated by writing assignments. You have so much you want to say, but you have trouble getting it all down on paper. Some of the difficulty may be due to your not knowing exactly what words to use. Another problem may be uncertainty about the proper way to convey your thoughts accurately. As a result, you find yourself using a small group of words over and over again. Relying on words with which you are comfortable is a good thing, as long as the words don't crop up so often that your text becomes boring and repetitive. In order to become a better writer, you need to use a wide variety of words. Luckily for you, the *Scholastic Pocket Dictionary of Synonyms, Antonyms & Homonyms* will help you expand your vocabulary and make your writing more lively.

To improve your writing, you not only need to be familiar with many words, but you also need to know how to use them properly. For instance, if you were writing a mystery and wanted to express the thought that the detective took some evidence, it is up to you to pick the way in which that thought is expressed. *Took* is not a very precise word and could mean several different things.

Using this as an opportunity to expand your horizons, you grab the *Scholastic Pocket Dictionary of Synonyms, Antonyms & Homonyms* out of your book bag. You look up the word *take* and check out your options. Synonyms, words that have similar meanings, are listed directly after the main word. Words that have opposite meanings, antonyms, are located in parentheses after the synonyms.

Now you have a list of options from which to choose. Which word most precisely expresses what you want to say? It all depends on what you see in your head. How, exactly, did the detective obtain the evidence? It is completely up to you to choose the word that conveys the exact meaning you had in mind. Each synonym has a slightly different meaning. Do you want to express that the detective chose the evidence by saying, "The detective selected the evidence"? Or do you mean that the detective was holding the evidence? You could express that by saying, "The detective grasped the evidence." Or, do you truly mean that the detective received the evidence from another person? That could be stated by saying, "The detective accepted the evidence."

Accepted, *grasped*, and *selected* are all synonyms of *take*, yet they each have unique definitions. The one that you select will influence the way in which the reader interprets what you have written.

However you decide that the detective located the evidence, it will be a much more thoughtful and precise statement than before you started. You will have taken one step forward in becoming a better writer, and your audience will have a clearer understanding of your thoughts.

The second portion of this book is also an asset to creative writers. There are certain words that are notoriously difficult to differentiate from one another. For instance, *to*, *two*, and *too*; *stationary* and *stationery*. No matter how much you study, these can be a source of confusion. Pages 208–237 list all these potential problem words in alphabetical order. You can consult these lists to select the word you would like to use and be sure that it is correctly spelled.

So, no matter what you decide to write about and what words you choose to use, the *Scholastic Pocket Dictionary of Synonyms, Antonyms & Homonyms* will inspire, animate, excite, rouse, inflame, fire, encourage, foster, kindle, promote, advance, prompt, and stimulate your thoughts and writing.

SYNONYMS AND ANTONYMS

abandon leave, forsake, desert, renounce, cease, relinquish, discontinue, cast off, resign, retire, quit, forgo, forswear, depart from, vacate, surrender, abjure, repudiate. (*pursue, prosecute, undertake*)

abandoned profligate, wicked, vicious, unprincipled, reprobate, incorrigible, sinful, graceless, demoralized, dissolute, depraved, bad, licentious, corrupt. (*virtuous, conscientious, correct, upright*)

abbreviate shorten, reduce, abridge, contract, curtail, epitomize, condense, prune, compress. (*lengthen, prolong, extend, enlarge, produce, elongate*)

abdicate abandon, relinquish, resign, surrender, vacate. (*retain, maintain, claim, occupy, assert*)

abet aid, support, promote, countenance, uphold, assist, instigate, encourage, incite, advocate, sanction, subsidize, embolden. (*thwart, contradict, obstruct, oppose, baffle, confound, discourage, disapprove, disconcert, counteract, deter, dissuade, frustrate*)

abeyance suspension, reservation, dormancy, expectation, intermission. (*revival, renewal, operation, resuscitation, action, enjoyment, possession*)

abhor hate, abominate, detest, loathe, despise, dislike, eschew, nauseate. (*love, admire, enjoy*)

abide dwell, stay, inhabit, continue, rest, tarry, lodge, reside, live, wait, sojourn, remain, expect, endure, tolerate, anticipate, confront, await, bear, face, watch. (*deport, migrate, move, journey, proceed, resist, mislike, forfend, avoid, shun, reject, abandon, forfeit*)

ability power, cleverness, faculty, skill, capacity, talent, expertise, aptitude, dexterity, efficiency, competency, qualification. (*weakness, incapacity, imbecility, inability, unreadiness, maladroitness*)

abject degraded, outcast, miserable, vile, pitiable, worthless, despicable, groveling, fawning, squalid, base-minded, slavish, beggarly, servile, cringing, low, wretched, sordid. (*honorable, dignified, eminent, exalted, esteemed, worthy, venerable, noble, princely, illustrious, independent, self-assertive, self-reliant, vain, arrogant, insolent, haughty*)

abjure renounce, deny, apostatize, discard, recant, disclaim, disavow, repudiate, revoke, retract, disown. (*profess, assert, demand, vindicate, claim, cherish, advocate, retain, acknowledge, appropriate, embrace*)

able strong, powerful, clever, skillful, talented, capable, fitted, efficient, effective, learned, gifted, masterly, telling, nervous, vigorous. (*weak, inefficient, unskillful, incapable, ineffective, unqualified*)

abnormal irregular, erratic, peculiar, unusual, exceptional, monstrous, aberrant, devious, divergent, eccentric, strange. (*typical, normal, regular, ordinary, usual, natural, customary, illustrative*)

abode home, stay, place, residence, domicile, habitation, lodgings, berth, quarters. (*halt, perch, tent, bivouac, caravansary: with the idea of transience*)

abolish destroy, eradicate, invalidate, make void, obliterate, extirpate, abrogate, annul, subvert, cancel, revoke, quash, nullify, overthrow, annihilate, supersede, suppress, expunge. (*support, sustain, cherish, promote, continue, confirm, restore, repair, revive, reinstate, enact, institute, reenact*)

abominable abhorrent, foul, accursed, detestable, hateful, horrible, loathsome, odious, offensive, execrable, nauseous, impure. (*delectable, desirable, admirable, enjoyable, lovable, charming, delightful, grateful, pure*)

abortion failure, miscarriage, misadventure, downfall, mishap, misproduction, defect, frustration, blunder, mess. (*success, consummation, completion, achievement, realization, perfection, exploit, feat, development*)

abound stream, swell, flow, increase, overflow, superabound, luxuriate, teem, swarm, flourish, prevail, be plentiful, wanton, revel, multiply. (*fall, waste, dry, lack, wane, evaporate, drain, die, decay, vanish, lessen, decrease*)

about almost, with respect to, near, nearly, touching, concerning, surrounding, relative to, relating to, in relation to, approximately, touching, roughly, generally. (*afar, away from, precisely, exactly*)

above over, beyond, exceeding. (*below, within, beneath*)

abridge abbreviate, diminish, shorten, lessen, curtail, restrict, contract, condense, epitomize, compress. (*amplify, expand, spread out*)

abrupt sudden, steep, precipitous, craggy, coarse, curt, blunt, violent, harsh, unceremonious, rugged, rough. (*undulating, easy, gliding, polished, smooth, blending, courteous*)

absent *a.* not present, gone away, elsewhere, inattentive, thoughtless, listless, preoccupied. (*present, in this place, here, attentive*)

absent *v.* keep away, depart, withdraw. (*be present, stay, remain*)

absolute perfect, complete, unconditional, irrelative, irrespective, supreme, despotic, autocratic, certain, authoritative, unqualified, unequivocal, irresponsible, arbitrary. (*imperfect, incomplete, conditional, conditioned, contingent, relative, dependent, constitutional, dubious, accountable, responsible*)

absorb swallow, drown, consume, imbibe, engross, drink in, suck up, engulf, monopolize, exhaust. (*eject, emit, exude, disgorge, dissipate, distract, distil, disperse*)

abstain refrain, forbear, refuse, demur, avoid, cease, stop, keep back, desist, discontinue, withhold, scruple. (*indulge, exceed, reveal, wanton*)

abstemious abstinent, moderate, self-denying, sober, temperate, sparing, frugal. (*sensual, self-indulgent, gluttonous, greedy, intemperate*)

abstract separate, detach, part, eliminate, draw away, remove, take away, appropriate, purloin, steal, thieve, draw from. (*add, unite, conjoin, adduce, impose, restore, surrender, return*)

absurd irrational, ridiculous, monstrous, senseless, asinine, stupid, chimerical, unreasonable, preposterous, silly, nonsensical, foolish. (*sensible, rational, reasonable, consistent, sound, substantial, logical, wise, sagacious, reflective, philosophical*)

abundant plentiful, copious, plenteous, large, ample, overflowing, teeming, full, lavish, luxuriant, liberal, rich. (*rare, scarce, scant, deficient, short, insufficient, niggardly, sparing, dry, drained, exhausted, impoverished*)

abuse *v.* injure, damage, spoil, maltreat, treat ill, ill-use, ill-treat, revile, scandalize, disparage, reproach, upbraid, asperse, malign, slander, vituperate, prostitute, defame, pervert, misuse, misemploy, vilify. (*tend, protect, conserve, consider, regard, shield, cherish, praise, extol, laud, vindicate, respect*)

abuse *n.* mistreatment, invective, ill-treatment, opprobium, scurrility, vituperation, ribaldry, obloquy, reproach, insolence, misusage, ill usage. (*good usage, good treatment, kindness, praise, deference, respect*)

accelerate hasten, urge, expedite, quicken, speed, urge on, press forward, hurry, promote, dispatch, facilitate. (*delay, obstruct, impede, clog, retard, hinder, shackle, drag*)

accent stress, rhythm, pulsation, beat, emphasis. (*smoothness, inaccentuation, monotony, equableness, babble, flow*)

accept welcome, hail, admit, recognize, avow, acknowledge, take, accede to, receive, assent to. (*refuse, decline, reject, disown, disavow, ignore, repudiate*)

acceptable grateful, pleasant, welcome, agreeable, pleasurable, seasonable, gratifying.

accessory assistant, additive, additional, auxiliary, supplementary, conducive, accomplice, ally, associate, abettor, colleague, confederate, helper. (*essential, inherent, immanent, incorporate, superfluous, irrelevant, malapropos, obstructive, cumbersome*)

accident chance, fortuity, disaster, incident, adventure, casualty, hazard, contingency, calamity, misadventure, mishap. (*law, purpose, appointment*)

accommodate convenience, oblige, adapt, supply, reconcile, suit, fit, adjust, furnish, serve, harmonize. (*inconvenience, disoblige, disturb, misfit*)

accommodating kind, unselfish, obliging, polite, considerate, yielding, conciliatory. (*disobliging, selfish, churlish, rude, imperious, dictatorial, exacting*)

accomplice abettor, confederate, accessory, ally, associate, partner, colleague, coadjutor, assistant, *particeps criminis*. (*rival, foe, adversary, antagonist*)

accomplish execute, perfect, perform, fulfil, do, carry out, attain, realize, consummate, achieve, finish, complete. (*fail of, frustrate, defeat, disconcert, destroy, baffle, mar, spoil*)

accord agree, consent, harmonize, tally, answer, comport, consist, conform, grant, concede, surrender, allow. (*disagree, differ, misfit, miscomport*)

accordingly agreeably, suitably, conformably, hence, consequently.

account *n.* narration, report, rehearsal, story, statement, narrative, recital, relation, description, motive, value, importance, advantage, ground, reason, profit. (*silence, suppression, disadvantage, concealment*)

account *v.* deem, esteem, consider, regard, hold, judge, rate, estimate, value, reckon, explain, solve. (*disesteem, misestimate, mystify, underrate, undervalue, perplex, darken*)

accountable responsible, liable, amenable, punishable, answerable, accredited, delegated, subordinate. (*autocratic, independent, irresponsible*)

accredit believe, trust, entrust, delegate, depute, commission, authorize. (*disbelieve, distrust*)

accumulate collect, garner, grow, mass, heap, store, bring together, hoard, gather, agglomerate, husband, augment, amass, increase. (*dissipate, disperse, diminish, scatter, expend, waste*)

accumulation heap, collection, store, mass, aggregation, hoard, pile. (*segregation, separation*)

accurate careful, exact, faithful, precise, correct, close, truthful, strict, just, actual, nice. (*careless, inexact, faulty, incorrect, inaccurate, loose, defective*)

accuse charge, incriminate, impeach, arraign, tax, taunt, censure, cite, summon, criminate. (*defend, vindicate, discharge, acquit, absolve, condone*)

accustom habituate, familiarize, form, inure, train, reconcile. (*disaccustom, dishabituate, estrange, wean, alienate*)

achieve accomplish, do, gain, perform, execute, effect, fulfil, finish, attain, win. (*fail, lose, miss*)

achievement exploit, feat, attainment, accomplishment, performance. (*failure, lack in completion*)

acknowledge avow, admit, recognize, own, accept, profess, endorse, grant, concede, concern. (*disavow, disclaim, disown, repudiate, ignore, deny*)

acme summit, zenith, climax, apex, pitch, culmination, meridian. (*base, floor, ground, foundation, nadir, depth, depression, foot, root*)

acquaint advertise, inform, impart, make known, divulge, teach, notify, apprize, advise, tell. (*misinform, deceive, delude, mislead, misguide*)

acquaintance knowledge, intimacy, familiarity, experience, companionship. (*ignorance, unfamiliarity, inexperience*)

acquiesce assent, concur, repose, agree, yield, be resigned, comply. (*dissent, demur, object*)

acquit discharge, exonerate, absolve, exculpate, release, dismiss, liberate, pardon. (*charge, accuse, impeach, constrain, implicate, bind, compel, condemn*)

acquittance release, receipt, discharge. (*bond, claim, charge, obligation*)

across athwart, against, transversely, opposed. (*lengthwise, along, concurrently, parallel*)

act deed, performance, action, movement, proceeding, exercise, operation, play. (*inaction, rest, repose, cessation, suspension, quiet, immobility*)

active nimble, agile, lively, sprightly, brisk, quick, expert, dexterous, supple, wide-awake, prompt, busy, industrious, diligent. (*slow, inactive, indolent, sluggish, heavy*)

actual developed, positive, unquestionable, demonstrable, certain, real, authentic. (*potential, undeveloped, hypothetical, suppositious, possible, virtual*)

acute pointed, penetrating, sagacious, perspicacious, keen, astute, piercing, sharp, shrewd, keen-sighted, severe, distressing. (*dull, blunt, obtuse*)

adapt fit, accommodate, suit, adjust, conform, admeasure, harmonize, attune. (*misfit, misconform, misapply*)

add adduce, adjoin, increase, extend, enlarge, sum up, cast up, subjoin, amplify, annex. (*deduct, subtract, dissever, abstract*)

addicted given, accustomed, prone, inclined, disposed, habituated. (*disinclined, unaccustomed, indisposed, averse, free*)

addition accession, enlargement, increase, extension, accretion, appendage. (*deduction, detraction, drawback, decrement, deterioration*)

address *n.* tact, manners, speech, abode. (*awkwardness, unmannerliness*)

address *v.* accost, greet, salute, approach, apostrophize, appeal, hail, woo, court. (*elude, avoid, shun, ignore, pass*)

adept expert, adroit, handy, master, performer, professor, artist. (*awkward, clumsy, inexpert, tyro*)

adequate equal, sufficient, fit, satisfactory, full, competent, capable, able. (*unequal, insufficient*)

adherence adhesion, attachment, devotion, fidelity, cleaving to, constancy, endearment. (*separation, disunion, unfaithfulness, desertion, treachery*)

adherent follower, supporter, ally, disciple, admirer, backer, aid, partisan. (*opponent, deserter, adversary, renegade, antagonist*)

adieu good-bye, farewell, leave-taking, parting, valediction. (*greeting, welcome, recognition, salutation*)

adipose obese, corpulent, sebaceous, oleaginous. (*leathery, skinny, bony, thin*)

adjacent near, neighboring, contiguous, close, bordering, conterminous. (*remote, distant*)

adjoin annex, add, connect, append, supplement, attach, unite, border, neighbor, touch, abut, approximate, verge, trench. (*disjoin, dismember, disconnect, detach, disintegrate, disunite, part, separate, recede, return, diverge, be distant, removed*)

adjourn postpone, suspend, defer, prorogue, delay, protract, put off. (*expedite, dispatch, urge*)

adjunct addition, attachment, appendage, auxiliary, appurtenance, aid, acquisition, advantage, help. (*essence, substance, body, clog*)

adjust harmonize, collocate, arrange, localize, adapt, affix, right, suit, classify, set in order, reconcile, accommodate, compose. (*dislocate, disarrange, disturb, confound, dismember, disorder*)

administer distribute, award, accord, dole, give, impart, afford, discharge, dispense, execute, perform, furnish, contribute, conduct. (*withdraw, withhold, refuse, retain, assume, resume, resign, deny*)

admirable wonderful, excellent, surprising, astonishing, praiseworthy, pleasing. (*commonplace, mediocre, ridiculous, abominable, displeasing*)

admissible allowable, permissible, probable, reasonable, just, proper, fair, right, qualified. (*inadmissible, improper, unreasonable*)

admit receive, pass, permit, accept, grant, concede, allow, acknowledge, confess, own, avow, suffer. (*exclude, debar, disallow, reject, deny, discharge, dismiss, eject, extrude, repudiate, disavow*)

admonish remind, forewarn, advise, warn, dissuade, caution, counsel, reprove, censure, rebuke. (*encourage, instigate, abet, incite, urge, applaud*)

adopt assume, select, affiliate, take, elect, arrogate, choose, endorse, avow, appropriate. (*reject, decline, repudiate, disavow, discard, renounce*)

adore admire, hallow, glorify, praise, venerate, reverence, worship, idolize. (*abhor, despise, disesteem, abominate, execrate, blaspheme*)

adulation flattery, compliment, sycophancy, courtship, incense, praise, blandishment, fawning, cringing. (*detraction, obloquy, defamation, calumny, traducement, sarcasm, ridicule, satire, bespatterment*)

advance propel, elevate, promote, further, lend, propagate, progress, increase, prosper, rise. (*retard, hinder, withhold, withdraw, recall, depress, degrade*)

advantage gain, success, superiority, help, assistance, benefit, good, avail, interest, utility, service, profit, acquisition. (*loss, disappointment, defeat, frustration, inferiority, obstacle, obstruction*)

adventurous bold, brave, daring, enterprising, courageous, gallant, fearless, venturesome, rash, chivalrous, hazardous. (*timid, unenterprising, unadventurous, cowardly, nervous, hesitating, cautious*)

adversary antagonist, foe, enemy, rival, assailant. (*accessory, abettor, aider, friend, helper, assistant, ally, accomplice*)

adversity ill luck, misfortune, misery, calamity, disaster, distress, unsuccess, failure, ruin, trouble, affliction, sorrow. (*good luck, prosperity, happiness*)

advertent attentive, regardful, mindful, watchful, thoughtful, observant, considerate. (*inattentive, inadvertent, casual, thoughtless, heedless, inobservant, inconsiderate*)

advertise publish, inform, advise, circulate, announce, notify, proclaim, promulge. (*suppress, hush, conceal, ignore, hoodwink, misguide, mislead*)

advise admonish, warn, deliberate, counsel, persuade, urge, prompt, instigate, incite, instruct, acquaint, inform. (*dissuade, deter, expostulate, remonstrate, prohibit, inhibit, restrain, curb, mislead, misadvise, hoodwink, deceive, delude, misinform*)

advocate pleader, counselor, upholder, propagator, promoter, supporter, countenancer, defender, maintainer. (*opponent, adversary, discountenancer*)

affable courteous, accessible, condescending, conversable, gracious, sociable, gentle, complaisant, urbane, polite, easy, approachable. (*exclusive, discourteous, distant, inaccessible, unapproachable, inconversable, haughty, contemptuous, supercilious*)

affect like, desire, favor, seek, assume, move, influence, concern, interest, feign, pretend. (*dislike, eschew, shun, repel, repudiate*)

affectation pretense, artifice, hypocrisy, assumption, simulation, mannerism, euphuism, airs. (*genuineness, naturalness, unaffectedness, simplicity, artlessness*)

affection influence, condition, state, inclination, bent, mood, humor, feeling, love, desire, propensity. (*insensibility, indifference, repugnance, disaffection*)

affinity relationship, relation, kindred, conformity, connection, alliance, similarity, analogy, homogeneity, harmony, correlativeness, sympathy, interdependence, interconnection, intercommunity. (*dissimilarity, discordance, disconnection, independence, antagonism, antipathy, repugnance, repulsion*)

affirm assert, swear, testify, tell, aver, propound, asseverate, depose, state, declare, endorse, maintain. (*deny, dispute, doubt, demur, negative*)

affliction trouble, trial, grief, pain, disease, misery, hardship, sorrow. (*consolation, relief, alleviation, assuagement, boon, blessing, gratification, pleasure*)

afford produce, supply, give, yield, grant, confer, bestow, impart, administer, extend. (*withhold, deny, withdraw, retain, stint, grudge*)

affront outrage, provocation, insult, ill-treatment, abuse, wrong, offense, indignity. (*homage, salutation, courtesy, apology, amends, compliment*)

afloat adrift, abroad, at sea, abroach, loose, distracted, dazed. (*ashore, snug, fight, close, fast, collected, concentrated*)

afoot working, launched, afloat, agoing, inaugurated, started, instituted, established. (*uncommenced, incomplete, projected, proposed, contemplated, designed*)

afraid fearful, apprehensive, timid, timorous, cowardly, fainthearted, cautious, careful, frightened, alarmed, terrified, suspicious, distrustful, anxious. (*fearless, unsolicitous*)

afresh anew again, frequently, repeatedly, intermittently. (*continuously, uniformly, uninterruptedly, connectedly*)

after behind, following, succeeding. (*before, afore, introducing, preceding*)

again anew, afresh, repeatedly, frequently. (*continuously, uniformly, uninterruptedly, once*)

against over, opposite, abutting, opposing, resisting, despite, across, athwart, counter. (*with, for, accompanying, aiding, suiting, promoting*)

age period, generation, era, epoch, date, century, antiquity, senility, eldership, seniority. (*youth, infancy, boyhood, childhood, moment, instant*)

agent doer, performer, actor, force, means, instrument, influence, cause, promoter, operator. (*counteragent, counteractor, counteraction, opponent*)

aggravate exasperate, provoke, wound, heighten, intensify, irritate, make worse, increase, enhance, embitter, magnify. (*soothe, conciliate, assuage, diminish, palliate, neutralize, soften, lessen*)

agile nimble, active, fleet, brisk, alert, featly, lithe, prompt, ready, quick, supple, swift, sprightly. (*slow, heavy, awkward, inert, clumsy, bulky, ponderous, elephantine*)

agitate disturb, trouble, excite, ruffle, stir, fluster, oscillate, instigate, convulse, shake. (*calm, compose, allay, pacify, smooth*)

agony pain, torture, torment, distress, woe, throe, suffering, pang, excruciation. (*assuagement, comfort, peace, ease, relief, gratification, enjoyment*)

agree suit, tally, accord, fit, harmonize, combine, assent, concur, acquiesce, admit, consent, conform, consort, comport, coincide. (*differ, disagree, revolt, protest, decline, refuse, dissent, demur*)

agreeable obliging, pleasant, accommodating, grateful, acceptable, welcome, suitable, consistent, consonant, amiable, gratifying, pleasing, good-natured, complaisant. (*disobliging, unpleasant, unaccommodating, disagreeable, obnoxious, ungrateful*)

agreement contract, compact, bond, concord, concurrence, conformity, harmony, unison, consonance, bargain, covenant, obligation, undertaking, treaty. (*disagreement, informal understanding or promise, parole*)

aid help, assist, succor, support, befriend, cooperate, contribute, favor, foster, protect, abet, encourage, instigate, subsidize. (*oppose, resist*)

ailment complaint, sickness, illness, disease. (*recovery, convalescence, sanity, health, robustness*)

aim *n.* tendency, intent, aspiration, bent, drift, object, scope, goal, purpose, mark, end, design, intention. (*shunning, disregarding, disaffecting*)

aim *v.* seek, level, propose, design, affect, intend, mean, purpose. (*shun, disregard, disaffect, ignore*)

akin related, agnate, cognate, homogeneous, similar, consanguineous, congenial, allied, sympathetic. (*unrelated, unconnected, foreign, alien, heterogeneous, uncongenial, hostile, unallied, antagonistic*)

alacrity quickness, readiness, briskness, activity, cheerfulness, compliance, willingness, promptitude. (*slowness, reluctance, repugnance*)

alarming terrible, fearful, frightful, portentous, ominous, threatening. (*soothing, assuring, encouraging, inviting, propitious, hopeful, alluring*)

alert active, brisk, nimble, prepared, prompt, vigilant, ready, wakeful, watchful, on the watch, lively. (*slow, sleepy, lazy, absent, unready, oblivious*)

alien foreign, strange, undomesticated, inappropriate, irrelevant, impertinent. (*pertinent, essential, proper, appropriate, relevant, germane, akin*)

alike resembling, similar, together, twin-fellow, analogous, identical, equal, equivalent, same, homogeneous, akin, equally. (*unlike, heterogeneous*)

alive quick, living, breathing, warm, lively, vivacious, alert, existing, existent, safe, subsisting, active, brisk, animated. (*dead, departed, cold, lifeless, defunct, inanimate, dispirited, dull*)

allege declare, affirm, assert, asseverate, depose, plead, cite, quote, assign, advance, maintain, say. (*contradict, gainsay, refute, deny, disprove, neutralize*)

allegiance subjection, obedience, loyalty, fealty, homage. (*disloyalty, rebellion, resistance, disaffection, malcontentment, treason*)

alleviate lighten, lessen, assuage, mitigate, soothe, moderate, relieve, remit, diminish. (*aggravate, enhance, increase, embitter, augment*)

alliance compact, treaty, cooperation, union, connection, partnership, league, combination, coalition, confederation, friendship, relation, relationship. (*disunion, enmity, divorce, discord, disruption*)

allot assign, grant, award, give, apportion, deal, dispense, parcel, distribute, divide, mete out, portion out. (*refuse, withhold, retain, appropriate*)

allow concede, apportion, allot, assign, afford, tolerate, authorize, grant, remit, recognize, acknowledge, avow, confess, admit, permit, suffer, sanction, yield. (*withhold, withdraw, resume, refuse*)

alloy admixture, deterioration, adulteration, drawback, diminution, decrement, impairment, debasement, depreciation, disparagement. (*purity, genuineness, enhancement, integrity*)

allude point, indicate, suggest, hint, signify, insinuate, refer, imply, intimate. (*specify, demonstrate, declare, mention, state*)

ally friend, companion, supporter, aider, abettor, accomplice, assistant, confederate, helper, associate, accessory, colleague, coadjutor. (*foe, enemy, opponent, adversary, baffler, counteractor*)

aloud audibly, loudly, clamorously, sonorously, vociferously, obstreperously. (*softly, silently, inaudibly, suppressedly*)

alter substitute, change, vary, modify, exchange, diversify, remodel. (*retain, perpetuate, conserve, stereotype, arrest, solidify, stabilitate*)

alternative choice, resource, opinion. (*compulsion, quandary, necessity, fix*)

altogether collectively, combined, in one, totally, entirely, wholly, fully, completely, utterly, thoroughly. (*separately, individually, partially*)

amass collect, accumulate, aggregate, heap, gather, store up, hoard, pile up. (*divide, dissipate, waste, scatter, disperse, parcel, portion, spend*)

amazement astonishment, awe, wonder, bewilderment, surprise, stupefaction, marvel. (*expectation, preparation, anticipation, familiarity*)

ambiguous equivocal, vague, doubtful, enigmatical, uncertain, obscure, unintelligible, perplexing, indistinct, dubious. (*univocal, obvious*)

ameliorate improve, raise, better, advantage, promote, advance, amend, rectify, meliorate. (*debase, depress, deteriorate, injure, impair, vitiate*)

amend improve, mend, repair, correct, rectify, better, ameliorate, reform. (*deteriorate, degenerate, neglect, aggravate, tarnish, blemish, spoil, corrupt*)

amiable lovable, good, kind, benevolent, charitable, delectable, engaging, fascinating, agreeable, lovely, pleasing, charming, attractive. (*churlish, disagreeable, hateful, abominable, ill-natured, ill-conditioned, unamiable*)

amiss wrong, untrue, wide, bad, false, defective, short, inappropriate, inopportune, injudicious, untimely, abortive. (*right, true, good, complete, effective, successful, satisfactory, consummate, expedient, appropriate, opportune*)

amnesty pardon, acquittal, remission, condonation, oblivion, dispensation, absolution. (*penalty, retaliation, punishment, retribution, requital, visitation, infliction, exaction, trial, account*)

ample large, bountiful, liberal, copious, spacious, roomy, diffusive, full, complete, sufficient, plentiful, abundant. (*narrow, niggardly, insufficient, stingy, scant, mean, stint, bare*)

amplify enrich, enlarge, increase, augment, multiply, dilate, develop, swell, expatiate, expand, discuss, unfold, extend. (*retrench, amputate, curtail, condense, abbreviate, epitomize, gather, collect*)

analogy relation, resemblance, proportion, similarity, similitude, coincidence, affinity, comparison, parity. (*disproportion, dissimilarity, disharmony*)

analysis dissection, separation, anatomy, segregation, decomposition, resolution, partition. (*composition, synthesis, aggregation, combination, coalition, amalgamation, coherence*)

anarchy disorder, tumult, rebellion, riot, misgovernment, insubordination. (*order, subjection*)

anatomy dissection, division, segregation, analysis, resolution, dismemberment. (*synthesis, collocation, organization, union, construction, structure*)

ancient old, antiquated, old-fashioned, antique, obsolete, old-time, aged, primeval, primordial, immemorial, time-honored. (*new, young, modern*)

anger *n.* ire, incensement, vexation, grudge, pique, exasperation, indignation, enmity, displeasure, irritation, passion, spleen, gall, resentment, rage, animosity, fury, choler, wrath. (*peace, peacefulness, peaceableness, appeasement, forgiveness*)

anger *v.* enrage, vex, kindle, fret, ruffle, chafe, infuriate, exasperate, provoke, irritate, incense, wound, inflame, embitter. (*appease, compose, forbear, allay, soothe, calm, conciliate, heal*)

animosity hatred, antipathy, dissension, aversion, acrimony, feud, strife, rancor, antagonism, bitterness, acerbity, hostility, enmity, malice, anger, malevolence, ill will, malignity, feeling against. (*congeniality, companionship, friendship*)

annex add, attach, fasten, affix, subjoin, append, connect, unite. (*withdraw, detach, disconnect*)

annihilate abolish, destroy, bring to naught, uproot, eradicate, nullify, exterminate, end, extinguish, demolish, obliterate, efface. (*keep, conserve, preserve, foster, tend, protect, cherish, develop*)

announce declare, propound, give notice, enunciate, advertise, publish, report, notify, make known, give out, reveal, herald, proclaim, intimate, promulge. (*conceal, suppress, hush, stifle, withhold*)

annoy tease, vex, irritate, disturb, affront, molest, pain, disquiet, incommode, tantalize, bother, weary, inconvenience, plague, discommode, harass, chafe, trouble. (*soothe, conciliate, appease, regard*)

anomaly irregularity, abnormity, exception, informality, peculiarity, eccentricity. (*conformity, regularity, illustration, conformance, exemplification*)

anonymous nameless, unattested, authorless, unidentified, unauthenticated. (*authenticated, attested, identified, authorized, verified, signed*)

answer reply, response, counterargument, confutation, acceptance (as of a challenge), tally, solution, vindication, apology, exculpation, defense, rejoinder, repartee, retort. (*challenge, question, defiance, summons, interrogation*)

antecedent prior, foregoing, previous, precursive, precedent, earlier, introductory, preliminary, former. (*posterior, later, subsequent, consequent*)

anticipate forestall, prejudge, expect, foretaste, apprehend, prevent, prearrange, prepare, meet, obviate, intercept, forecast. (*remember, recollect, remedy, recall, undo, cure, misapprehend*)

anticipation expectation, awaiting, preoccupation, preconception, foresight, forethought, foretaste, prevention, forestallment, contemplation, hope, trust, prospect, forecast, provision. (*surprise, unpreparedness, unexpectedness*)

anxiety care, trouble, eagerness, disquiet, apprehension, carefulness, diffidence, solicitude, misgiving. (*carelessness, ease, confidence, contentment*)

anxious solicitous, careful, uneasy, concerned, restless, watchful, disturbed, unquiet. (*without care, careless, inert, ease, unconcerned, calm, composed*)

apathy indifference, insensibility, unfeelingness in company, insusceptibility, unconcern, sluggishness, hebetude. (*anxiety, care, eagerness, interest, sensibility, susceptibility, sensitivity, irritability, curiosity*)

ape mimic, imitate, simulate, personate, represent. (*not to imitate, vary, modify, change*)

apiece distributively, individually, separately, severally, analytically. (*collectively, together, accumulatively, indiscriminately, confusedly, synthetically*)

apology defense, justification, plea, exculpation, excuse, vindication, acknowledgment, confession. (*charge, imputation, impeachment, offense, incrimination, injury, accusation, wrong, insult*)

appall affright, alarm terrify, scare, daunt, cow, shock, frighten, discourage, dishearten, horrify, dismay, astound. (*encourage, rally, assure, embolden*)

apparel clothes, robes, vesture, vestments, raiment, garniture, habiliments, habit, dress, clothing, caparison, trappings, housings. (*nudity, divestiture, dishabille, tatters, rags*)

apparent obvious, plain, conspicuous, manifest, appearing, unmistakable, clear, probable, seeming, presumable, likely, patent, ostensible, visible, evident, indubitable, notorious, certain. (*uncertain, dubious, inapparent, minute, unobservable, improbable, hidden, real*)

appeal accost, address, apostrophize, invite, cite, invoke, urge, refer, call upon, entreat, request, resort. (*deprecate, repudiate, protest, disavow, disclaim, defy, abjure*)

appearance advent, coming, arrival, presence, apparition, aspect, manifestation, probability, likeness, exhibition, mien, manner, semblance, air, show, look, pretense, likelihood, presumption. (*departure, disappearance, unlikelihood, nonappearance, concealment, evanition*)

append affix, supplement, subjoin, attach. (*separate, disengage, disconnect, detach*)

appetite passion, desire, propensity, proclivity, inclination, propension, appetency, want, craving, disposition, tendency, proneness. (*repugnance, aversion, antipathy, loathing, indifference, apathy*)

applause praise, plaudit, laudation, encomium, commendation, approbation, acclamation, approval, eulogy, acclaim. (*obloquy, condemnation, denunciation, dissatisfaction, contempt, censure, blame*)

applicable available, ancillary, convenient, useful, pertinent, conducive, appropriate. (*useless, unavailable, inconducive, inapplicable, irrelevant*)

appoint fix, determine, install, allot, order, prescribe, institute, employ, apportion, apply, designate, assign, intrust, invest, ordain, arrange. (*reverse, cancel, recall, withdraw, reserve, withhold*)

apportion assign, deal, allot, grant, share, divide, dispense, administer, distribute, appoint. (*reserve, retain, refuse, withhold, assume, resume*)

appreciate esteem, recognize, acknowledge, respect, value, prize, regard, reckon, estimate. (*undervalue, misconceive, misjudge, ignore, depreciate*)

apprehend comprehend, understand, take, expect, seize, conceive, arrest, fancy, dread, imagine, presume, anticipate, fear, conjecture. (*ignore, miss, lose, misconjecture, misconceive, misapprehend*)

approach access, avenue, entrance, adit, vestibule, arrival, approximation, advent, nearing, admission, appropinquation, admittance, mode, path, way, advance, similarity. (*exit, egress, debouchure, outlet, departure, recession, distance*)

approve like, comment, sanction, praise, support, second, promote, encourage, authorize. (*disapprove, dislike, censure, blame, disown, disavow*)

approximate approach, resemble, border, abut, near, trench. (*separate, differ, vary, recede, diverge*)

apt fit, apposite, clever, meet, liable, becoming, appropriate, ready, fitting, suitable, pertinent, qualified, prompt, adapted, likely. (*unfitted, ill-timed, awkward, unlikely, inapt*)

arbitrary tyrannical, despotic, harsh, dictatorial, imperious, unforbearing, overbearing, selfish, absolute, irresponsible, tyrannous, domineering, peremptory. (*mild, modest, lenient, considerate*)

arbitrate settle, adjust, compose, decide, determine, accommodate, adjudicate. (*dispute, claim*)

ardent longing, passionate, aspiring, warm, eager, fervent, excited, fiery, glowing, zealous, fervid, fierce, keen, vehement, hot, affectionate, impassioned, burning, heated. (*cool, cold, indifferent, dispassioned, apathetic, passionless, phlegmatic, platonic*)

argue discuss, debate, prove, question, evidence, establish, imply, sift, dispute, persuade, controvert, contend, demonstrate, reason. (*dictate, assert, propound, command*)

argument reasoning, controversy, evidence, discussion, topic, dispute. (*assertion, assumption*)

arid dry, parched, sterile, unproductive. (*moist, dewy, watered, fertile, luxuriant, exuberant, verdant*)

aright right, well, rightly, correctly, truly, properly, uprightly, unexceptionably, justly, suitably, appropriately. (*wrongly, awry, incorrectly, improperly, defectively, erroneously*)

arouse stir, excite, disturb, animate, wake up, stimulate, alarm, provoke, cheer. (*allay, assuage*)

arraign summon, accuse, censure, indict, charge, impeach. (*acquit, condone, discharge, release*)

arrange order, put in order, group, array, place, adjust, range, locate, dispose, assort, deal, sort, parcel, classify. (*derange, disarrange, confuse, disturb, disperse, jumble, disorder*)

array *v.* vest, deck, equip, decorate, rank, adorn, dress, accoutre, invest, attire, place, arrange, draw up, marshal, set in order, dispose. (*disarray, disarrange, confuse, jumble, divest, denude, strip*)

array *n.* arrangement, order, disposition, sight, exhibition, show, parade. (*disarray, disorder, confusion, confusedness, jumble*)

arrest seize, take, stop, capture, withhold, restrain, hold, detain, apprehend. (*release, dismiss*)

arrive reach, attain, come to, enter, get to, land. (*embark, depart, start*)

arrogance haughtiness, overbearingness, contemptuousness, hauteur, browbeating, loftiness, self-conceit, stateliness, vainglory, insolence, self-importance, assumption, discourtesy. (*bashfulness, servility, considerateness, deference, courtesy, modesty, shyness, diffidence, politeness*)

artful cunning, designing, maneuvering, sharp, knowing, subtle, sly, crafty, wily, shrewd. (*simple, undesigning, artless, open, innocent, unsophisticated*)

artificial invented, fabricated, fictitious, constructed, manufactured, pretended, simulated, false, assumed, concocted, contrived, deceptive, artful, affected, unnatural, constrained. (*natural, inartificial, genuine, spontaneous, transparent, artless, unaffected*)

ascertain prove, verify, find out, discover, confirm, detect, determine, learn, discern. (*guess, conjecture, surmise, suppose, presume*)

ascribe assign, attribute, impute, refer, render, allege, charge. (*deny, refuse, exclude, dissociate*)

aspiration longing, desire, aim, wish, craving, ambition, endeavor, hope, effort, eagerness. (*apathy, indifference, aimlessness, dullness, inertia, callousness, carelessness, aversion, avoidance*)

assembly meeting, concourse, assemblage, multitude, group, synod, conclave, conference, convocation, unison, company, congregation, collection, crowd, gathering, convention, aggregate. (*dispersion, dissipation, disunion, disruption*)

assent coincidence, agreement, concert, acknowledgment, consent, acquiescence, approval, concurrence, approbation, compliance. (*dissent, disagreement, difference, disavowal, repudiation*)

assign attribute, apportion, allege, refer, specify, consign, entrust, commit, point out, allot to, adduce, advance, appoint, convey. (*withhold, withdraw, resume, retain, refuse, disconnect, dissociate*)

assist help, succor, aid, support, relieve, befriend, second, cooperate with, back, benefit, further. (*hinder, resist, oppose, antagonize, counteract, clog, prevent*)

assistant helper, aider, attendant, coadjutor, auxiliary, ally, associate, contributor, partner, confederate. (*hinderer, opposer, rival, foe, antagonist*)

association union, connection, conjunction, consortment, companionship, alliance, familiarity, community, membership, society, company, denomination, partnership, fellowship, fraternity, friendship. (*disunion, disconnection, estrangement*)

assortment collection, disposition, distribution, class, quantity, selection, stock, miscellany, lot, variety. (*disarrangement, displacement, misplacement*)

assume take, appropriate, arrogate, wear, exhibit, postulate, suppose, presume, usurp, claim, pretend, feign, affect. (*waive, allow, doff, render, surrender, concede, grant, demonstrate, abandon*)

assure advise, advertise, promise, inform, rally, console, encourage, countenance, aid, support, convince, uphold, certify. (*misinform, misadvise*)

astonish startle, surprise, confound, amaze, astound, fill with wonder, stupefy, alarm, terrify, electrify, scare, dumbfound. (*rally, encourage*)

astray loose, abroad, missing, about, at large, wrong, erring, wandering. (*right, close, at home*)

athletic strong, vigorous, powerful, stalwart, brawny, muscular, able-bodied, lusty, sinewy, robust. (*weak, puny, nerveless, strengthless, unbraced*)

atrocious monstrous, nefarious, wicked, outrageous, villainous, enormous, shameful, heinous, cruel, flagrant, facinorous, flagitious. (*laudable, noble, honorable, generous, humane, admirable*)

attach fasten, apply, append, add, fix, subjoin, annex, unite, conciliate, tie, connect, conjoin, attract, win, bind. (*unfasten, loose, disunite, untie*)

attack *v.* assail, assault, invade, encounter, charge, besiege, impugn, contravene. (*defend, resist, repel, protest, withstand on one's own part or for another, support, aid, shield, uphold, vindicate*)

attack *n.* invasion, assault, onset, aggression, onslaught. (*defense, resistance, repulse, protection*)

attain reach, extend, master, arrive at, earn, win, achieve, accomplish, get, obtain, acquire, gain, secure. (*lose, fail, forfeit, miss, abandon, resign*)

attempt try, endeavor, strive, undertake, seek, essay, attack, violate, force. (*disregard, abandon, pretermit, dismiss, neglect, shun, drop*)

attend listen, heed, notice, observe, wait on, serve, mind, watch, accompany, consort, follow, imply, involve. (*wander, disregard, leave, forsake*)

attention observation, notice, regard, watchfulness, heed, consideration, circumspection, study, vigilance, care. (*disregard, inadvertence, remission, indifference, carelessness, abstraction, distraction*)

attest vouch, aver, assert, certify, witness, vouch for, affirm, testify, evidence, support, confirm, suggest, prove, involve, demonstrate, establish, imply, bespeak. (*deny, controvert, contradict, contravene, disprove, disestablish, exclude, neutralize*)

attire robes, garment, clothing, vestments, habiliment, habit, raiment, clothes, garb, apparel, accoutrements, livery, uniform, costume. (*nudity, divestment, exposure, denudation, bareness, disarray*)

attract influence, induce, dispose, incline, tempt, prompt, allure, charm, fascinate, invite, entice. (*repel, deter, indispose, disincline, estrange, alienate*)

attractive winning, alluring, tempting, inviting, engaging, captivating, fascinating, enticing, interesting, charming, pleasant, beautiful, agreeable. (*unattractive, repugnant, repulsive, uninteresting, disagreeable, unpleasant, deformed, ugly, deterrent*)

attribute *v.* refer, assign, associate, apply, ascribe, charge, impute, connect. (*divorce, disconnect, dissociate, dissever*)

attribute n. property, quality, characteristic, attainment, sign, mark, indication, manifestation, symbol.

attrition sorrow, repentance, affliction, penitence, compunction, remorse, self-reproach. (*impenitence, callousness, obduracy, reprobation, relentlessness*)

audacious insolent, adventurous, presumptuous, valiant, rash, bold, daring, reckless, enterprising. (*timid, cowardly, cautious, inadventurous, unenterprising*)

audacity boldness, rashness, temerity, recklessness, hardihood. (*caution, self-preservation, timidity, calculation, forethought, foresight, diffidence*)

augment increase, enlargement, amplification, enrichment, supply, enhancement, addition, acquisition, improvement. (*deduction, detraction, diminution, contraction, withdrawal, reservation, expenditure, loss, waste, detriment, deterioration, impoverishment, reduction, curtailment*)

augury prophecy, prediction, divination, conjecture, omen, prognostication. (*experience, science*)

august majestic, dignified, stately, noble, pompous, imposing, grand, solemn, exalted. (*mean, undignified, unimposing, common, vulgar, despicable, paltry, unnoticeable, beggarly, commonplace*)

auspicious propitious, lucky, favorable, encouraging, satisfactory, successful, hopeful, promising, happy, golden, fortunate, opportune, prosperous. (*unpropitious, unfavorable, discouraging, unsatisfactory, inauspicious, unpromising, abortive*)

austere hard, rigid, stern, severe, morose, unrelenting, unyielding, strict, rigorous, harsh, sour, relentless. (*mild, affable, kindly, tender feeling*)

authentic genuine, veritable, reliable, real, original, trustworthy, not spurious, true, legitimate, certain, accepted, current, received. (*unreliable, spurious, false, apocryphal, disputed, exploded, rejected, counterfeit, unfounded, unauthorized, baseless*)

authoritative decisive, sure, conclusive, authentic, powerful, firm, potent, dictatorial, imperious, arbitrary, arrogant, imperative, dogmatic, commanding. (*weak, inconclusive, vague, indeterminate, indefinite, vacillating, undecisive, bland, conciliatory*)

authority ground, justification, authenticity, genuineness, conclusiveness, decisiveness, control, direction, jurisdiction, government, regulation, power, right, rule, sway, sufferance, supremacy, dominion. (*groundlessness, spuriousness, indecision, inconclusiveness, inoperativeness, incompetency, weakness, usurpation, wrong*)

autocratic independent, arbitrary, despotic, irresponsible, absolute. (*dependent, subordinate, responsible, constitutional, limited*)

auxiliary helpful, abetting, aiding, accessory, promotive, conducive, assistant, ancillary, assisting, subsidiary, helping. (*unassisting, unconducive, unpromotive, redundant, superfluous, obstructive*)

avail suffice, hold, stand, endure, answer, tell, profit, help, benefit, advantage, service, use, utility. (*fail, fall, disappoint, betray*)

available useful, appropriate, convertible, attainable, handy, conducive, applicable, procurable, advantageous, helpful, profitable, suitable, serviceable. (*useless, inappropriate, inapplicable, unprocurable, inconducive, irrelevant, inoperative, unavailable*)

avarice greed, cupidity, rapacity, penuriousness, niggardliness, miserliness, stinginess, covetousness, acquisitiveness, griping, greediness. (*large-heartedness, unselfishness, liberality, bountifulness*)

aver assert, asseverate, affirm, depose, avouch, protest, oblige, declare. (*deny, contradict, contravene, disavow, disclaim, repudiate, gainsay, oppugn*)

avidity cupidity, avarice, desire, greed, longing, rapacity, eagerness. (*coldness, indifference, apathy, insensibility, antipathy, nausea, aversion, repugnance, loathing*)

avoid quit, shun, abandon, desert, forsake, relinquish, fly, eschew, elude, dodge, escape, shirk. (*seek, court, approach, accost, address, affect*)

award assign, apportion, attribute, accord, grant, distribute, divide, allot, give, determine, decree, order, adjudge. (*refuse, withhold, withdraw*)

aware conscious, sensible, informed, certified, assured, known, apprized, cognizant. (*unconscious, insensible, ignorant, unaware, uninformed*)

awful fearful, direful, appalling, terrible, alarming, dreadful, horrible, solemn, portentous, horrific. (*innocuous, informidable, unimposing, unastonishing*)

awkward ungainly, clownish, clumsy, maladroit, unhandy, uncouth, rough, boorish, bungling, gawky. (*neat, clever, dexterous, skillful, adroit*)

axiom self-evident truth, aphorism, truism, apopthegm, maxim. (*nonsense, absurdity, stultiloquy, absurdness*)

babble prate, prattle, dribble, chatter, gabble, twaddle, blab, cackle. (*enunciate, vociferate, hush*)

babel hubbub, confusion, clamor, jargon, din, discord, clang. (*elocution, articulation, monotony, distinctness, consecutiveness, intonation, enunciation*)

baffle frustrate, counteract, estop, disconcert, elude, mock, thwart, confound, defeat, perplex, restrain, upset, foil, mar, balk, neutralize, dodge, counterfoil. (*point, aid, abet, enforce, promote*)

bait morsel, snare, decoy, enticement, allurement, inducement. (*warning, scarecrow, dissuasive, deterrent, prohibition, intimidation, threat*)

balance weigh, poise, pit, set, counterpoise, counteract, neutralize, equalize, estimate, redress, adjust. (*upset, tilt, cant, subvert, mispoise, overbalance*)

balderdash gasconade, flummery, rhodomontade, bombast, fustian, froth. (*sense, wisdom*)

balk estop, bar, thwart, frustrate, foil, stop, prevent, hinder, neutralize, nullify, mar, counteract, disappoint, defeat, baffle. (*aid, abet, promote*)

banish expel, abandon, dispel, eject, extrude, exclude, relegate, expatriate, repudiate, disclaim. (*cherish, foster, protect, consider, encourage, locate*)

banquet feast, festivity, treat, entertainment, festival, carousal, carouse, regalement, cheer. (*fast, abstinence, starvation*)

banter badinage, chaff, mockery, derision, ridicule, irony, jeering, raillery. (*discussion, discourse*)

bargain transaction, negotiation, business, profit, speculation, higgling, gain, hawking, chaffer, haggling. (*loss, misprofit*)

base vile, dishonorable, low, sordid, ignoble, worthless, mean, infamous, shameful, groveling, disingenuous, disesteemed, cheap, corrupt, deep. (*lofty, exalted, refined, noble, esteemed, honored*)

bashful modest, diffident, shy, retiring, reserved. (*bold, impudent, forward, unreserved, pert, conceited, ostentatious, egotistic*)

battle fight, conflict, contest, combat, engagement, encounter, action. (*peace, truce, pacification, arbitrament, council, mediation*)

bawl shout, vociferate, halloo, roar, bellow. (*whisper, mutter, babble, mumble*)

beach shore, coast, strand, seacoast, seaboard, seashore. (*sea, ocean, deep, main*)

beaming shining, gleaming, bright, radiant, beautiful, transparent, translucid. (*dull, opaque, dingy, beamless, wan*)

bear carry, lift, transport, convey, maintain, uphold, suffer, undergo, support, tolerate, waft, yield, sustain, hold, harbor, entertain, fill, enact, endure, admit, produce, generate. (*drop, refuse*)

beat strike, pound, batter, surpass, thrash, cudgel, overcome, defeat, conquer, worst, whack, belabor, vanquish. (*defend, protect, shield, fall*)

beauty loveliness, grace, fairness, seemliness, comeliness, picturesqueness, exquisiteness, adornment, embellishment. (*foulness, ugliness, deformity, hideousness, bareness, unattractiveness*)

because owing, consequently, accordingly. (*irrespectively, independently, inconsequently, unconnectedly*)

beck nod, sign, signal, symbol, token, indication, authority, orders, instruction, subserviency, influence, call, command, control, mandate. (*independence, unsubservience*)

becoming beseeming, neat, fit, proper, decorous, comely, seemly, befitting, graceful, decent, suitable, improving. (*unbeseeming, unseemly, uncomely, unbecoming, unbefitting, ungraceful, indecent*)

befitting fitting, decent, becoming, suitable, appropriate, proper, consistent, expedient, desirable. (*obligatory, compulsory, unbefitting, indecent*)

before precedently, anteriorly, antecedently. (*after, afterward, subsequently, posteriorly, later*)

beg ask, request, entreat, supplicate, beseech, implore, pray, petition, crave. (*insist, exact, extort, require, demand*)

beggarly miserable, poor, stinted, wretched, niggardly, stingy, scant, illiberal. (*noble, princely, stately, prodigal, sumptuous, liberal, profuse, gorgeous, magnificent*)

begin initiate, commence, prepare, start, originate, arise, inaugurate. (*achieve, complete, terminate, conclude, consummate, finish, close, end*)

beginning commencement, start, origin, rise, initiation, preparation, preface, prelude, inauguration, inception, threshold, opening, source, outset, foundation. (*end, close, termination, conclusion, consummation, completion*)

behavior conduct, bearing, demeanor, proceeding, comportment, action, manner, deportment. (*misdemeanor, misbehavior, misconduct*)

belief assent, faith, trust, credence, avowal, assurance, admission, conviction, opinion, permission, creed, reliance, concession, confidence. (*dissent, unbelief, distrust, denial, misgiving, disavowal*)

belonging related, connected, appertaining, cognate, congenial, obligatory, accompanying. (*unrelated, unconnected, irrelevant, impertinent, alien*)

bend curve, deviate, incline, tend, swerve, diverge, mold, persuade, influence, bias, dispose, direct, lower, subordinate to, lean, deflect, bow, condescend, yield, stoop, submit. (*proceed, continue, extend, advance, stand, stiffen, break, crush*)

benediction blessing, commendation, approval, benison, gratitude, thankfulness, thanksgiving. (*curse, malediction, disapproval, censure, obloquy*)

benefactor friend, supporter, contributor, upholder, well-wisher, favorer, well-doer, patron. (*foe, opponent, disfavor, antagonist, rival, back-friend, oppressor*)

beneficial profitable, salutary, advantageous, wholesome, salubrious. (*prejudicial, noxious, hurtful, unprofitable, detrimental*)

benefit boon, behoof, service, utility, avail, use, good, advantage, profit, favor, blessing. (*evil, low, disadvantage, detriment, damage, calamity*)

bequeath give, grant, will to, bestow, impart, leave to. (*withhold, alienate, transfer, disinherit, dispossess*)

bereavement destitution, affliction, deprivation, loss. (*gift, blessing, donation, benefaction, compensation, reparation, restoration, reinstatement*)

besotted intoxicated, steeped, stupefied, drunk, drenched, doltish, gross, prejudiced. (*sober, temperate, clear, unbiased, unprejudiced, enlightened*)

bespeak betoken, foreorder, forestall, provide, prearrange, indicate, evidence. (*belie, resign*)

betimes early, beforehand, prepared, readily. (*behindhand, slowly, sluggishly, belatedly*)

betray deceive, delude, dupe, circumvent, ensnare, dishonor, manifest, indicate, reveal. (*protect, preserve, guard, conserve, foster, cherish, fence*)

better meliorate, improve, amend, emend, ameliorate, rectify, reform. (*make worse*)

beware care, refrain, consider, heed, look, fear, avoid. (*ignore, overlook, neglect, incur, brave, dare*)

bewilder daze, dazzle, confound, mystify, puzzle, embarrass, astonish, perplex, confuse, mislead. (*guide, inform, lead, instruct, enlighten*)

bewitch enchant, fascinate, charm, captivate, entrance. (*exorcise, disillusion, disenchant*)

bid tell, request, instruct, direct, order, proffer, charge, command, propose, offer. (*forbid, deter*)

bide wait, remain, tarry, stay, await, expect, anticipate, continue, bear, abide, endure. (*quit, depart, migrate, move, resist, resent, repel, abjure*)

big large, great, wide, huge, bulky, proud, arrogant, pompous, fat, massive, gross. (*little, small, narrow, minute, slight, lean, affable, easy*)

binding restrictive, obligatory, restraining, stringent, styptic, costive, astringent. (*loosening, opening, enlarging, distending*)

birth parentage, extraction, nativity, family, race, origin, source, rise, lineage, nobility. (*death, extinction, plebeianism*)

bitter harsh, sour, sharp, tart, acrimonious, sarcastic, severe, sad, afflictive, intense, stinging, pungent, acrid, cutting. (*sweet, mellow, pleasant*)

blacken bespatter, befoul, bedaub, defame, decry, calumniate, dishonor, asperse, traduce, vilify, slander, malign. (*vindicate, clear, eulogize*)

blackguard scoundrel, rascal, rapscallion, blackleg, villain. (*gentleman*)

blame censure, chide, rebuke, reproach, vituperate, dispraise, disapprove, condemn, reprehend, reprobate, reprove. (*acquit, exculpate, exonerate, encourage, praise, approve*)

bland soft, mild, gentle, complaisant, courteous, affable, gracious, tender, benign. (*harsh, abrupt*)

blast *n.* breeze, explosion, blight, burst, blaze, frustration, destruction, squall, gale, tempest, hurricane. (*zephyr, gentle breeze*)

blast *v.* blight, shrivel, destroy, wither. (*restore, expand, swell*)

bleak blank, bare, open, cold, exposed, stormy, nipping. (*warm, sheltered, verdant, luxuriant*)

blemish spot, blur, blot, flaw, speck, fault, imperfection, stain, daub, tarnish, defacement, discoloration, disfigurement, disgrace, dishonor, defect. (*purity, unsulliedness, honor, intactness*)

blend mix, harmonize, unite, combine, fuse, merge, amalgamate, mingle, commingle, coalesce. (*run, separate, divide, dissociate, confound*)

bless felicitate, endow, enrich, gladden, rejoice, cheer, thank. (*deprive, sadden, impoverish, ignore*)

blind sightless, unseeing, eyeless, depraved, undiscerning, ignorant, prejudiced, uninformed, unconscious, unaware. (*farsighted, penetrating, sensitive, keen, discriminating, clear-sighted, pure-minded, aware, conscious*)

blink wink, ignore, connive, overlook. (*notice, visit, note, mark*)

bliss blessedness, joy, ecstasy, rapture. (*condemnation, accursedness, suffering, misery, woe*)

blithe light, merry, joyous, happy, bright, elastic, gladsome, bonny, vivacious, lively, cheerful, blithesome, gay. (*heavy, dull, dejected, sullen*)

blockhead dolt, dunderhead, jolterhead, dunce, ninny, numskull, dullard, simpleton, booby, loggerhead, ignoramus. (*sage, adept, luminary, schoolman, philosopher, savant*)

blooming flourishing, fair, flowering, blossoming, young, beautiful. (*fading, waning, blighted*)

blot obscure, tarnish, spoil, sully, spot, discolor, pollute, obliterate, erase, blur, stain, blotch, smear, smudge. (*elucidate, clear, absterge, perpetuate*)

blow puff, blast, breath, stroke, infliction, wound, disappointment, affliction, knock, shock, calamity, misfortune. (*assuagement, consolation, relief, comfort, blessing, sparing*)

bluff bare, open, bold, abrupt, frank, plainspoken, blunt, surly, rude, blustering, swaggering, brusque, hectoring, coarse, discourteous, rough, bullying. (*undulating, inclined, inabrupt, courteous*)

blunder error, mistake, misunderstanding, fault, oversight, inaccuracy, delusion, slip. (*accuracy, truthfulness, exactness, correctness, faultlessness*)

blush bloom, color, carnation, complexion, aspect, shame, confusion, guiltiness, self-reproach. (*innocence, purity, guiltlessness, unconsciousness*)

boast vaunt, brag, swagger, swell, bluster, vapor, triumph, glory.

body substance, mass, whole, substantiality, collectiveness, assemblage, collection, matter, association, organization. (*spirit, soul, individual*)

boggle halt, hesitate, dubitate, falter, blunder, blotch, botch, spoil, mar. (*encounter, face, advance*)

bold courageous, fearless, adventurous, brave, self-confident, forward, intrepid, dauntless, valiant, daring, audacious, lionhearted, doughty. (*timid, fearful, unadventurous, shy, bashful, retiring*)

bombast bluster, inflatedness, pomposity, boastfulness, exaggeration, fustian. (*truthfulness, moderation, restraint, modesty, humility*)

bond tie, fastening, chain, association, manacle, fetter, compact, obligation, security. (*freedom, option, discretion, honor, parole*)

bondsman slave, serf, prisoner, captive, vassal. (*freeman, yeoman, gentleman, lord, master*)

bonny fair, pretty, pleasant, lively, cheerful, shapely, buxom. (*dull, unseemly, ill-favored*)

border limit, boundary, brink, rim, verge, brim, edge, edging, band, hem, enclosure, confine. (*land, tract, interior, substance, space, center*)

border on be contiguous to, be adjacent to, conterminous with, adjoin, adjacent to. (*remote from, away from*)

botch patch, cobble, blunder, clump, disconcert, spoil, jumble, mess, bungle, mar, blacksmith. (*fine-draw, trim, harmonize, mend, beautify, embroider*)

bother fuss, worry, pester, excitement, stir, plague, vex, annoy, tease, confusion, vexation, flurry, trouble. (*calm, composure, orderliness*)

boundless unbounded, immeasurable, infinite, unlimited, illimitable, unmeasurable. (*narrow, restricted, limited, confined, circumscribed*)

bounty liberality, bounteousness, benevolence, munificence, donation, gift, generosity, charity, benignity. (*illiberality, closeness, hardness, churlishness, stinginess, niggardliness*)

brag boast, vaunt, swagger, bully. (*cringe, whine, whimper*)

branch member, bifurcation, bough, limb, offspring, shoot, spray, sprig, twig, ramification, offshoot, relative, scion. (*trunk, stock, stem, race*)

break fracture, rupture, shatter, shiver, destroy, tame, curb, demolish, tear asunder, rend, burst, sever, smash, split, subdue, violate, infringe. (*heal, piece, conjoin, protect, conserve, encourage*)

breath respiration, inspiration, expiration, inhalation, exhalation. (*cessation, passing, departure*)

breeding nurture, education, training, discipline, instruction, manners, air, demeanor, decorum. (*ill manners, ill training, ill behavior, ignorance*)

brevity shortness, closeness, conciseness, succinctness, terseness, compendiousness, pointedness, abbreviation, abridgment. (*length, protraction, elongation, extension, prolixity, diffuseness, interminableness, tediousness*)

bright shining, brilliant, burnished, luminous, lucid, sparkling, limpid, clever, happy, witty, joyous, cheerful, radiant. (*opaque, dull, dead, muddy*)

brilliant flashing, radiant, shining, lustrous, highly intelligent, sparkling. (*dull, stupid*)

bring fetch, procure, convey, carry, bear, adduce, import, produce, cause, induce. (*export, remove, abstract, subtract, prevent, exclude, debar*)

brisk quick, lively, vivacious, active, alert, nimble, sprightly, spirited, animated, prompt, effervescent. (*slow, heavy, dull, inactive, indolent*)

broad wide, extensive, expansive, ample, liberal, comprehensive, unreserved, indelicate, coarse, generic. (*narrow, restricted, confined, limited*)

brotherhood fraternity, association, fellowship, society. (*division, disunity, individual*)

brutal savage, inhuman, rude, unfeeling, merciless, ruthless, brutish, barbarous, sensual, beastly, ignorant, stolid, dense, cruel, violent, vindictive, bloodthirsty, intemperate. (*humane, civilized, generous, intelligent, polished, chivalrous, conscientious*)

bubble trifle, toy, fancy, conceit, vision, dream, froth, trash. (*acquisition, prize, treasure, reality*)

bugbear hobgoblin, goblin, gorgon, ghoul, spirit, spook, specter, ogre, scarecrow.

building edifice, architecture, construction, erection, fabric, structure. (*ruin, dilapidation, dismantlement, demolition*)

bulk mass, whole, entirety, integrity, majority, size, magnitude, extension, body, volume, bigness, largeness, massiveness, dimension. (*tenuity, minority, dismemberment, disintegration, diminution, portion, contraction, section, atom, particle*)

bungler botcher, clown, lubber, fumbler, novice. (*adept, adroit, master, artist, workman, proficient, professor*)

buoyant sprightly, spirited, vivacious, lively, light, floating, hopeful, cheerful, elastic, joyous. (*heavy, depressed, cheerless, joyless, dejected, moody*)

burden load, weight, incubus, obstruction, oppression, grief, difficulty, affliction. (*ease, lightness, airiness, expedition, facility, acceleration, abjugation, liberation, lightheartedness, alleviation*)

burn ignite, kindle, brand, consume, cauterize, rage, glow, smoulder, blaze, flash, cremate, incinerate. (*extinguish, stifle, cool, wane, subside*)

bury inter, inhume, conceal, repress, suppress, obliterate, cancel, entomb, compose, hush. (*disinter, exhume, bruit, excavate, expose, resuscitate*)

business occupation, profession, vocation, transaction, trade, calling, office, employment, interest, duty, affair, matter, concern. (*stagnation, leisure, inactivity*)

bustle business, activity, stir, commotion, energy, excitement, haste, hurry, eagerness, flurry. (*idleness, vacation, inactivity, indolence, indifference*)

busy industrious, diligent, assiduous, engaged, occupied. (*idle, slothful, lazy, indolent, unoccupied*)

but save, except, barring, yet, beside, excluding, still, excepting, notwithstanding. (*with, including, inclusive, nevertheless, however, notwithstanding*)

calamity disaster, misfortune, mishap, catastrophe, misadventure, trouble, visitation, affliction, reverse, blight. (*godsend, blessing, boon*)

calculate estimate, consider, weigh, number, count, apportion, proportion, investigate, reckon, rate, compute. (*guess, conjecture, hit, chance, risk*)

calculation estimation, consideration, balance, apportionment, investigation, reckoning, computation, anticipation, forethought, regard, circumspection, watchfulness, vigilance, caution, care. (*inconsiderateness, inconsideration, incaution, indiscretion, miscalculation, misconception, exclusion, exception, omission, carelessness, supposition*)

caliber gauge, diameter, ability, capacity, force, quality, character. (*weakness, incapacity*)

called named, designated, denominated, yclept, termed. (*unnamed, undesignated, misnamed, misdesignated*)

calm smooth, pacify, compose, allay, still, soothe, appease, assuage, quiet, tranquilize. (*stir, excite, agitate, disconcert, ruffle, lash, heat, discompose*)

calumny slander, defamation, detraction, libel, traducement, backbiting, opprobrium, aspersion. (*vindication, clearance, eulogy, panegyric*)

cancel efface, blot out, annul, expunge, nullify, quash, rescind, repeal, revoke, abrogate, obliterate, discharge, erase, abolish, countervail. (*enforce, enact, reenact, confirm, perpetuate, contract*)

candid fair, honest, open, sincere, frank, artless, impartial, plain, straightforward, aboveboard, transparent, unreserved, ingenious. (*unfair, close*)

candidate aspirant, petitioner, canvasser, applicant, claimant, solicitor. (*waiver, decliner, abandoner, resigner, abjurer, noncompetitor*)

canvass question, investigate, challenge, test, dispute, solicit, sift, examine, discuss, apply for, request. (*pretermit, allow, ignore, disregard, admit*)

capacity space, size, volume, tonnage, caliber, ability, faculty, capability, cleverness, talents, magnitude, parts, competency, comprehensiveness, accommodation. (*narrowness, restriction, incapacity, coarctation, contractedness*)

capital chief, excellent, important, cardinal, principal, consummate, high. (*inferior, unimportant, subordinate, minor, defective, mean*)

capricious wayward, uncertain, fanciful, freakish, fitful, fickle, changeful, whimsical, humorous, inconstant, crotchety. (*firm, unchanging, inflexible, decided, unswerving, constant*)

captivated taken, charmed, smitten, fascinated, enslaved, captured, enthralled. (*free, unaffected, uninfluenced, unscathed, insensible, insensitive*)

care attention, pains, anxiety, concern, trouble, circumspection, regard, solicitude, caution, prevention, custody, preservation, thrift, heed, foresight, wariness, economy, prudence. (*inattention, neglect*)

career course, success, walk, line, progress, history, way of life, passage, race. (*misproceeding, misdeportment, unsuccess, miscarriage*)

caress endearment, blandishment, wheedling, fondling, stroking. (*vexation, irritation, annoyance*)

caricature mimicry, parody, travesty, burlesque, extravagance, exaggeration, hyperbole, monstrosity, farce. (*portraiture, representation, resemblance, justice, fidelity, truthfulness*)

carnival revel, rout, festivity, masquerade. (*fast, mortification, lent, retirement*)

carpet table, board, consideration, consultation. (*shelf, rejection, disposal, oblivion*)

carriage transportation, conveyance, bearing, manner, conduct, demeanor, walk, gait, mien, behavior, deportment, vehicle. (*misconveyance, miscarriage, misconduct, misconsignment*)

case occurrence, circumstance, contingency, event, plight, predicament, fact, subject, condition, instance. (*hypothesis, supposition, fancy, theory*)

cast *v.* hurt, send down, throw, fling, pitch, impel, project, construct, mold, frame. (*raise, elevate*)

cast *n.* mold, stamp, kind, figure, form, aspect, mien, air, style, manner, character. (*malformation, deformity, abnormity*)

caste order, class, rank, lineage, race, blood, dignity, respect. (*degradation, taboo, disrepute*)

casual accidental, occasional, incidental, contingent, unforeseen, fortuitous. (*regular, ordinary*)

catastrophe revolution, disaster, calamity, misfortune, misadventure, reverse, blow, visitation. (*blessing, victory, triumph, felicitation, achievement*)

cause source, origin, producer, agent, creator, purpose, inducement, reason, account, principle, motive, object, suit, action. (*effect, result, accomplishment, end, production, issue, preventive*)

cease intermit, stop, desist, abstain, discontinue, quit, refrain, end, pause, leave off. (*ceaseless, never-ending, everlasting, constant, incessant*)

celebrated famed, renowned, illustrious, eminent, glorious, famous, noted, distinguished, notable, exalted. (*unrenowned, obscure, undistinguished*)

celebrity fame, honor, glory, star, reputation, distinction, renown, notability, eminence, notoriety. (*obscurity, meanness, ingloriousness, ignominy, disgrace, contempt, cipher, nobody*)

celestial heavenly, ethereal, atmospheric, supernal, angelic, radiant, eternal, immortal, seraphic, divine, godlike, elysian. (*earthly, terrestrial, terrene*)

censure blame, stricture, reproach, reprobate, inculpate, reprove, condemn, reprehend, chide, berate, scold, upbraid, disapproval, remonstrance, rebuke, reprimand, dispraise. (*praise, eulogy, approbation, encouragement, commendation*)

ceremonial official, ministerial, functional, pompous, imposing, sumptuous, scenic. (*ordinary, private, unimposing, unostentatious, undramatic*)

certain true, fixed, regular, established, incontrovertible, undoubtful, indubitable, infallible, unmistakable, sure, unfailing, real, actual, undeniable, positive, convinced, assured. (*uncertain, dubious, exceptional, irregular, casual, occasional*)

certify acknowledge, aver, attest, vouch, avow, avouch, testify, protest, declare, demonstrate, prove, evidence, inform, assure. (*disprove, disavow, misinform, misadvise*)

challenge defy, summon, dare, question, investigate, brave, canvass. (*pass, allow, grant, concede*)

chance accident, fortuity, hazard, haphazard, fortune, random, casualty, luck. (*law, rule, sequence, consequence, causation, effectuation*)

changeless regular, settled, steady, firm, stationary, consistent, resolute, reliable, undeviating, uniform, immutable, immovable. (*irregular, unsettled, unsteady, wavering, fluctuating, capricious*)

character symbol, letter, nature, type, disposition, genius, temperament, cast, estimation, repute, office, reputation, part, capacity, class, order, sort, stamp, kind, quality, species, sign, tone, mark, figure, record. (*vagueness, anonymity, nondescription, disrepute*)

characteristic distinction, peculiarity, diagnosis, idiosyncrasy, specialty, individuality, personality, singularity. (*nondescription, abstractedness, generality, miscellany*)

charitable kind, benign, benevolent, beneficent, liberal, considerate, forgiving, compassionate, placable, inexacting, inextreme. (*uncharitable, unkind, harsh, selfish, churlish, illiberal, censorious*)

charm *v.* bewitch, enchant, fascinate, lay, soothe, mesmerize, delight, enrapture, transport, entice, allure, entrance, captivate, subdue. (*disenchant, rouse, disturb, annoy, irritate*)

charm *n.* spell, incantation, enchantment, fascination, attraction, allurement. (*disenchantment, repulsion, fear*)

chaste pure, modest, uncontaminated, spotless, immaculate, undefiled, virtuous, incorrupt, simple, unaffected, nice. (*impure, corrupt, meretricious*)

cheap common, inexpensive, uncostly, mean, vile, worthless, low-priced. (*rare, costly, worthy*)

cheat *v.* overreach, fleece, silence, trick, gull, cozen, juggle, defraud, swindle, dupe, beguile, deceive, deprive, hoodwink, prevaricate, dissemble, shuffle, inveigle. (*enlighten, guide, remunerate*)

cheat *n.* deception, fraud, imposition, trick, artifice, illusion, impostor, swindle, finesse, deceit, lie, fiction. (*truth, reality, verity, fact, certainty*)

cheer hope, happiness, comfort, hospitality, plenty, conviviality. (*dejection, sullenness, gloom, starvation, niggardliness, dearth, inhospitableness*)

cheerful lively, gay, bright, happy, bonny, merry, joyful, pleasant, buoyant, sunny, enlivening, in good spirits, sprightly, blithe, joyous. (*lifeless, dull, gloomy, unhappy, dejected, depressed, sullen*)

childish weak, silly, puerile, infantile, imbecile, foolish, trifling, paltry, trivial. (*strong, resolute, wise, judicious, sagacious, chivalrous*)

chivalrous courageous, generous, knightly, gallant, heroic, adventurous, valiant, spirited, handsome, high-minded. (*unhandsome, dirty, sneaking*)

choice option, adoption, selection, election, preference, alternative. (*compulsion, necessity, rejection, refusal, unimportance, indifference, refuse*)

chuckle grin, crow, cackle. (*cry, wail, grumble, whimper, whine*)

cipher nonentity, dot, nothing, trifle, button, straw, pin, rush, molehill. (*somebody, bigwig, something, notability, celebrity, triton, colossus*)

circumstance detail, feature, point, event, occurrence, incident, situation, position, fact, topic, condition, particular, specialty. (*deed, case, transaction*)

civil well-mannered, political, courteous, well-bred, complaisant, affable, urbane, polite, obliging, accommodating, respectful. (*disobliging, unaccommodating, disrespectful, boorish, clownish, churlish*)

claim *v.* demand, ask, require, insist, pretend, request, maintain. (*forgo, waive, disclaim, abjure, disavow, abandon*)

claim *n.* assertion, vindication, pretension, title, right, privilege, arrogation, demand. (*waiver, abjuration, disclaimer, surrender*)

claimant assertor, vindicator, appellant, litigant. (*relinquisher, resigner, conceder, waiver*)

classification order, species, nature, character, cast, stamp, group, kind, section, sect, category, assortment, designation, description, genus. (*individuality, specialty, isolation, alienation, division*)

clause portion, paragraph, stipulation, provision, article, condition, chapter, section, passage. (*document, instrument, muniment*)

clear *v.* clarify, disencumber, disentangle, disembarrass, vindicate, liberate, set free, release, exonerate, exculpate, justify, retrieve, acquit, absolve, whitewash, extricate, eliminate. (*befoul, contaminate, pollute, clog, encumber, embarrass*)

clear *a.* open, pure, bright, transparent, free, disencumbered, disentangled, disengaged, absolved, acquitted, serene, unclouded, evident, apparent, distinct, manifest, conspicuous, unobstructed, plain, obvious, intelligible, lucid. (*thick, muddy*)

clever able, ready, talented, quick, ingenious, dexterous, adroit, expert, gifted, quick-witted, skillful, well-contrived. (*weak, dull, stupid, slow*)

cling fasten, hold, adhere, embrace, stick, cleave, hang, twine, hug. (*drop, recede, secede, apostatize, abandon, relax, forgo, swerve, surrender*)

cloak conceal, disguise, mask, veil, hide, cover, palliate, screen, mitigate, extenuate. (*exhibit, propound, promulge, portray, aggravate, expose, demonstrate, reveal*)

close narrow, limited, restricted, condensed, packed, secret, compressed, solid, firm, compact, reserved, niggardly, shut, fast, dense. (*wide, open*)

clownish rustic, boorish, bucolic, foolish, awkward, clumsy, cloddish, untutored, rude. (*polite, civil, urbane, affable, graceful, polished, refined*)

clumsy awkward, inexpert, uncouth, maladroit, botching, bungling, unskillful, unwieldy, unhandy, ill-shaped. (*neat, workmanlike, artistic, handy*)

coarse common, ordinary, indelicate, vulgar, gross, unrefined, immodest, rough, rude, unpolished. (*fine, refined, gentle, polished, delicate, choice*)

cognizance notice, observation, recognition, knowledge, experience. (*inadvertence, neglect, ignorance, inexperience, oversight, connivance*)

coherent consecutive, consistent, complete, sensible, compact, logical, close. (*inconsecutive, rambling, disunited, inconsistent, discursive, loose*)

coincidence chance, fortuity, casualty, concurrence, correspondence, contemporaneousness, commensurateness, harmony, agreement, consent. (*design, purpose, adaptation, asynchronism, anachronism, disharmony, incommensurateness, discordance, variation, difference*)

colleague helper, companion, associate, ally, confederate, coadjutor, partner, assistant, adjutant, assessor. (*co-opponent, corival, counter-agent, co-antagonist, competitor*)

collect collate, gather, glean, sum, infer, learn, congregate, assemble, convoke, convene, muster, amass, garner, accumulate. (*classify, arrange, distribute, dispose, dispense, divide, sort, deal*)

collection assembly, assemblage, store, gathering, collation. (*dispersion, distribution, dispensation, division, arrangement, disposal, classification*)

color hue, tint, complexion, pretense, speciousness, tinge, garbling, falsification, distortion, perversion, varnish. (*achromatism, paleness, nakedness, openness, genuineness, transparency, truthfulness*)

combination union, association, consortment, concert, confederacy, alliance, league, coalition, cabal, synthesis, cooperation. (*division, disunion*)

comfortable snug, satisfied, pleasant, agreeable, cozy, commodious, convenient, consoled. (*uncomfortable, dissatisfied, troubled, miserable, wretched*)

commerce trade, traffic, merchandise, barter, exchange, business, communication, dealing, intercourse. (*stagnation, exclusion, inactivity, interdict*)

commodious ample, easy, convenient, spacious, suitable, comfortable. (*inconvenient, incommodious, narrow, ill-contrived, incommensurate, discommodious*)

common ordinary, familiar, habitual, everyday, frequent, coarse, vulgar, low, mean, universal. (*unusual, exceptional, scarce, rare, uncommon, refined, partial, infrequent, sporadic, egregious, excellent*)

community aggregation, association, commonwealth, coordination, society, sympathy, order, class, brotherhood, fraternity, polity, unity, nationality, similarity, homogeneity. (*segregation, secession, independence, dissociation, disconnection*)

company aggregation, association, union, sodality, order, fraternity, guild, corporation, society, community, assemblage, assembly, crew, posse, gang, troop, audience, congregation, concourse. (*rivalry, opposition, disqualification, antagonism*)

compass encompass, surround, enclose, environ, circumscribe, embrace, achieve, effect, effectuate, consummate, complete, circumvent. (*expand, dispand, unfold, amplify, display, dismiss, liberate, discard, fail, bungle, batch, misconceive, mismanage*)

compatible consistent, consentaneous, harmonious, coexistent, correspondent, congruous, accordant, agreeable, congenial, consonant. (*incompatible, impossible, inconsistent, discordant, hostile, adverse, antagonistic, incongruous*)

compel force, oblige, drive, constrain, necessitate, make, coerce, bind. (*persuade, convince, coax*)

compensation remunerative, equivalent, wages, pay, allowance, restoration, restitution, satisfaction, atonement, expiation, indemnification, amercement, damages. (*deprivation, injury, non-payment, gratuity, donation, fraudulence, damage*)

competition rivalry, emulation, race, two of a trade. (*association, colleagueship, alliance, joint-stock, copartnership, confederation*)

complacent pleased, satisfied, content, pleasant, affable, kind, mannerly, acquiescent, amiable. (*dissatisfied, irritated, churlish, unmannerly, morose*)

complaint murmur, discontent, repining, grievance, annoyance, remonstrance, expostulation, lamentation, sickness, disease. (*congratulation, rejoicing, approbation, complacency, boon, benefit*)

complement completion, fulfilment, totality, supply, counterpart, correlative. (*deficiency, deficit, insufficiency, abatement, detraction, defalcation*)

complete full, perfect, finished, adequate, entire, consummate, total, exhaustive, thorough, accomplished. (*incomplete, partial, imperfect, unfinished, inadequate*)

complexion face, aspect, color, look, feature, appearance, character, hue, interpretation, indication. (*unindicativeness, concealment, reticence, inexpression, heart, core*)

complicated confused, intricate, involved, perplexed, entangled. (*clear, simple, uninvolved, lucid*)

compliment homage, courtesy, flattery, praise. (*insult, discourtesy, contempt*)

complimentary commendatory, laudatory, panegyrical, eulogistic, encomiastic, lavish of praise. (*disparaging, condemnatory, damnatory, denunciatory, reproachful, abusive, objurgatory, vituperative*)

composition compound, conformation, structure, mixture, combination, compromise, adjustment, settlement, commutation. (*analysis, segregation, examination, criticism, discussion, disturbance, aggravation, perpetuation*)

comprehend comprise, embody, grasp, understand, conceive, apprehend, enclose, include, involve, embrace. (*exclude, except, misunderstand*)

comprehensive wide, ample, general, extensive, large, broad, all-embracing, generic, significant, capacious, inclusive, compendious, pregnant. (*narrow, restricted, shallow, exclusive, adversative*)

compromise arbitrate, adjust, compose, settle, endanger, implicate, involve. (*aggravate, excite, foster, perpetuate, exempt, enfranchise, disengage*)

conceal hide, secrete, disguise, keep secret, dissemble, screen, suppress. (*reveal, manifest, exhibit, avow, confess, expose, promulgate, publish*)

concentrate assemble, converge, muster, congregate, convene, draw, conglomerate, condense, localize, centralize. (*disperse, scatter, dismiss, decentralize*)

concerning about, of, relating, regarding, touching, in relation to, respecting, with respect to, with regard to, with reference to, relative to. (*omitting*)

concert union, combination, concord, harmony, agreement, association, cooperation. (*dissociation, counteraction, opposition*)

condescension affability, graciousness, favor, stooping. (*haughtiness, arrogance, pride, superciliousness, disdain, scorn*)

condition state, case, mood, term, mode, qualification, requisite, stipulation, predicament, proviso, situation, circumstances, plight. (*relation*)

conditionally provisionally, relatively, provided, hypothetically, contingently. (*absolutely, unconditionally, categorically, positively*)

conducive contributive, promotive, subsidiary, causative, effective, productive. (*preventive, counteractive, contrariant, repugnant, destructive*)

conduct lead, bring, carry, transfer, direct, guide, control, manage, administer. (*mislead, miscarry, mismanage, misconduct, misadminister*)

confer compare, collate, discuss, deliberate, converse, consult, give, present. (*dissociate, contrast, hazard, conjecture, withhold, withdraw*)

confession creed, catechism, articles, doctrine, tenets, profession, declaration, subscription. (*heresy, apostasy, protest, condemnation, refutation*)

confidant confessor, adviser, confederate. (*traitor, betrayer, rival*)

confident positive, assured, sure, certain, impudent, bold, sanguine. (*unsure, afraid, timid*)

confidential private, secret, trustworthy, intimate. (*public, open, patent, official, treacherous*)

confirm strengthen, stabilize, establish, substantiate, settle, prove, fix, perpetuate, sanction, corroborate, ratify. (*weaken, shake, upset, cancel*)

confront oppose, face, encounter, resist, intimidate, menace. (*rally, encourage, abet, countenance*)

confused abashed, embarrassed, perplexed, disconcerted, disorganized, promiscuous, chaotic, complex, involved, disarranged, disordered. (*unabashed, unembarrassed, systematic, unconfused*)

congress parliament, council, conclave, assembly, synod, legislature, convention. (*cabal, conclave, mob*)

conjecture guess, divination, hypothesis, theory, notion, surmise, supposition. (*computation, calculation, inference, reckoning, proof, deduction*)

connection junction, conjunction, union, association, concatenation, relation, affinity, relevance, intercourse, communication, kinsman, relationship, kindred. (*disconnection, disjunction, dissociation*)

conquer subdue, vanquish, surmount, overcome, overpower, overthrow, defeat, crush, master, subjugate, prevail over. (*fail, fall, retreat, succumb, fly, submit, surrender, lose, forfeit, sacrifice*)

conscious aware, cognizant, sensible. (*unaware, unconscious, insensible*)

consecutive orderly, arranged, coherent, continuous. (*disordered, undigested, incoherent*)

consent submit, agree, acquiesce. (*resist, disagree, dissent, decline, refuse*)

consequence effect, issue, result, inference, coherence, deduction, conclusion, outcome, importance, note, moment, dignity. (*cause, causation, antecedence, premise, origin, datum, postulate*)

consider attend, revolve, meditate, think, reflect, investigate, regard, observe, judge, opine, infer, deduce, weigh, cogitate, deliberate, ponder, deem. (*disregard, ignore, pretermit, despise, guess*)

considerate thoughtful, attentive, forbearing, unselfish, judicious, serious, prudent, circumspect, reflective, careful, cautious. (*thoughtless, inconsiderate, inattentive, rude, overbearing, selfish, injudicious, rash, careless*)

consistency consistence, congruity, composition, substance, material, amalgamation, compound, mass, density, solidity, closeness, compactness, coherence, uniformity, harmony, analogy, proportion. (*volatility, vaporousness, subtility, tenuity, sublimation, incoherence, inconsistency, incongruity, disproportion, contrariety, contradiction*)

consistent congruous, accordant, consonant, agreeing, compatible, harmonious. (*incongruous, at variance with, not agreeing with, incompatible*)

conspicuous visible, easily seen, prominent, distinguished, manifest, eminent, famous, noted, salient, observable, noticeable, magnified. (*invisible, inconspicuous, inobservable, noticeable, microscopic*)

constant uniform, regular, invariable, perpetual, continuous, firm, fixed, steady, immutable, faithful, true, trustworthy. (*irregular, exceptional*)

constitution temperament, frame, temper, character, habit, nature, government, polity, state, consistence, composition, substance, organization, structure, regulation, law. (*accident, habituation, modification, interference, anarchy, despotism, tyranny, rebellion, revolution, dissipation, disorganization, demolition, destruction*)

construction composition, fabrication, explanation, rendering, erection, fabric, edifice, reading, understanding, interpretation, view. (*dislocation, dismemberment, demolition, displacement, misplacement, misconstruction, misunderstanding, misconception, misinterpretation*)

consult interrogate, canvass, question, deliberate, confer, advise with, regard, consider, ask advice of, care for, promote. (*resolve, explain, expound, direct, instruct, dictate, counteract, contravene*)

consumption decline, decay, expenditure, waste, decrement, lessening, decrease. (*growth, development, enlargement, augmentation*)

contact touch, contiguity, continuity, apposition, adjunction. (*proximity, adjacence, interruption, disconnection, separation, distance, isolation*)

contagious catching, epidemic, infectious, pestilential, communicated, transferred, transmitted, infectious. (*sporadic, endemic, preventive, antipathetic*)

contaminate defile, taint, corrupt, sully, befoul, soil. (*purify, cleanse, lave, clarify, sanctify, chasten*)

contemplate meditate, behold, observe, ponder, study, purpose, design, intend, project. (*ignore, overlook, waive, abandon*)

contemptible despicable, mean, vile, pitiful, disreputable, paltry, trifling, trivial. (*important, grave, weighty, honorable, respectable, venerable*)

content full, satisfied, pleased, gratified, contented, willing, resigned. (*unsatisfied, dissatisfied*)

contentious litigious, perverse, wayward, splenetic, cantankerous, exceptious. (*pacific, obliging*)

contingent dependent, incidental, resultant, coefficient, hypothetical, uncertain, conditional. (*positive, absolute, independent, unmodified, unaffected, uncontrolled, irrespective*)

continually constantly, persistently, always, ever, perpetually, unceasingly, repeatedly, frequently, continuously. (*casually, occasionally, contingently, sometimes, rarely, fitfully, intermittently*)

contract *n.* covenant, agreement, compact, bond, pact, stipulation, bargain. (*promise, assurance, parole*)

contract *v.* abridge, abbreviate, narrow, lessen, reduce, compress, decrease, retrench, curtail, form, agree. (*expand, amplify, dilate, elongate*)

contradict oppose, dissent, negative, controvert, deny, disprove, confute, refute, gainsay, contravene. (*state, propound, maintain, argue, confirm, affirm*)

contrary opposed, opposite, repugnant, antagonistic, adverse, incompatible, inconsistent. (*agreeing, consentaneous, compatible, kindred, coincident*)

contribute conduce, add, subscribe, give, cooperate, assist, tend, supply. (*refuse, withhold*)

contrive plan, design, arrange, fabricate, adapt, manage, scheme, devise, concert, adjust. (*hit, hazard, run, chance, venture, bungle, over-vault*)

control check, curb, moderate, repress, guide, regulate, restrain, coerce, manage, administer, govern. (*neglect, abandon, license, liberate, mismanage, misconduct*)

convenient handy, apt, adapted, fitted, suitable, helpful, commodious, useful, timely, seasonable, opportune. (*inconvenient, awkward, obstructive, useless, superfluous, unseasonable, untimely*)

conventional customary, usual, ordinary, stipulated, prevalent, social. (*unusual, unsocial, legal*)

conversant familiar, acquainted, proficient, experienced, versed, learned. (*unfamiliar, unacquainted, ignorant, unversed, unlearned, strange*)

convertible identical, commensurate, conterminous, equivalent, equipollent. (*variant, incommensurate, unequivalent, contrary, contradictory*)

conviction assurance, persuasion, belief. (*doubt, misgiving, disbelief*)

cooperate assist, abet, contribute, concur, work together, help, conspire. (*thwart, oppose*)

copy imitation, portraiture, facsimile, counterfeit, duplicate, image, likeness, transcript. (*original, prototype, model, example, pattern*)

cordial warm, earnest, sincere, reviving, invigorating, affectionate, hearty. (*cold, distant, formal*)

corner cavity, hole, nook, recess, retreat. (*coin, abutment, prominence, salience, angle, protrusion, elbow, protection, convexity*)

corpulent stout, burly, fat, portly, gross, lusty, plethoric, fleshy. (*lean, thin, attenuated, slight*)

correct *a.* true, exact, faultless, accurate, proper, decorous, right. (*false, untrue, incorrect*)

correct *v.* chasten, punish, rectify, amend, reform, emend, redress, set right, improve. (*spare, falsify, corrupt*)

correction amendment, discipline, emendation, chastisement, punishment. (*deterioration, debasement, retrogradation, reward, recompense*)

correspond match, tally, fit, answer, agree, suit, harmonize. (*vary, differ, disagree, jar, clash*)

correspondence fitness, agreement, adaptation, congruity, answerableness, match, congeniality, communication, letter, writing, dispatches. (*conversation, colloquy, confabulation, reservation, withdrawal, withholding, nonintercourse, difference*)

corrupt defiled, polluted, vitiated, decayed, depraved, putrid, rotten, infected, tainted, profligate, contaminated. (*pure, uncorrupt, undefiled*)

corruption decomposition, decay, putrescence, adulteration, depravity, rottenness, defilement, deterioration, perversion, debasement, taint, contamination, putrefaction. (*vitality, organization*)

cost *v.* require, consume, absorb. (*bring, produce, yield, afford, fetch, return*)

cost *n.* expenditure, outlay, disbursement, payment, compensation, price, worth, expense, charge, outgoings. (*receipt, income, emolument*)

costly valuable, expensive, high-priced, rich, precious, sumptuous. (*valueless, cheap, low-priced, mean, worthless, beggarly, paltry*)

council cabinet, bureau, chamber, consultation, conclave, parliament, congress, synod, company, assembly, meeting, conference, convention, convocation. (*league, conspiracy, cabal, intrigue, mob*)

counsel advice, instruction, monition, admonition, warning, recommendation. (*misguidance, misinstruction, betrayal*)

count compute, reckon, enumerate, estimate, number, sum, calculate. (*hazard, conjecture, guess*)

countenance *v.* help, aid, abet, favor, sanction, patronize, support, encourage. (*oppose, confront, discourage, discountenance, browbeat*)

countenance *n.* aid, abet, encourage, support. (*discountenance*)

counteract counterinfluence, counterfoil, foil, baffle, neutralize, oppose, rival, thwart, hinder. (*aid, help, abet, promote, conserve, cooperate, subserve*)

counterpart match, fellow, tally, brother, twin, copy, correlative, complement, supplement. (*opponent, counteragent, reverse, obverse, opposite, antithesis, contrast, contradiction*)

countryman rustic, clown, boor, compatriot, swain, yeoman, husbandman, farmer, agriculturist, laborer, peasant, fellow countryman, fellow subject, fellow citizen, subject, citizen, inhabitant, native. (*oppidan, townsman, cockney, foreigner, alien*)

couple bracket, link, conjoin, unite, splice, buckle, button, clasp, pair, yoke, connect, tie, brace. (*loose, part, isolate, separate, detach, divorce, uncouple*)

courage bravery, boldness, valor, pluck, fortitude, resolution, gallantry, fearlessness, intrepidity. (*timidity, cowardice, pusillanimity, poltroonery, dastardliness*)

course order, sequence, continuity, direction, progress, line, way, mode, race, career, road, route, series, passage, succession, round, manner, plain, conduct, method. (*disorder, discursion, solution, interruption, deviation, hindrance, error, conjecture*)

courtly dignified, polished, refined, aristocratic, high-bred, mannerly. (*undignified, rough, unpolished, coarse, unrefined, plebeian, awkward, boorish, rustic, unmannerly*)

covetous acquisitive, avaricious, greedy, grasping, rapacious. (*unselfish, liberal, self-sacrificing*)

coward craven, dastard, recreant, poltroon, renegade. (*champion, hero, daredevil, desperado*)

coxcomb fop, dandy, puppy, prig, pedant. (*genius, savant, authority, celebrity, philosopher, sage*)

coy shy, reserved, bashful, shrinking, retreating, modest. (*bold, forward, rompish, hoydenish*)

crabbed sour, morose, cross-grained, petulant, churlish, irritable, crusty. (*pleasant, open, easy, genial, conversable, warm, cordial, hearty*)

craft art, artifice, cunning, guile, stratagem, maneuver, wiliness, trickery, duplicity, chicanery, intrigue, underhandedness, dodge. (*openness, fairness, candor, honesty, frankness, sincerity, artlessness*)

cram stuff, choke, squeeze, ram, pack, gorge. (*disgorge, vent, discharge, unload, unpack, eviscerate*)

crash jar, clang, clash, resonance. (*murmur, whisper, babble, rumbling, reverberation, din*)

cream marrow, pith, gist, acme. (*refuse, offal, dregs, dross, garbage*)

credential, or **credentials** missive, diploma, title, testament, seal, warrant, letter, vouchers, certificates, testimonials. (*self-license, self-constitution, self-appointment, autocracy*)

credit relief, trustworthiness, reputation, security, honor, praise, merit, confidence, faith. (*disbelief, distrust, untrustworthiness, shame, insecurity*)

creed belief, catechism, articles, confession, subscription. (*protest, abjuration, recantation, retractation, disbelief, nonsubscription*)

criminal illegal, felonious, vicious, culpable, wrong, iniquitous, sinful, immoral, guilty, nefarious, flagitious. (*lawful, virtuous, right, just, innocent*)

critical nice, delicate, exact, fastidious, discriminating, censorious, accurate, dubious, precarious, ticklish, crucial, important, momentous, hazardous. (*inexact, popular, loose, easy, undiscriminating, safe, determined, decided, settled, retrieved, redressed*)

criticism stricture, censure, animadversion. (*approval, praise*)

cross-grained perverse, wayward, peevish, morose, cantankerous, ill-conditioned. (*genial, pleasant, agreeable, jolly, obliging, accommodating*)

crude raw, undigested, unconsidered, half-studied, harsh, unshaped, unchastened, unfinished, unrefined, ill-prepared. (*well-prepared, well-digested, well-considered, well-studied, ripe, well-adapted, well-proportioned, well-expressed, classical*)

cruel savage, barbarous, pitiless, inexorable, unrelenting, ruthless, truculent, hardhearted, harsh, unmerciful, brutal, inhuman, maleficent, malignant. (*humane, forbearing, generous, merciful, forgiving, benevolent, beneficent*)

crush pulverize, triturate, pound, bray, crumble, overpower, demolish. (*consolidate, compact*)

cuff slap, box, smack, punch, pummel, hustle buffet. (*cudgel, flagellate, thrash, cane, strap, lash*)

cultivate promote, foster, study, improve, fertilize, till, advance, refine, improve, civilize, nourish, cherish. (*neglect, desert, abandon, stifle, prevent*)

cupidity avarice, acquisitiveness, covetousness, stinginess. (*prodigality, extravagance, liberality*)

cure remedy, alleviation, restorative, heal-all, amelioration, reinstatement, restoration, renovation, convalescence. (*aggravation, confirmation*)

curiosity inquisitiveness, interest, wonder, marvel, interrogativeness, rarity, phenomenon, celebrity, oddity, lion. (*indifference, heedlessness, disregard, abstraction, absence, weed, drug, dirt, cipher*)

curious inquiring, inquisitive, scrutinizing, prying, meddling, singular, searching, interrogative, peeping, peering, rare, unique, odd, recondite. (*indifferent, uninquiring, incurious, uninterested*)

current running, prevalent, ordinary, present, popular, general, floating, exoteric, vulgar. (*rejected, obsolete, exploded, confined, private, secret*)

custody keeping, guardianship, conservation, care. (*neglect, betrayal, exposure, abandonment*)

cynical sarcastic, snarling, snappish, sneering, cross-grained, currish, carping. (*genial, lenient*)

daft silly, innocent, idiotic, lunatic, light-headed, cracked. (*sane, sound, sensible, practical*)

dainty choice, rare, refined, tasty, exquisite, luxurious, epicurean. (*common, coarse, unrelishing, nasty, dirty, omnivorous, greedy, gluttonous*)

damp cool, blunt, dishearten, quench, slack, moderate, humid, wet, moist, discourage, discountenance, repress. (*urge, inflame, incite, fan*)

dapper spruce, neat, natty, smart. (*slovenly, awkward, unwieldy, untidy*)

daring adventurous, dashing, bold, courageous, venturesome, dauntless, foolhardy, fearless, brave, intrepid, valorous. (*cautious, timid, inadventurous*)

dark black, dusky, sable, swarthy, opaque, obscure, enigmatical, recondite, abstruse, unintelligible, blind, ignorant, besotted, benighted, dim, shadowy, inexplicable, secret, mysterious, hidden, murky, nebulous, cheerless, dismal, dim, gloomy, somber, joyless, sorrowful. (*white, fair, cheerful*)

dash hurl, cast, throw, subvert, detrude, drive, rush, send, fly, speed, dart, scatter, strike, course. (*raise, reinstate, erect, creep, crawl, lag, hobble*)

daunt terrify, scare, frighten, cow, dishearten, appall, intimidate, confront. (*countenance, encourage, rally, inspirit*)

dawdle lag, dally, idle. (*haste, speed, dash*)

dead defunct, deceased, departed, gone, inanimate, lifeless, insensible, heavy, unconscious, dull, spiritless, cheerless, deserted, torpid, still. (*vital, living, animate, vivacious, susceptible, alive, joyous*)

deadly mortal, fatal, malignant, baleful, pernicious, noxious, venomous, destructive, baneful, implacable. (*vital, life-giving, healthful, wholesome*)

deaf surd, hard of hearing, disinclined, averse, inexorable, insensible, rumbling, inaudible, heedless, dead. (*acute, listening, disposed, interested*)

dear high-priced, costly, expensive, beloved, precious, loved. (*cheap, inexpensive, misliked, vile*)

death departure, demise, decease, dissolution, mortality, fall, failure, termination, cessation, expiration, release, exit. (*birth, rise, life, growth*)

debatable dubious, doubtful, inestimable, uncertain, problematical, floating, unsettled, disputable. (*certain, sure, unquestionable, indisputable*)

debauchery riot, revel, excess, orgies, gluttony. (*moderation, frugality, asceticism*)

debt debit, liability, default, obligation, claim, score, something due. (*liquidation, assets, credit, trust, grace, favor, obligation, accommodation, gift*)

decay *v.* decline, wane, sink, dwindle, rot, wither, perish, waste, ebb, decrease. (*rim, grow, increase*)

decay *n.* declension, waning, sinking, wasting, decrease, corruption, decadence, putrefaction, rottenness, dry rot, consumption, decline. (*rise, growth, birth, increase, fertility, exuberance, luxuriance, prosperity*)

deceit cheat, imposition, trick, fraud, deception, double dealing, delusion, circumvention, guile, beguilement, treachery, sham, insidiousness, indirection, duplicity, cunning, artifice. (*enlightenment, instruction, guidance, reality, verity, fair dealing, honesty, openness*)

deceitful deceptive, delusive, fraudulent, fallacious. (*open, fair, honest, truthful, veracious*)

deceive trick, cheat, beguile, delude, gull, dupe, take in, overreach, mislead, betray, ensnare, entrap, circumvent. (*enlighten, advise, illumine, guide, disabuse, deliver*)

decide determine, fix, settle, adjudicate, terminate, resolve. (*waver, raise, moot, drop, doubt*)

decipher read, spell, interpret, solve, unravel, explain, unfold. (*cipher, symbolize, mystify*)

declaration avowal, exhibition, manifestation, statement, ordinance, assertion, affirmation, profession. (*denial, concealment, suppression*)

decompose analyze, segregate, individualize, resolve, dissolve. (*compound, concoct, mix, organize*)

decorum seemliness, propriety, dignity, order, decency, good manners, good behavior, modesty. (*impropriety, bad manners or behavior*)

decrease diminish, lessen, subside, abate, lower, decline, retrench, curtail, reduce, wane. (*increase, grow, amplify, expand, augment, extend*)

decrepit infirm, weak, crippled, superannuated, effete, broken down, enfeebled, tottering, aged. (*strong, straight, young*)

dedicate devote, consecrate, offer, set, apportion, assign, apply, separate, hallow, set apart. (*alienate, misapply, desecrate, misconvert, misuse*)

deed act, action, commission, achievement, perpetration, instrument, document, muniment, exploit, feat. (*omission, failure, abortion, false witness, innocent, canceling, disproof, invalidation*)

deep profound, subterranean, submerged, designing, abstruse, recondite, learned, low, sagacious, penetrating, thick, obscure, mysterious, occult, intense, heartfelt. (*shallow, superficial, artless*)

deface mar, spoil, injure, disfigure, deform, damage, mutilate, destroy. (*decorate, adorn*)

default lapse, forfeit, omission, defect, delinquency, absence, want, failure. (*maintenance, appearance, plea, satisfaction, forthcoming, supply*)

defeat *n.* frustration, overthrow, discomfiture. (*victory, triumph, success*)

defeat *v.* conquer, overcome, worst, beat, baffle, rout, overthrow, vanquish, frustrate, foil. (*secure, promote, insure, speed, advance, establish*)

defect shortcoming, omission, fault, imperfection, flaw, blemish, want. (*supply, sufficiency*)

defective faulty, imperfect, insufficient, deficient, wanting, short. (*correct, complete, sufficient*)

defense resistance, protection, vindication, plea, justification, excuse, rampart, bulwark, apology, shelter, excuse. (*abandonment, surrender*)

defer delay, postpone, waive, adjourn, prorogue, put off, retard, procrastinate, protract, hinder, prolong. (*expedite, hasten, quicken, press*)

deference respect, consideration, condescension, contention, regard, honor, veneration, submission, reverence, obedience, homage, allegiance. (*disrespect, contumely, contumacy, disregard, slight*)

definite clear, specified, determined, definitive, restricted, specific, certain, ascertained, precise, exact, fixed, limited, bounded, positive. (*vague, unspecified, undetermined, indefinite, obscure, confused, intermingled*)

definition determination, limitation, specification, restriction. (*confusion, vagueness, acceptation*)

defray meet, liquidate, pay, settle, bear, discharge, quit. (*dishonor, repudiate, dissatisfy, misappropriate, embezzle*)

defy scorn, challenge, provoke, oppose, brave. (*accept, give in, concede*)

degree grade, rank, stage, step, extent, measure, mark, rate, position, quality, class, station, range, quantity, amount, limit, order. (*space, mass, magnitude, size, numbers*)

deliberate *v.* consider, meditate, consult, weigh, reflect, ponder, debate, perpend. (*shelve, burke, discard, hazard, chance, risk*)

deliberate *a.* grave, purposed, intentional, designed, determined, resolute, earnest, unbiased, unprejudiced. (*playful, jocose, facetious, irresolute*)

delicious exquisite, luxurious, delightful, dainty, choice. (*coarse, common, unsavory, unpalatable, nauseous, loathsome*)

delight enjoyment, pleasure, happiness, transport, ecstasy, joy, gratification, gladness, rapture, bliss. (*pain, suffering, sorrow, trouble, misery, displeasure, dissatisfaction, disappointment, discomfort*)

delinquent criminal, culprit, offender. (*worthy, paragon, pattern*)

deliver liberate, free, save, utter, set free, surrender, yield, transmit, concede, give up, rescue, pronounce, hand, give, entrust, consign. (*confine, capture, suppress, retain, betray, withdraw, assume*)

democratic popular, leveling, radical, subversive, unlicensed, anarchical, destructive, republican. (*regal, imperial, aristocratic, oligarchical, constitutional, conservative, tyrannical, despotic, autocratic*)

demonstrate prove, show, exhibit, manifest, evince, illustrate. (*disprove, conceal*)

demure sedate, staid, grave, modest, downcast, sober, dispassionate, prudish, discreet. (*lively, vivacious, facetious, wanton, wild, noisy, boisterous*)

denomination name, designation, description, kind, class, order. (*nondescription, misnomer*)

dense slow, thick, stupid, stolid, solid, stout, compact, consolidated, condensed, close, thickset. (*quick, clever, intelligent, rare, rarefied, sparse*)

deny refuse, reject, withhold, negative, contradict, gainsay, disclaim, disavow, disown, oppose. (*grant, accept, concede, admit, affirm, confirm, afford*)

department section, division, portion, function, office, branch, province, line. (*institution, establishment, art, science, literature, service, state, whole*)

dependent hanging, resting, contingent, trusting, relying, subject, relative. (*independent, irrelative, irrespective, absolute, free*)

depression lowering, degradation, debasement, dejection, discouragement, hollow, valley, dip. (*raising, elevation, exaltation, promotion, preferment*)

deprive strip, bereave, despoil, rob, divest, dispossess, abridge, depose, prevent, hinder. (*invest, endow, compensate, enrich, supply, present, reinstate*)

derision scorn, contempt, mockery, irony, sarcasm, contumely, disrespect. (*respect, regard, admiration, reverence*)

descendant offspring, progeny, stock, scion, seed, branch, issue, house, family, lineage. (*author, founder, parent, ancestor, progenitor, stock, root*)

describe draw, delineate, portray, explain, illustrate, define, picture, depict, represent, relate, narrate, recount. (*confound, confuse, mystify, misrepresent, caricature, distort*)

desert wild, waste, wilderness, solitude, void. (*enclosure, field, pasture, garden, oasis*)

design *v.* contemplate, purpose, intend, plan, prepare, project. (*hit, risk, guess, conjecture*)

design *n.* contemplation, purpose, intention, plan, preparation, draft, delineation, sketch, drawing, artifice, cunning, artfulness, guile, contrivance, intent, project, scheme. (*execution, performance, result, issue, construction, structure, candor, fairness*)

desirable expedient, advisable, valuable, acceptable, proper, judicious, beneficial, profitable, good, enviable, delightful. (*undesirable, inadvisable, inexpedient, objectionable, improper, injudicious, unprofitable, evil*)

desire longing, affection, propension, craving, concupiscence, appetency. (*loathing, hate, repugnance, disgust, aversion, abomination, horror*)

despair hopelessness, despondency, desperation. (*hopefulness, elation, anticipation, hilarity, confidence, sanguineness, expectation*)

desperate wild, daring, audacious, determined, reckless, abandoned, rash, furious, frantic, despairing, regardless, mad, desponding, hopeless, inextricable, irremediable. (*cool, calm, cautious*)

despotic autocratic, domineering, arbitrary, arrogant, imperious, self-willed, irresponsible, absolute, cruel, tyrannical. (*limited, constitutional*)

destination purpose, intention, design, consignment, object, end, fate, doom, arrival, application, use, scope, appointment, point, location, goal, aim. (*operation, tendency, exercise, action, movement, design, initiation, project, effort*)

destiny fate, decree, lot, fortune, predestination, necessity, doom, end. (*will, volition, choice, deliberation, freedom, free will*)

destroy demolish, annihilate, subvert, ruin, overthrow, undo, waste, consume. (*restore, reinstate, repair, fabricate, make, construct, create*)

destructive detrimental hurtful, noxious, injurious, deleterious, baleful, baneful, ruinous, subversive. (*wholesome, conservative, preservative, beneficial, reparatory, subsidiary, restorative*)

detraction diminution, deterioration, depreciation, slander, backbiting, derogation. (*augmentation, improvement, enhancement, eulogy, compliment*)

detriment loss, harm, hurt, injury, deterioration, impairment, disadvantage, prejudice, damage, inconvenience. (*enhancement, improvement, remedy, reinstatement, repair, augmentation*)

detrimental injurious, hurtful, pernicious. (*beneficial, profitable, augmentative*)

develop educe, enucleate, eliminate, enunciate, lay open, disclose, unravel, unfold, clear, amplify, expand, enlarge. (*envelop, wrap, obscure, mystify*)

device artifice, expedient, design, plan, stratagem, project, symbol, emblem, show, invention, contrivance, cognizance. (*fair dealing, openness*)

devil satan, lucifer, fiend, arch-fiend, foul fiend, demon. (*archangel, angel, seraph, cherub*)

devise contrive, plan, maneuver, concert, manage. (*miscontrive, mismanage*)

devoid void, wanting, destitute, unendowed, unprovided. (*furnished, supplied, replete, provided*)

devotion piety, devoutness, religiousness, dedication, self-abandonment, consecration, ardor, self-surrender, self-sacrifice, love, attachment. (*impiety, profanity, selfishness, aversion, alienation*)

devour eat, consume, swallow, gorge, gobble, bolt, absorb. (*disgorge, vomit*)

dictate prompt, suggest, enjoin, order, direct, prescribe, decree, instruct, propose, command. (*follow, repeat, obey, echo, answer*)

dictation imperative, imperious, domineering, arbitrary. (*condescending, affable, indulgent, modest, unassuming, suppliant, supplicatory, precatory*)

die expire, depart, perish, decline, decease, disappear, wither, languish, wane, sink, fade, decay, cease. (*begin, originate, rise, live, develop*)

difference separation, destruction, dissimilarity, unlikeness, disagreement, dissonance, discord, contrariety, dissent, distinction, dissimilitude, estrangement, variety. (*community, consociation*)

difficult hard, intricate, involved, perplexing, enigmatical, obscure, trying, arduous, troublesome, uphill, unmanageable, unamenable, reserved, opposed. (*easy, plain, straight, simple, lucid, categorical, tractable, amenable, unreserved, favorable*)

digest sort, arrange, dispose, order, classify, study, ponder, consider, prepare, assimilate, incorporate, convert, methodize, tabulate. (*displace, confound, complicate, derange, disorder, discompose*)

dilemma fix, hobble, quandary, doubt, difficulty, scrape. (*extrication, rebutment, freedom, advantage, superiority, escape, solution, retort*)

diligence care, assiduity, attention, application, heed, industry. (*indifference, carelessness, neglect*)

dingy dull, dusky, rusty, bedimmed, soiled, tarnished, dirty, dim, colorless, obscure, dead, somber. (*bright, burnished, glossy, high-colored*)

diplomacy embassage, ministry, ambassadorship, representation, tact, contrivance, management, negotiation, outwitting, circumvention. (*cancel, recall, conge, miscontrivance, mismanagement*)

diplomatic judicious, knowing, wise, prudent, well-contrived, clever, astute, politic, discreet, well-planned, well-conceived, sagacious, well-managed. (*injudicious, bungling, stultifying, ill-managed, undiplomatic*)

direction course, tendency, inclination, line, control, command, bearing, superscription, order, address. (*misdirection, deviation, miscontrol, misinstruction, aberration*)

directly straightly, straightaway, immediately, undeviatingly, at once, promptly, quickly, instantly. (*indirectly, by-and-by, interveniently*)

disability disqualification, impotency, unfitness, incapacity, forfeiture, incompetency. (*qualification, recommendation, fitness, deserving, merit*)

disappoint betray, deceive, frustrate, baffle, delude, vex, mortify, defeat, foil. (*realize, justify*)

discernible visible, conspicuous, manifest, palpable, apparent, plain, perceptible, evident. (*invisible, inconspicuous, obscure, indiscernible, impalpable, microscopic, minute*)

discipline order, strictness, training, government, instruction, drilling, control, coercion, punishment, organization. (*disorder, confusion, rebellion, mutiny, encouragement, reward, disorganization*)

discomfort disquiet, vexation, annoyance, trouble, unpleasantness, disagreeableness. (*comfort, ease, pleasantness, agreeableness*)

disconcert abash, confuse, confound, upset, baffle, derange, discompose, thwart, disturb, defeat, fret, interrupt, vex, ruffle, disorder, unsettle, frustrate, discomfit. (*encourage, rally, countenance*)

discreet discerning, wise, prudent, circumspect, cautious, wary, regulative, sensible, judicious. (*undiscerning, blind, foolish, imprudent, indiscreet, unrestrained, reckless*)

discrimination penetration, sagacity, acuteness, nicety, shrewdness, judgment, discernment, insight, distinction. (*dullness, confusedness, indiscriminateness, shortsightedness, hebetude, indiscernment*)

disease complaint, disorder, illness, indisposition, distemper, ailment, malady, sickness. (*health, convalescence, sanity, salubrity*)

disgust nausea, loathing, abomination, aversion, dislike, repugnance, abhorrence, distaste. (*desire, liking, partiality, predilection, relish, fondness, longing, avidity*)

dismal dreary, ominous, foreboding, lonesome, cheerless, gloomy, sad, depressed, lugubrious, funereal, sorrowful, melancholy, tragic, blank. (*gay, propitious, promising, cheerful, lively, elated*)

dispatch expedite, send, accelerate, hasten, execute, conclude, get rid of. (*retard, detain, obstruct, impede, retain*)

dispel disperse, scatter, dissipate, drive away, dismiss. (*collect, recall, summon, convene, congregate, conglomerate, mass, accumulate*)

disperse dispel, scatter, disseminate, separate, break up, spread abroad, deal out, distribute, dissipate. (*collect, summon, recall, gather, concentrate*)

dispute argue, question, canvass, contest, contend, challenge, debate, controvert, controversy, difference, gainsay, impugn, quarrel, altercation. (*waive, concede, allow, forgo*)

dissemble disguise, conceal, repress, smother, restrain, cloak. (*exhibit, manifest, protrude, vaunt*)

disseminate spread, propagate, preach, proclaim, publish, promulgate, scatter, circulate. (*repress, suppress, stifle, discountenance, extirpate*)

dissolute abandoned, profligate, loose, licentious, wanton, vicious. (*upright, conscientious*)

distance interval, removal, separation, interspace, remoteness, absence, space, length. (*proximity, nearness, adjacency, contiguity, neighborhood*)

distinct separate, independent, unconnected, detached, disjoined, unlike, definite, obvious, different, dissimilar, clear, conspicuous, plain, perspicuous. (*united, consolidated, conjoined, one*)

distinction difference, separation, dignity, eminence. (*unity, identity, debasement, insignificance*)

distinguish discern, descry, perceive, characterize, make famous, know, discriminate, see, discover, separate, divide, dissimilate, differentiate. (*miss, overlook, confound, confuse*)

distinguished illustrious, noted, celebrated, conspicuous, eminent, marked, famous. (*obscure, inconspicuous, hidden, not famous*)

distress harass, embarrass, trouble, grieve, annoy, vex, mortify, pain, disturb, afflict, worry. (*soothe, compose, please, gratify, gladden, console*)

disturb derange, discompose, disorder, discommode, plague, confuse, rouse, agitate, annoy, trouble, interrupt, incommode, worry, vex, molest, disquiet. (*order, collocate, arrange, pacify, soothe*)

diversion detour, divergence, deviation, recreation, amusement, pastime, sport, enjoyment. (*continuity, directness, procedure, business, task*)

divide separate, dissect, bisect, portion, part, divorce, segregate, sever, sunder, deal out, disunite, keep apart, part among, allot, distribute, multiply. (*unite, collocate, classify, convene, congregate, conglomerate, conglutinate, commingle, join, consociate*)

divorce separate, disconnect, dissever, divert, alienate. (*conjoin, unite, connect, apply, reconcile*)

do work, act, accomplish, execute, achieve, transact, finish, enact, perform, produce, complete. (*undo, mar, neglect, omit*)

docile compliant, amenable, easily managed, yielding, gentle, quiet, pliant, tractable, teachable, tame. (*intractable, stubborn, obstinate, self-willed*)

dogmatic doctrinal, theological, imperious, dictatorial, authoritative, arrogant, magisterial, self-opinionated, positive. (*practical, active, moderate*)

doleful dolorous, rueful, melancholy, piteous, somber, sorrowful, woebegone, dismal. (*merry, joyful, gay, blithe, beaming*)

dominion power, authority, rule, tyranny, despotism, government, control, empire, sway, realm, territory, jurisdiction. (*weakness, submission, subjugation, inferiority, servitude*)

dormant sleeping, slumbering, latent, undeveloped, quiescent, inert. (*vigilant, wakeful, active*)

doubt dubiousness, dubitation, scruple, hesitation, suspense, distrust, suspicion, perplexity, uncertainty, ambiguity, difficulty, indecision. (*certainty, clearness, precision, determination, decision*)

drain draw, strain, drip, percolate, drop, exhaust, empty, dry. (*replenish, fill, supply, pour*)

draw drag, pull, attract, induce, haul, entice, inhale, sketch, delineate, describe. (*push, carry, propel, throw, repel, drive, compel, impel, thrust*)

dreadful fearful, shocking, monstrous, dire, terrible, frightful, terrific, horrible, alarming, awful. (*encouraging, inspiriting, assuring, promising*)

dreamy fanciful, visionary, speculative, abstracted, absent, foggy. (*collected, earnest, attentive, awake, active, energetic, practical*)

dregs refuse, sediment, offal, lees, off-scouring, dross, trash. (*cream, flower, pink, pickings, bouquet*)

dress garniture, preparation, arrangement, clothing, habiliments, accoutrements, vestments, uniform, raiment, apparel, attire, clothes, array, garments, livery, costume, garb, investiture. (*nudity, disorder, disarrangement, undress, deshabille*)

drift tendency, direction, motion, tenor, meaning, purport, object, intention, purpose, scope, aim, result, issue, inference, conclusion, end, course. (*aimlessness, pointlessness, vagueness, unmeaningness, indefiniteness, confusedness, aberrancy*)

drink imbibe, swallow, quaff, absorb, drain, draught. (*disgorge, replenish, pour, exude, water*)

drivel fatuity, nonsense, trifling, snivel, babble. (*soundness, coherence, substance, solidity*)

droll whimsical, comical, odd, queer, amusing, laughable, funny, comic, fantastic, farcical. (*sad, lamentable, tragic, lugubrious, funereal*)

drop ooze, emanate, distill, percolate, fall, decline, descend, faint, droop. (*evaporate, rally, rise*)

drown sink, immerse, swamp, overwhelm, engulf, deluge, inundate, submerge. (*dry, drain*)

dry arid, parched, moistureless, juiceless, barren, tame, sarcastic, vapid, lifeless, dull, tedious, uninteresting, monotonous. (*moist, fresh, juicy*)

dull stupid, stolid, doltish, insensible, callous, heavy, gloomy, dismal, cloudy, turbid, opaque, dowdy, sluggish, sad, tiresome, commonplace, dead. (*sharp, clew, lively, animated, sensible, cheerful*)

durable lasting, permanent, stable, persistent, abiding, constant, continuing. (*evanescent, transient, impermanent, unstable*)

duty obligation, part, business, responsibility, allegiance, function, office, province, calling, trust, commission, service. (*freedom, exemption, immunity, license, dispensation, desertion, dereliction*)

dwindle pine, waste, diminish, decrease, fall off, decline, melt. (*expand, enlarge, increase, grow*)

e

early soon, betimes, forward, shortly, quickly, erelong, anon, matutinal, beforehand. (*late, tardily, backward, vespertinal, belated*)

earn merit, acquire, achieve, obtain, win, gain, deserve. (*forfeit, forgo, waste, lose, spend, squander*)

earnest eager, serious, intent, determined, strenuous, solemn, grave, warm, fervent, intense, ardent. (*indifferent, idle, playful, desultory, irresolute, sportive, jesting, flippant*)

easy quiet, comfortable, manageable, indulgent, facile, lenient, unconstrained, gentle, not difficult, unconcerned, self-possessed. (*uneasy, disturbed, uncomfortable, difficult, unmanageable, hard, exacting*)

economy administration, dispensation, management, rule, arrangement, distribution, husbanding. (*maladministration, waste, misrule, mismanagement*)

ecstasy rapture, inspiration, fervor, frenzy, transport, emotion, joy, delight, enthusiasm, happiness. (*indifference, coolness, dullness, weariness*)

edifice structure, building, tenement, fabric. (*ruin, heap, demolition, dismantlement*)

educate instruct, nurture, discipline, train, teach, develop, ground, school, initiate. (*miseducate*)

effective powerful, conducive, operative, cogent, telling, able, potent, talented, efficacious, efficient, serviceable, effectual. (*weak, ineffective*)

effort trial, attempt, endeavor, exertion. (*failure, misadventure, unsuccess, frustration, futility*)

egotism conceit, vanity, self-assertion, self-conceit, self-praise, self-exaltation, conceitedness. (*consideration, deference, self-abnegation*)

elastic ductile, extensile, alterable, resilient, modifiable, flexible, buoyant, springy. (*tough, unchangeable, rigid, unflexible, inelastic, crystallized*)

elated cheered, joyed, inspirited, overjoyed, proud, inflated. (*depressed, dispirited, disappointed*)

elegance beauty, grace, refinement, symmetry, gracefulness, taste. (*deformity, awkwardness, inelegance, disproportion, ungracefulness, coarseness*)

elegant graceful, lovely, well formed, well made, symmetrical, accomplished, polished, refined, handsome. (*inelegant, deformed, unsymmetrical, ill-proportioned, ungraceful, coarse, rude*)

elementary physical, material, natural, primary, rudimentary, simple, inchoate, component, constituent, ultimate. (*immaterial, incorporeal, impalpable, compound, collective, aggregate*)

eligible capable, suitable, worthy, desirable, preferable, choice, prime. (*undesirable, worthless*)

elude escape, avoid, baffle, shun, eschew, evade, parry, fence, mock, frustrate. (*encounter, meet, confront, court, dare, defy*)

embalm conserve, preserve, treasure, store, enshrine, consecrate. (*expose, desecrate, abandon*)

embarrass entangle, disconcert, trouble, perplex, confuse, hamper, clog, distress, puzzle, encumber. (*extricate, liberate, expedite, facilitate*)

embezzle appropriate, confuse, falsify, peculate, misappropriate. (*square, balance, clear*)

embody express, methodize, systematize, codify, incorporate, aggregate, integrate, compact, introduce, enlist, combine. (*eliminate, segregate*)

embrace clasp, comprehend, include, hug, comprise, contain, close, embody, incorporate. (*exclude, reject, except*)

emergency crisis, conjuncture, pitch, embarrassment, strait, necessity, exigency, casualty, difficulty. (*rescue, deliverance, solution, subsidence*)

emotion passion, feeling, excitement, agitation, perturbation, trepidation, tremor. (*indifference, lack of feeling*)

emphatic earnest, forcible, strong, energetic, impressive, positive, important, special, egregious, consummate. (*mild, unemphatic, cool, unimpassioned, unimportant, ordinary, unnoticeable*)

employ use, apply, economize, occupy, engage, engross. (*discard, dismiss, misuse, misemploy*)

empower enable, commission, encourage, qualify, delegate, warrant, sanction, direct, authorize. (*hinder, prevent, discourage, disable, disqualify*)

empty vacant, void, unencumbered, unobstructed, unoccupied, waste, uninhabited, unfrequented, devoid, vacuous, destitute, unfilled, unfurnished, untenanted, evacuated, deficient, weak, silly, idle, senseless. (*full, occupied, encumbered, obstructed, cultivated, colonized, inhabited, informed, well-instructed, experienced, sensible, significant, forcible, important, substantial*)

enamor captivate, fascinate, enslave, charm, endear, bewitch, enchain. (*repel, disgust, estrange*)

enclose shut, encircle, environ, include, circumscribe, envelop, wrap, afforest. (*open, disclose, exclude, bare, expose, develop*)

encourage embolden, rally, enhearten, cheer, incite, stimulate, foster, cherish, promote, urge, impel, advance, countenance, forward, reassure, animate, inspirit, prompt, abet. (*deter, discourage*)

endanger imperil, expose, peril, jeopardize, hazard, risk. (*cover, defend, protect, shield, screen*)

endear attach, conciliate, gain. (*estrange, alienate, embitter*)

endless interminable, illimitable, unending, unceasing, boundless, deathless, imperishable, everlasting, perpetual, eternal, infinite. (*terminable*)

endorse sanction, approve, subscribe, accept. (*protest, repudiate, cancel, abjure, renounce*)

endowment gift, provision, benefit, benefaction, capacity, attainment, qualification. (*impoverishment, spoliation, disendowment, incapacity*)

enforce urge, compel, require, exact, exert, strain. (*relax, waive, forgo, remit, abandon*)

engage promise, undertake, vouch, employ, occupy, hire, gain, attract, enlist, stipulate, pledge, agree, buy, adopt, involve. (*decline, refuse, withdraw, dismiss, discard, extricate, disengage*)

enigmatical puzzling, perplexing, obscure, mystic. (*lucid, explanatory, plain, self-evident*)

enlarge amplify, expand, augment, broaden, swell, stretch out, extend, stretch, dilate, increase. (*narrow, lessen, contract, restrict, diminish, curtail*)

enlighten illumine, edify, instruct, illuminate, inform, teach. (*mislead, darken, confound, obscure*)

enlist enter, register, enroll, incorporate, embody. (*withdraw, erase, expunge, dismiss, disband*)

enmity discord, hate, hostility, malevolence, maliciousness, aversion, malignity, ill-feeling, animosity, opposition, bitterness, acrimony, asperity. (*friendship, love, affection, esteem, friendliness, cordiality*)

enormous huge, immense, gigantic, colossal, elephantine, vast, gross, monstrous, prodigious. (*diminutive, insignificant, trivial, venial, average*)

enough sufficient, ample, plenty, abundance. (*bare, scant, insufficient, inadequate, short*)

ensue follow, accrue, supervene, befall. (*precede, threaten, premonish, forewarn*)

ensure fix, determine, secure, seal. (*imperil, hazard, jeopardize, forfeit*)

enterprising active, bold, daring, adventurous, speculative, dashing, venturesome. (*inactive, timid, inadventurous, cautious*)

entertain harbor, maintain, conceive, foster, receive, recreate, amuse. (*eject, exclude, deny, debar, annoy, weary, bore, tire.*)

enthusiasm excitement, frenzy, sensation, inspiration, transport, rapture, warmth, fervor, fervency, zeal, ardor, vehemence, passion, devotion. (*coldness, callousness, indifference, disaffection, repugnance, alienation, contempt*)

entire whole, complete, unimpaired, total, perfect, all, full, solid, integral, undiminished. (*partial*)

entitle qualify, empower, fit, enable, name, style, denominate, designate, characterize. (*disqualify, disentitle, disable, not designate, not characterize*)

entreat implore, obsecrate, beg, beseech, importune, crave, solicit, supplicate, pray, ask, urge, petition. (*command, insist, bid, enjoin*)

enumerate specify, name, number, recount, detail, reckon, compute, calculate, call over. (*confound, miscount, misreckon*)

ephemeral transient, evanescent, fleeting, fugacious, fugitive, momentary. (*abiding, persistent*)

equable uniform, regular, proportionate, even, smooth, easy. (*irregular, desultory, variable, fitful,*

equal uniform, commensurate, coordinate, adequate, alike, equivalent, even, equable, sufficient, impartial, coextensive, smooth. (*unequal, incommensurate, incoordinate, inadequate, disparate*)

equitable fair, just, proportionate, impartial, upright, proper, reasonable, evenhanded, honest. (*unfair, unjust, disproportionate, partial*)

erase obliterate, efface, expunge, blot, cancel. (*mark, write, delineate*)

erect elevate, raise, establish, plant, uplift, construct, build, found, institute, set up. (*lower, supplant, subvert, depress, remove, destroy, demolish*)

erratic desultory, aberrant, abnormal, flighty, changeful, capricious. (*regular, normal, methodical, calculable, unalterable, steady, undeviating*)

error fault, mistake, blunder, falsity, deception, fallacy, untruth, hallucination. (*correction, correctness, truth, accuracy, soundness, rectification*)

escape elude, decamp, abscond, fly, flee, evade, avoid. (*incur, confront, encounter, meet, suffer*)

essential innate, inherent, requisite, necessary, vital, immanent, indispensable, leading. (*accidental, qualitative, quantitative, promotive, regulative, induced, imported, adventitious*)

establish plant, fix, settle, found, demonstrate, organize, confirm, institute, prove, substantiate. (*supplant, unsettle, break up, disestablish*)

esteem price, value, consider, deem, judge, believe, estimate, think, regard, affect, appreciate, revere, honor, respect, admire, venerate, prize, love, like. (*disregard, disaffect, dislike, undervalue, underrate, decry, deprecate*)

eternal infinite, endless, everlasting, deathless, imperishable, never-dying, ceaseless, ever-living, perpetual, undying, unceasing. (*ephemeral, transient, temporal, fleeting, evanescent, sublunary*)

etiquette manners, breeding, fashion, conventionality. (*boorishness, rudeness, misobservance*)

evaporate melt, colliquate, liquefy, vaporize, disappear, dissolve, exhale, distill. (*consolidate, compact, solidify, indurate, crystallize*)

event occurrence, circumstance, episode, adventure, issue, accident, result, fact, incident. (*cause, antecedent, operation, inducement, contribution, convergence, predisposition, tendency*)

eventful remarkable, memorable, signal, important, marked, noted, critical, stirring, notable. (*ordinary, unmarked, unimportant, eventless, uninteresting, characterless, trivial*)

evidence manifestation, attraction, averment, testimony, disposition, declaration, appearance, sign, token, proof, indication, exemplification, illustration. (*surmise, conjecture, counterevidence, disproof, refutation, concealment, suppression, misindication, fallacy*)

evident plain, visible, conspicuous, manifest, indisputable, obvious, clear, palpable, incontrovertible. (*doubtful, obscure, questionable, uncertain, dubious*)

evil ill, noxious, deleterious, wrong, bad, mischievous, hurtful, sinful, unhappy, adverse, unpropitious, wicked, corrupt, harmful, unfair, notorious, miserable, sorrowful. (*wholesome, beneficial, right, virtuous, holy, pure, happy, fortunate*)

exactly precisely, accurately, correspondently. (*loosely, inadequately, incorrectly, differently, otherwise*)

exaggerate amplify, enlarge, heighten, magnify, overstate, overdraw, strain, overpaint, overestimate. (*disparage, attenuate, palliate, understate*)

examine weigh, ponder, investigate, perpend, test, scrutinize, criticize, prove, study, discuss, inquire, search, overhaul, explore, inspect. (*discard, conjecture, guess, slur, misconsider, misinvestigate*)

example sample, specimen, pattern, model, copy, illustration, instance, issue, development. (*stock, material, substance, law, rule, character*)

except exclude, save, bar, segregate, negative. (*count, include, reckon, state, classify, propound*)

exceptional rare, peculiar, uncommon, irregular, unusual, abnormal. (*common, regular, normal, usual, ordinary*)

excessive enormous, undue, exorbitant, over-much, superabundant, superfluous, unreasonable, immoderate, inordinate, extravagant. (*insufficient, scant, inadequate*)

excuse exculpate, absolve, pardon, forgive, overlook, condone, remit, indulge, justify, vindicate, defend, acquit, mitigate, extenuate, release, exempt, exonerate. (*charge, inculpate, condemn*)

execrable detestable, loathsome, accursed, cursed, villainous, diabolical, hateful, abominable, damnable. (*desirable, eligible, respectable, laudable*)

exemplary laudable, praiseworthy, conspicuous, honorable, wary, meritorious, worthy, excellent. (*detestable, objectionable, exceptionable*)

exempt free, irresponsible, unamenable, clear, liberated, privileged, absolved. (*subject, responsible, liable, amenable*)

exercise exertion, use, practice, application, training, employment, drill. (*rest, ease, relaxation*)

exhaust empty, spend, consume, debilitate, waste, void, drain, weaken, weary. (*fill, replenish*)

existence being, entity, creature. (*nonentity, nonexistence, chimera*)

expand swell, dilate, spread, extend, open, diffuse, develop, unfold, enlarge, amplify. (*contract, curtail, attenuate, restrict, condense*)

expect anticipate, await, forecast, forebode, wait for, rely on, look for, foresee. (*welcome, hail, recognize, greet, realize*)

expediency utility, advantage, interest. (*inexpediency, disadvantage, inutility, detriment*)

expend spend, disburse, lay out, waste, consume, use. (*save, husband, economize*)

expense price, cost, charge, payment, expenditure, outlay. (*income, profit, receipt*)

experience *n.* experiment, trial, test, proof, habit, knowledge. (*ignorance, inexperience*)

experience *v.* try, feel, undergo, encounter, endure. (*evade, escape, miss, lose*)

explain expound, teach, illustrate, clear up, interpret, elucidate, decipher. (*mystify, obscure*)

explanation exposition, explication, interpretation, sense, description. (*mystification, obscuration, confusion, misinterpretation*)

explicit plain, detailed, inobscure, declaratory, categorical, stated, distinctly stated, express, definite, determinate. (*implicit, implied, hinted*)

expression countenance, look, indication, phrase, term, face, feature, lineament. (*falsification, misstatement, solecism, enigma, suppression*)

exquisite choice, rare, refined, delicate, perfect, matchless, intense, consummate, delicious. (*common, coarse, ordinary*)

extend prolong, stretch, expand, enlarge, increase, augment, reach, spread, amplify, avail, apply. (*curtail, contract, restrict, narrow, limit*)

extent degree, distance, quantity, space, size. (*diminution, restriction, limitation*)

extinguish abolish, destroy, extirpate, eradicate, kill, quench, annihilate, put out. (*implant, replenish, cherish, promote, invigorate, propagate, establish, confirm, secure*)

extortionate hard, closefisted, severe, rigorous, exorbitant, preposterous, monstrous, exacting. (*liberal, indulgent, bountiful, reasonable, fair, moderate*)

extraordinary unwonted, uncommon, peculiar, unusual, unprecedented, wonderful, marvelous, prodigious, monstrous, remarkable, strange, preposterous. (*wonted, common, usual, ordinary*)

extravagant wild, monstrous, preposterous, absurd, prodigal, wasteful, reckless, excessive, lavish, profuse, abnormal. (*sound, sober, consistent, rational, fair, economical, frugal, careful*)

extreme terminal, final, remote, utmost, farthest, last, extravagant, immoderate, most violent, distant, ultimate. (*initial, primal, moderate, judicious*)

fable apologue, fiction, parable, allegory, romance, invention, fabrication, untruth, novel, falsehood. (*history, narrative, fact*)

facetious witty, funny, humorous, jocular, waggish, playful, droll, jocose. (*heavy, matter-of-fact, dull, grave, serious, lugubrious, somber, saturnine*)

facile docile, tractable, manageable, indulgent, weak, irresolute, easy, affable, flexible, characterless, pliable. (*sturdy, obstinate, determined, resolute, pigheaded, crusty, inflexible, self-willed, independent, self-reliant*)

facility ease, address, readiness, quickness, adroitness, dexterity, pliancy. (*labor, awkwardness, difficulty*)

fact truth, deed, occurrence, certainty, circumstance, event, reality. (*fiction, supposition, falsehood, unreality, lie, delusion, chimera, invention, romance*)

fade fall, fail, decline, sink, droop, dwindle, vanish, change, pale, bleach, set, etiolate. (*rise, increase, grow, bloom, flourish, abide, stand, last*)

faint weak, languid, fatigued, unenergetic, timid, irresolute, feeble, exhausted, halfhearted, obscure, dim, pale, faded, inconspicuous. (*strong, vigorous, energetic, fresh, daring, resolute, prominent*)

fair open, clear, spotless, unspotted, untarnished, reasonable, unblemished, serene, beautiful, just, honorable, equitable, impartial. (*lowering, dull, foul, disfigured, ugly, unfair, dishonorable*)

faithful true, firm, attached, loyal, accurate, close, consistent, correspondent, exact, equivalent, staunch, incorruptible. (*false, fickle, capricious*)

fallacy sophistry, error, blunder, misconception, bugbear, fiction, delusion, chimera. (*truth, verity*)

false untrue, erroneous, fallacious, sophistical, spurious, deceptive, fabrication, counterfeit, mendacious, sham, mock, bogus, unfaithful, fib, falsity, fiction, dishonorable, faithless. (*true, correct*)

falsify mistake, misinterpret, misrepresent, belie, betray, garble, cook. (*verify, correct, rectify*)

falter halt, hesitate, hobble, slip, dubitate, stammer, demur, waver, flinch, vacillate. (*proceed, run, speed, flow, discourse, determine, persevere, resolve, career*)

familiar household, common, free, frank, affable, everyday, well-acquainted, accustomed, conversant, intimate. (*uncommon, rare, strange*)

famous renowned, glorious, celebrated, illustrious, far-famed. (*unknown, obscure, unsung, inglorious*)

fanciful grotesque, chimerical, unreal, imaginary, quaint, eccentric, freakish, humorous, erroneous, capricious, whimsical, erratic, absurd, fitful. (*natural, literal, regular, real, sober, ordinary, truthful, accurate, correct, orderly, calculable*)

fancy thought, belief, idea, supposition, imagination, caprice, notion, conceit, vagary, inclination, whim, humor, predilection, desire. (*object, subject, fact, reality, order, law, truth, system, verity*)

fashion form, shape, guise, style, appearance, character, figure, mold, mode, custom, practice, usage, manner, way, ceremony. (*person, work, dress, speech, formlessness, shapelessness, derangement, eccentricity, strangeness, outlandishness*)

fast firm, secure, fixed, constant, steadfast, stable, unyielding, unswerving, rapid, accelerated, wild, reckless, dissipated, gay. (*loose, insecure*)

fastidious critical, overnice, overrefined, censorious, punctilious, particular, squeamish, dainty. (*easy, indulgent, uncritical, coarse, omnivorous*)

fat corpulent, fleshy, brawny, pursy, rich, luxuriant, portly, stout, fertile, unctuous, obese, oleaginous. (*lean, slender, attenuated, emaciated*)

fatal calamitous, deadly, destructive, mortal, lethal. (*beneficial, wholesome, nutritious, vitalizing, salubrious, restorative, slight, superficial, harmless.*)

fate necessity, destiny, lot, end, fortune, doom. (*will, choice, decision, freedom, independence*)

fault defect, error, imperfection, flaw, misdeed, failure, omission, want, drawback. (*sufficiency, correctness, completeness, perfection*)

favor permission, grace, concession, predilection, gift, civility, benefit, kindness, goodwill, regard, condescension, preference, boon, countenance, patronage. (*refusal, denial, prohibition*)

favorable permissive, indulgent, propitious, concessive, partial, fond, liberal, advantageous, auspicious, friendly. (*reluctant, unpropitious, unfavorable, impartial*)

fear apprehension, solicitude, alarm, fright, dread, terror, trepidation, dismay, consternation, misgiving, horror, timidity, awe. (*assurance, confidence, courage, fearlessness, trust, boldness*)

feeble wretched, weak, poor, frail, debilitated, dull, forceless, puny, nerveless, enfeebled, enervated, faint, infirm, incomplete, vain, fruitless, scanty, pitiable. (*strong, robust, active, effective*)

feeling touch, sensation, contact, pathos, tenderness, impression, consciousness, sensibility, emotion, sentiment, passion, sensitiveness. (*insensibility, callousness, imperturbability, inexcitability, coldness, insensateness*)

felicitous happy, timely, successful, opportune, joyous. (*unfortunate, unhappy, untimely, unsuccessful, disastrous, inopportune, sad*)

feminine female, womanish, womanly. (*manly, masculine, manful*)

fertile rich, luxuriant, teeming, productive, exuberant, causative, conducive, pregnant, fraught, prolific, fecund, fruitful, ingenious, inventive. (*poor, sterile, barren, unproductive, ineffective, inconducive, fruitless, inoperative, uninventive, unimaginative*)

fickle fanciful, fitful, capricious, irresolute, changeable, vacillating, mutable, unreliable, veering, shifting, variable, restless, inconstant, unstable. (*sober, orderly, reliable, well-regulated, calculable, trustworthy, steady, uniform*)

fiction invention, fabrication, creation, figment, fable, falsehood, romance, myth. (*fact, truth*)

fidelity fealty, attachment, truthfulness, allegiance, accuracy, closeness, exactness, faithfulness, integrity, loyalty, honesty. (*treachery, disloyalty*)

fiery hot, vehement, ardent, fervent, fierce, passionate, irascible, choleric, excited, enkindled, glowing, fervid, impassioned, irritable, hot-brained. (*cold, icy, indifferent, phlegmatic, passionless, unimpassioned, mild, quenched, extinguished, tame*)

fight battle, contention, struggle, conflict, combat, contest, action, engagement, encounter. (*pacification, reconciliation*)

figure aspect, shape, emblem, type, image, condition, appearance, form, symbol, metaphor, likeness, delineation, illustration. (*misrepresentation, deformity, disfigurement*)

fill replenish, content, supply, satisfy, gorge, glut, occupy, appoint, stuff, store, rise, swell, glow, expand, increase. (*exhaust, deprive, drain, dissatisfy, stint, vacate, misappoint, subside, shrink*)

final terminal, last, latest, conclusive, definite, developed, ultimate, decisive. (*initiative, open*)

find meet, confront, ascertain, experience, perceive, discover, furnish, invent. (*miss, elude, overlook, lose, withhold, withdraw, miscontrive*)

fine thin, minute, slender, delicate, pure, smooth, filmy, gauzy, keen, artistic, choice, finished, high, grand, noble, sensitive, refined, generous, honorable, excellent, superior, pretentious, handsome, pretty, beautiful, showy, elegant, ostentatious, presumptuous, nice, casuistical, subtle. (*coarse, large, rough, blunt, rude, unfinished, mean*)

finical affected, overnice, dandyish, dallying, foppish, spruce, factitious, euphuistic. (*unaffected, effective, practical, energetic, real, genuine, natural*)

finish complete, perfect, accomplish, conclude, achieve, end, shape, terminate. (*begin, commence, start, undertake, fail, miscontrive, mismanage, botch*)

first leading, primary, pristine, original, foremost, primitive, principal, primeval, highest, chief, earliest, onmost. (*subsequent, secondary*)

fit decent, befitting, meet, apt, fitting, adapted, seemly, appropriate, becoming, decorous, qualified, congruous, peculiar, particular, suitable, prepared, adequate, calculated, contrived, expedient, proper, ripe. (*awkward, ungainly, misfitting, ill-suited*)

fix place, settle, fasten, link, locate, attach, consolidate, tie, plant, root, establish, secure, determine, decide. (*displace, unsettle, disarrange, remove, uproot, transfer, transplant, disestablish*)

flat dull, tame, insipid, vapid, spiritless, level, horizontal, absolute, even, downright, mawkish, tasteless, lifeless. (*exciting, animated, interesting*)

flexible pliant, lithe, supple, elastic, easy, indulgent, ductile, flexible, yielding, pliable. (*tough, rigid, inelastic, inflexible, hard, inexorable*)

flimsy gauzy, poor, thin, transparent, trifling, trivial, puerile, insane, slight, superficial, weak, shallow. (*solid, sound, irrefragable, substantial*)

flippant pert, forward, superficial, thoughtless, saucy, malapert. (*flattering, servile, obsequious*)

flock herd, congregate, throng, assemble, crowd. (*disperse, scatter, separate, segregate*)

flood deluge, inundation, abundance. (*drought, drain, ebb, scarcity, subsidence*)

florid rubicund, flowery, sanguine, ornate, overwrought, meretricious. (*pallid, exsanguineous, bare, unadorned, nude, sober, chaste*)

flounder roll, blunder, bungle, boggle, wallow, tumble. (*emerge, flow, course, career, speed, rise*)

flourish prosper, thrive, speed, triumph, brandish, wave. (*fail, fade, decline, miscarry, founder*)

flow stream, issue, progress, glide, course, career, run. (*halt, stick, stickle, stop, hesitate, fail*)

flurry agitate, excite, worry, ruffle, fluster. (*soothe, compose, quiet, calm, mesmerize*)

foible peccadillo, failing, fault, weakness, infirmity. (*crime, atrocity, enormity, sin*)

follow pursue, chase, accompany, obey, imitate, succeed, result, ensue, attend, shadow, observe, copy. (*avoid, elude, quit, disobey, precede*)

folly madness, nonsense, misconduct, imprudence, silliness, foolishness, weakness, absurdity, imbecility. (*sense, wisdom, sanity, judgment, prudence, sobriety*)

foment excite, cherish, fan, propagate, encourage. (*allay, extinguish, discourage, extirpate*)

fond loving, attached, affectionate, foolish, silly, weak, doting, empty, enamored, devoted. (*unloving, averse, unaffectionate, strong-minded*)

foolish senseless, idiotic, crazed, shallow, weak, silly, injudicious, irrational, absurd, contemptible, objectionable, witless, brainless, imbecile, preposterous, ridiculous, nonsensical, simple. (*sensible, sane, deep, clear-sighted, sound, sagacious*)

forbidding repulsive, deterrent, prohibitory, offensive. (*attractive, encouraging, alluring, seductive, permissive*)

force power, strength, agency, instrumentality, compulsion, cogency, vigor, might, dint, vehemence, pressure, host, army, coercion, validity, violent. (*feebleness, weakness, counteraction, neutralization*)

foreign strange, exotic, outlandish, alien, irrelevant, extraneous. (*domestic, native, congenial, pertinent, germane*)

forfeit fine, penalty, mulct, amercement, damages, loss. (*premium, bribe, douceur, remuneration, compensation, reward, gratuity*)

forge work, frame, produce, elaborate, fabricate, counterfeit, feign, falsify, form, shape, make falsely. (*shatter, batter, shiver, blast, fuse, detect*)

forget lose, pretermit, unlearn, obliviate, overlook. (*acquire, learn, remember, recollect, mind*)

form shape, mold, fashion, constitute, arrange, frame, construct, contrive, make, produce, create, devise. (*deform, dislocate, distort, dissipate*)

formal regular, complete, shapely, sufficient, correct, stately, dignified, ceremonious, pompous, stiff, precise, explicit, exact, affected, methodical. (*irregular, incomplete, informal, inadequate, incorrect, easy, unassuming, unceremonious*)

formality ceremony, parade, affectation, stateliness, punctiliousness, etiquette. (*informality, casualness, simplicity*)

former preceding, antecedent, previous, prior, earlier, ancient, bygone, anterior, first-mentioned, foregoing. (*succeeding, subsequent, posterior, latter, modern, coming, future*)

fortunate lucky, propitious, happy, felicitous, prosperous, auspicious, providential, successful. (*unlucky, unfortunate, unhappy, infelicitous*)

forward advanced, ready, eager, anxious, obtrusive, self-assertive, impertinent, progressive, onward, confident, bold, presumptuous. (*tardy, backward, reluctant, indifferent, slow, modest*)

found establish, institute, fix, set, build, set up, base, endow, rest, ground, plant, root. (*disestablish, subvert, supplant, uproot*)

foundation institution, establishment, footing, base, basis, origin, ground, groundwork, rudiments, substratum, underlying principle. (*disestablishment, superstructure*)

fragrant odorous, scented, perfumed, balmy, sweet-smelling, aromatic, sweet-scented, odoriferous, spicy. (*inodorous, scentless, fetid*)

frail irresolute, erring, mutable. (*resolute, virtuous, lasting*)

frank ingenuous, candid, open, unreserved, artless, free, familiar, honest, easy, sincere, outspoken, plain. (*disingenuous, close, reserved*)

freakish sportful, frisky, whimsical, fanciful, capricious, erratic. (*steady, sober, demure, unwhimsical, unfanciful, reliable, consistent, uniform*)

free detached, playing, operating, open, unoccupied, unobstructed, unimpeded, permitted, unhindered, exempt, gratuitous, unconditional, at liberty, clear, liberal, untrammeled, unconfined, careless, loose, easy, munificent, unreserved, frank, bountiful, generous, bounteous. (*subservient*)

frequent many, repeated, numerous, recurrent, general, continual, usual, common. (*few, solitary, rare, scanty, casual*)

fresh new, young, vigorous, cool, recent, renewed, unimpaired, untarnished, unfaded, blooming, ruddy, novel, untried, modern, unskilled. (*old, stale, jaded, weary, former, stagnant, ordinary*)

fretful irritable, fractious, peevish, impatient, petulant, waspish. (*patient, forbearing, contented*)

friction rubbing, grating, attrition, abrasion, contact. (*lubrication, detachment, isolation*)

friend associate, companion, acquaintance, familiar, ally, chum, messmate, coadjutor, confidant, adherent. (*opponent, foe, adversary, antagonist, enemy*)

friendly well-inclined, well-disposed, amicable, kindly, social, neighborly, sociable, affectionate, favorable, cordial. (*ill-inclined, ill-disposed, hostile, inimical, adverse, antagonistic*)

frightful terrible, horrible, alarming, ugly, hideous, monstrous, dreadful, direful, awful, shocking, horrid, terrific. (*pleasing, attractive, beautiful*)

frivolous trifling, silly, trivial, petty, worthless. (*serious, earnest, important, grave*)

frolic play, game, sport, festivity, entertainment, gambol, gaiety, lark, spree, merrymaking, prank. (*study, undertaking, purpose, engagement*)

frugal sparing, economical, parsimonious, abstinent, abstemious, temperate, saving, thrifty, provident. (*profuse, luxurious, extravagant, prodigal, self-indulgent, intemperate*)

fruitful productive, prolific, pregnant, fraught, causative, effectual, useful, successful, fertile, abundant, plenteous, fecund, plentiful. (*unproductive, sterile, barren, fruitless, ineffectual, useless*)

fulfill fill, complete, discharge, verify, accomplish, achieve, execute, effect. (*neglect, ignore*)

fulsome excessive, gross, loathsome, nauseous, sickening, fawning, offensive. (*chaste, sober, nice*)

function office, part, character, capacity, business, administration, discharge, operation, exercise, power, duty, employment. (*usurpation, maladministration, misconduct, misdemeanor*)

fundamental primary, important, indispensable, essential. (*secondary, unimportant, adventitious, ascititious, nonessential*)

funny sportive, droll, comical, laughable, humorous, jocose, ridiculous, ludicrous, diverting. (*dull, tedious, mournful, lugubrious, dismal, grave*)

furnish supply, provide, equip, afford, yield, bestow purvey, give. (*withhold, withdraw, dismantle*)

fuss stir, excitement, tumult, worry, ado, bustle, flurry, fidget. (*quiet, peace, sedateness, tranquillity*)

future forthcoming, coming, advenient. (*gone, bygone, past*)

gabble prate, jabber, jargon, stuff, babble, rattle, twaddle, gibber, chatter, gibberish. (*conversation, speech, eloquence, reticence, taciturnity*)

gain acquire, get, win, procure, obtain, profit, benefit, earn, attain, realize, achieve, reap, reach. (*lose, forfeit, suffer*)

gallant brave, chivalrous, intrepid, courteous, heroic, fearless, courageous, valiant, bold, splendid, showy, gay. (*cowardly, churlish, discourteous*)

game sport, recreation, pastime, amusement, frolic, diversion, play. (*study, toil, labor, business*)

garble misrepresent, misquote, mutilate, cook, dress, color, falsify, pervert, distort. (*quote, cite*)

gaudy tawdry, fine, meretricious, bespangled, glittering, showy, gay, garish. (*rich, simple*)

gauge measure, fathom, probe. (*survey, conjecture, view, scan, guess, observe, mismeasure*)

gawky awkward, ungainly, uncouth, clumsy, clownish. (*neat, handy, graceful, handsome*)

gay merry, blithe, lively, jolly, sportive, sprightly, smart, festive, gladsome, pleasuresome, cheerful. (*heavy, melancholy, grave, sad, somber*)

generous noble, chivalrous, liberal, disinterested, bountiful, magnanimous, openhearted, munificent, honorable. (*mean, ignoble, illiberal*)

genial warm, cordial, balmy, cheering, merry, festive, joyous, hearty, revivifying, restorative. (*cold, cutting, harsh, deleterious, noxious, deadly*)

genteel polite, well-bred, refined, courteous, fashionable, elegant, aristocratic, polished, graceful. (*rude, boorish, ill-bred, clownish, unfashionable, unpolished, inelegant, plebeian*)

gentle courteous, polite, high-bred, mild, bland, tame, docile, amiable, meek, soft, placid, tender. (*rough, rude, coarse, fierce, savage*)

genuine authentic, true, real, pure, unalloyed, natural, unaffected, sincere, unadulterated, veritable, sound. (*spurious, fictitious, adulterated*)

get gain, procure, acquire, earn, obtain, attain, secure, achieve. (*lose, forfeit, surrender, forgo*)

ghastly deathlike, wan, grim, cadaverous, spectral, pallid, hideous, shocking. (*blooming, fresh*)

giddy whirling, vertiginous, thoughtless, inconstant, unsteady, lofty, beetling, dizzy, harebrained, flighty. (*stationary, slow, ponderous, thoughtful*)

gift donation, present, grant, boon, gratuity, benefaction, endowment, talent, faculty, alms, douceur. (*reservation, refusal, wages, purchase*)

gist essence, pith, marrow, substance, kernel, force, main point. (*surplusage, redundancy, additament, environment, accessories, garb, clothing*)

give bestow, grant, confer, impart, yield, produce, surrender, concede, present, afford, communicate, furnish. (*withhold, withdraw, refuse*)

glad happy, joyous, pleased, gratified, blithesome, gleeful, gladsome, delighted, cheerful, elated, joyful. (*unhappy, sorrowful, disastrous*)

glare beam, shine, gleam, ray, radiate, glow. (*shimmer, scintillate, glitter, smolder, glimmer*)

glassy vitreous, smooth, polished, glacial, glabrous, brittle, transparent, crystalline, pellucid, limpid, glossy, silken. (*rough, uneven, rugged*)

glory brightness, radiance, effulgence, honor, fame, celebrity, pomp, luster, magnificence, splendor, renown. (*obscurity, ignominy, cloud, dishonor*)

glut *v.* gorge, fill, stuff, cram, satiate, cloy, surfeit. (*disgorge, empty, void*)

glut *n.* surplus, redundancy, superfluity, overstock. (*scarcity, drainage, exhaustion, dearth*)

go move, depart, pass, travel, vanish, reach, extend, proceed, stir, set out, budge. (*stand, stay*)

good *a.* right, complete, virtuous, sound, pious, benevolent, propitious, serviceable, suitable, efficient, sufficient, competent, valid, real, actual, considerable, honorable, reputable, righteous, proper, true, upright, just, excellent. (*wrong, imperfect, unsound, vicious, profane, niggardly*)

good *n.* boon, benefit, advantage, gain, blessing, mercy, virtue, prosperity, weal, profit, interest, welfare. (*hurt, injury, loss, detriment*)

goodly pleasant, desirable, excellent, fair, comely, considerable, graceful, fine. (*unpleasant*)

gorgeous magnificent, splendid, costly, rich, superb, grand, strong. (*poor, naked, bare, cheap*)

govern rule, direct, control, moderate, guide, supervise, manage, command, conduct. (*misrule, misdirect, miscontrol*)

grace favor, beauty, condescension, kindness, elegance, charm, excellence, pardon, mercy. (*disfavor, deformity, unkindness, pride, inelegance*)

gracious affable, courteous, benignant, kind, civil, condescending, merciful, friendly, tender, gentle, beneficent. (*haughty, discourteous, ill-disposed, ungracious, churlish*)

gradual slow, continuous, unintermittent, gradational, regular, step by step, progressive. (*sudden, momentary, instantaneous, periodic, recurrent*)

grand large, dignified, imposing, important, eventful, magnificent, grandly, majestic, august, exalted, stately, splendid, lofty, elevated, pompous, gorgeous, sublime, superb. (*little, undignified*)

graphic picturesque, illustrative, descriptive, pictorial, forcible, vivid, feeling, described, picturesquely. (*unpicturesque, unillustrative, undescriptive*)

grateful pleasant, acceptable, agreeable, thankful, obliged, welcome. (*unpleasant, disagreeable*)

gratify please, satisfy, indulge, humor. (*displease, dissatisfy, disappoint, stint, discipline, inure*)

gratitude thankfulness, gratefulness. (*unthankfulness, ingratitude, thanklessness, oblivion*)

grave sad, serious, momentous, weighty, pressing, sedate, demure, thoughtful, sober, somber, solemn, important, aggravated, heavy, cogent. (*joyous, merry, facetious, unimportant, ridiculous*)

great big, wide, huge, numerous, protracted, excellent, large, immense, bulky, majestic, gigantic, vast, grand, sublime, august, eminent, magnanimous, noble, powerful, exalted, noticeable. (*little, narrow, puny, scanty, few, short, mean, ignoble, weak, unimportant*)

greedy gluttonous, voracious, hungry, desirous, avaricious. (*abstemious, abstinent, indifferent, contented*)

grief trouble, tribulation, woe, mourning, regret, affliction, sorrow, sadness. (*joy, exultation*)

grieve trouble, burden, annoy, distress, bewail, wound, pain, sorrow, hurt, afflict, mourn, lament, complain, deplore. (*ease, console, soothe, please*)

grim fierce, ferocious, terrible, hideous, ugly, ghastly, sullen, stern. (*mild, docile, attractive*)

groan moan, whine, growl, grumble. (*giggle*)

groundless vain, suppositious, unfounded, baseless, fanciful, gratuitous, chimerical, false. (*well-founded, substantial, authoritative, actual, authentic*)

group cluster, bunch, knot, assemblage, collocation, class, collection, clump, order, assembly. (*isolation, individual, crowd, confusion, medley*)

grudge *v.* spare, retain, covet, envy, withhold. (*spend, impart, welcome, satisfy, gratify*)

grudge *n.* spite, grievance, aversion, rancor, hatred, pique, dissatisfaction, discontent, refusal. (*welcome, satisfaction, approval, contentment, complacency, bestowal, benefaction*)

gruff rough, surly, bearish, harsh, rude, blunt. (*smooth, mild, affable, courteous*)

guess conjecture, surmise, divine, suppose, suspect, fancy, imagine. (*examine, prove, investigate, establish, demonstrate, elaborate, deduce*)

guide lead, direct, conduct, pilot, regulate, superintend, influence, train, manage. (*mislead*)

gush burst, stream, flow, gush, spout, rush, pour out, flow out. (*drip, drop, dribble, trickle*)

habit habituation, custom, familiarity, association, inurement, usage, practice, way, manner. (*dishabituation, inexperience, inconversance, desuetude*)

habitual regular, ordinary, perpetual, customary, usual, familiar, accustomed, wonted. (*irregular, extraordinary, occasional, unusual, exceptional, rare*)

half moiety, bisection, dimidiation. (*integrity, entirety, totality, whole*)

halt stop, rest, limp, falter, hammer, stammer, demur, dubitate, pause, hold, stand still, hesitate. (*advance, decide, determine, speed, flow, career*)

handsome comely, good-looking, generous, liberal, beautiful, ample, pretty, graceful, lovely, elegant. (*uncomely, ill-looking, ungenerous, illiberal, unhandsome*)

handy near, convenient, useful, helpful, manageable, dexterous, ready, expert. (*remote, inconvenient, awkward, useless, cumbrous, unwieldy*)

happy lucky, fortunate, felicitous, successful, delighted, joyous, merry, blithesome, prosperous, glad, blissful. (*unlucky, unfortunate, infelicitous*)

hard firm, dense, solid, compact, unyielding, impenetrable, arduous, difficult, grievous, distressing, rigorous, oppressive, exacting, unfeeling, stubborn, harsh, forced, constrained, inexplicable, flinty, severe, cruel, obdurate, hardened, callous. (*soft, fluid, liquid, elastic, brittle, penetrable, easy*)

hardship trouble, burden, annoyance, grievance, calamity, infliction, endurance, affliction. (*pleasure, amusement, alleviation, recreation, gratification, relief, assuagement, facilitation, boon*)

hardy inured, robust, strong, resolute, stout-hearted, vigorous, intrepid, brave, manly, valiant. (*weak, uninured, delicate, irresolute, enervated, debilitated, tender, fragile*)

harm hurt, mischief, injury, detriment, damage, evil, wrong, misfortune, ill, mishap. (*benefit, boon, amelioration, improvement, reparation*)

harmonious congruous, accordant, proportioned, uniform, melodious, musical, dulcet, tuneful, consistent, peaceful, agreeable, amicable, friendly, concordant. (*incongruous, discordant*)

hasty speedy, rapid, superficial, hurried, irascible, impetuous, reckless, headlong, crude, incomplete, undeveloped, immature, swift, precipitate, fiery, passionate, slight, quick, excitable, rash, cursory. (*slow, leisurely, careful, close, reflective, developed, matured, complete, elaborate*)

hateful abominable, detestable, vile, odious, heinous, execrable, loathsome, repulsive. (*lovable*)

have own, possess, feel, entertain, accept, bear, enjoy, keep. (*want, need, lose, forgo, discard, reject, miss, desiderate, covet, desire*)

hazard peril, risk, jeopardy, danger, chance, imperil, dare. (*safety, security, protection, warrant, certainty, calculation, law*)

hazy foggy, nebulous, misty, filmy, gauzy, cloudy, murky, caliginous. (*diaphanous, clear*)

head top, crown, chief, leader, ruler, mind, source, section, divsion, topic, gathering, culmination, crisis, leadership, guide, commander, acme, summit. (*tail, bottom, follower, servant, retainer*)

heart core, nucleus, kernel, interior, center, character, disposition, courage, hardihood, nature, life, feeling, benevolence. (*exterior, hand, action*)

hearty healthy, robust, cordial, sound, warm, honest, earnest, genuine, well, sincere, heartfelt, hale. (*unhealthy, delicate, infirm, cold, insincere*)

heat warmth, ardor, passion, excitement, fever, ebullition, intensity. (*coolness, indifference, subsidence, calmness, composure, reflection*)

heavy weighty, ponderous, inert, slow, stupid, dull, impenetrable, stolid, cumbrous, grievous afflictive, oppressive, burdensome, sluggish, laborious, depressed. (*light, trifling, trivial, agile, active, quick, joyous, alleviative, consolatory, inspiriting, animating, buoyant*)

heighten exalt, increase, enhance, intensify, color, vivify, aggravate, raise, exaggerate, lift up, amplify. (*lower, depress, diminish, deteriorate*)

heinous hateful, flagrant, detestable, flagitious, atrocious, odious, abominable, execrable, enormous. (*excellent, laudable, meritorious, praiseworthy, distinguished, justifiable, excusable, palliable*)

help aid, succor, remedy, prevent, avoid, assist, promote, cooperate, relieve, second. (*oppose*)

hereditary inherited, ancestral, lineal. (*conferred, acquired, won*)

hesitate dubitate, waver, demur, scruple, falter, stammer, pause, doubt. (*decide, determine*)

hide conceal, secrete, mask, dissemble, store, protect, disguise, ensconce, screen, cover, burrow. (*expose, discover, exhibit, manifest, betray, strip*)

hideous frightful, unshapely, monstrous, horrid, horrible, ugly, grisly, grim, ghastly. (*graceful*)

high elevated, lofty, tall, eminent, excellent, noble, haughty, violent, proud, exalted. (*depressed, low, stunted, ignoble, mean, base, affable*)

hinder prevent, interrupt, obstruct, retard, debar, embarrass, impede, thwart, block, stop. (*accelerate, expedite, enable, promote, facilitate*)

hoarse harsh, grating, husky, raucous, rough, gruff. (*mellifluous, mellow, rich, sweet, melodious*)

hold keep, grasp, retain, support, restrain, defend, maintain, occupy, possess, sustain, regard, consider, cohere, continue, have. (*drop, abandon*)

hollow empty, concave, foolish, weak, faithless, insincere, artificial, unsubstantial, void, flimsy, transparent, senseless vacant, unsound, false. (*full, solid, well-stored, strong, firm, sincere, true*)

homely plain, coarse, uncomely. (*handsome, beautiful, refined, courtly*)

honest honorable, upright, virtuous, proper, right, sincere, conscientious. (*dishonest, dishonorable, vicious, improper, wrong, insincere*)

honor respect, reverence, nobility, dignity, eminence, reputation, fame, high-mindedness, spirit, self-respect, renown, grandeur, esteem. (*disrespect, contempt, irreverence, slight, obscurity*)

honorary gratuitous, unofficial, unremunerative, nominal, titular. (*official, remunerative, professional, jurisdictional*)

hope anticipation, prospect, vision, longing, confidence, desire, expectation, trust. (*despair, despondency, distrust, disbelief, abandonment, abjuration*)

horrible abominable, detestable, dreadful, fearful, hideous, ghastly, terrific, hateful, direful, horrid, awful, frightful. (*lovely, desirable, enjoyable*)

huge enormous, monstrous, colossal, vast, bulky, large, great, prodigious, immense, stupendous, gigantic. (*petty, undersized, pygmy, puny*)

humane benign, kind, tender, merciful, benevolent, compassionate. (*unkind, cruel, unmerciful*)

humble low, lowly, obscure, meek, modest, unassuming, unpretending, submissive. (*high, lofty, eminent, proud, boastful, arrogant, assuming, pretentious*)

humor disposition, temper, mood, caprice, jocoseness, pleasantry, frame, drollery, fun. (*nature, personality, mind, will, purpose, seriousness*)

hurt *v.* wound, bruise, harm, injure, damage, pain, grieve. (*heal, soothe, console, repair, reinstate, compensate, benefit*)

hurt *n.* harm, injury, damage, wound, detriment, mischief. (*benefit, pleasure*)

hurtful mischievous, injurious, pernicious, baleful, deleterious, baneful, noxious, detrimental, prejudicial. (*helpful, remedial*)

hypocritical pharisaical, sanctimonious, smug, smooth, mealy, unctuous, mincing. (*plain-spoken, candid, truthful, sincere, genuine, transparent*)

idea image, notion, conception, belief, doctrine, supposition, understanding, fiction, fancy, thought, opinion, impression, sentiment. (*object*)

ideal mental, notional, conception, intellectual, creative, spiritual, poetical, supposititious, fictitious, unreal, imaginary, chimerical, fanciful, imaginative. (*physical, visible, material, tangible*)

idle void, unoccupied, waste, vain, empty, unemployed, useless, inactive, lazy, indolent. (*tilled, occupied, populated, filled, employed, assiduous, industrious*)

ignoble mean, base, dishonorable, humble, plebeian, lowly. (*honorable, noble, eminent, exalted, lordly, grand, notable, illustrious*)

ignominious shameful, scandalous, dishonorable, infamous. (*honorable, reputable, creditable*)

ignorant untaught, uneducated, uninformed, unlearned, illiterate, unlettered. (*wise, learned*)

illusion dream, mockery, deception, delusion, hallucination, phantasm, vision, myth, false show, error, fallacy. (*form, reality, body, substance*)

illustrious renowned, glorious, brilliant, deathless, eminent, distinguished, celebrated, conspicuous, noble, famous. (*ignominious, disgraceful*)

ill will antipathy, hatred, malevolence, dislike, aversion. (*goodwill, beneficence*)

imaginative creative, conceptive, ideal, poetical, romantic, inventive, original. (*unimaginative, unpoetical, unromantic, prosaic, matter-of-fact*)

imagine conceive, suppose, surmise, understand, fancy, fabricate, deem, presume, think, apprehend. (*represent, exhibit, demonstrate, prove*)

imitate represent, copy, resemble, follow, portray, depict, repeat, pattern after, mock, ape, counterfeit, mimic. (*misrepresent, caricature, alter*)

immediate proximate, contiguous, present, direct, instant, next. (*distant, remote, future, mediate*)

impair deteriorate, injure, reduce, damage, enfeeble, vitiate, diminish, lessen. (*enhance, improve, augment, repair*)

impassible immaterial, immortal. (*passible*)

impediment hindrance, obstacle, obstruction, stumbling block. (*aid, aidance, help, assistance*)

imperative urgent, irresistible, dictatorial, inexorable, peremptorily, compulsory, obligatory. (*indulgent, lenient, mild, entreative, supplicatory*)

imperious arrogant, exacting, dictatorial, authoritative, domineering, haughty, lordly. (*yielding, submissive, compliant, docile, ductile, lenient*)

implement instrument, utensil, tool, appliance. (*labor, work, science, art, manufacture, agriculture*)

implicate connect, associate, charge, criminate, involve, entangle, infold, compromise. (*disconnect, dissociate, acquit, extricate*)

imply involve, mean, indicate, suggest, hint, import, denote, include. (*express, declare, state*)

importance weight, moment, consequence, significance, signification, avail, concern. (*unimportance, insignificance, nothingness, immateriality*)

important significant, expressive, relevant, main, leading, considerable, great, dignified, influential, weighty, momentous, material, grave, essential. (*insignificant, trivial, inexpressive, irrelevant, inconsiderable, petty, mean, uninfluential*)

impotent weak, powerless, useless, feeble, helpless, nerveless, enfeebled. (*strong, vigorous, powerful, virile*)

impressive forcible, solemn, affecting, imposing, important. (*weak, unimpressive, feeble, tame, jejune, dry, vapid, unimportant, insignificant*)

improvement advancement, amendment, progress, increase, correction, proficiency. (*degeneracy, deterioration, debasement, retrogression*)

impudent impertinent, insolent, saucy, shameless, brazenfaced, rude, bold, immodest. (*servile*)

impulse incentive, push, incitement, force, influence, instigation, feeling, sudden thought, motive. (*rebuff, premeditation, deliberation*)

inadvertence oversight, negligence, inattention, carelessness, blunder. (*carefulness, exactness, meticulousness*)

inaudible low, inarticulate, suppressed, muttering, mumbling, stifled, muffled. (*audible, outspoken, sonorous, articulate, clear, ringing, loud*)

incapable unqualified, unable, unfitted, weak, incompetent, feeble, disqualified, insufficient. (*qualified, able, fitted, strong, clever*)

incidental casual, occasional, appertinent, concomitant, concurrent, accidental, fortuitous. (*systematic, regular, independent, disconnected*)

incivility discourtesy, ill-breeding, ill-manners, uncourteousness. (*civility, urbanity, good manners*)

inclement harsh, tyrannical, cruel, unmerciful, severe, stormy, rough, rigorous. (*mild, benign*)

inclination leaning, slope, tendency, disposition, proneness, aptness, predilection, bias, bent, attachment, affection, liking, wish. (*inaptitude*)

incoherent unconnected, incongruous, inconsequential, loose. (*coherent, connected*)

incomparable matchless, unique, consummate, transcendent. (*common, ordinary, average*)

inconsolable cheerless, joyless, spiritless, melancholy, gloomy, disconsolate, comfortless, forlorn, heartsick, despairing. (*cheerful, hopeful, consolable*)

inconstant fickle, mutable, variable, fitful, unstable, undependable, changeable, capricious. (*stable, steadfast, dependable*)

incontestable indisputable, unquestionable, unassailable, impregnable. (*dubious, questionable*)

inconvenience incommode, discommode, distrust, molest. (*suit, aid, benefit, subserve, assist*)

increase advance, heighten, dilate, enhance, aggregate, pile up, raise, magnify, spread. (*lessen*)

incredible surpassing belief, fabulous, marvelous. (*credible, believable*)

inculcate impress, urge, enforce, infuse, instill, implant, press, teach. (*insinuate, suggest, disavow, abjure, denounce*)

incumbent pressing, binding, coercive, indispensable, urgent, devolvent, obligatory. (*optional, discretional*)

incurable irremediable, irredeemable, terminal. (*tractable, removable, remediable*)

indecent indelicate, immodest, improper.

indelible indestructible, indefeasible, ineffaceable, persistent, irreversible. (*mutable, evanescent, transient, effaceable*)

indescribable unaccountable, inexpressible, ineffable, unutterable. (*familiar, ordinary*)

indestructible imperishable, indiscerptible. (*perishable, destructible, dissoluble*)

indicate show, evidence, betray, evince, manifest, declare, specify, denote, point out, betoken, designate, mark. (*conceal, contradict, negative*)

indifference triviality, unimportance, insignificance, coolness, carelessness, apathy, insensibility, composure. (*importance, significance, weight, gravity, eagerness, interest, affection, ardor*)

indiscriminate mixed, confused, medley, promiscuous, ill-assorted, undiscerning, undistinguishing, undiscriminating. (*careful, sorted, select*)

indispensable necessary, essential, requisite, needful, expedient. (*unnecessary, unessential, inexpedient, dispensable*)

individual personal, specific, peculiar, indivisible, identical, singular, idiosyncratic, special, single, separate, particular. (*general, common*)

indivisible minute, atomic, ultimate. (*divisible*)

induce produce, cause, prompt, persuade, instigate, impel, actuate, urge, influence, move, prevail on. (*slave, prevent, disincline, dissuade*)

indulge spoil, pamper, humor, gratify, cherish, bask, revel, grovel, foster, favor, allow. (*thwart*)

indulgent compliant, tender, tolerant. (*harsh*)

industrious diligent, laborious, busy, assiduous, active, hardworking. (*lazy, shiftless, idle*)

ineffable inexpressible, inconceivable, insurpassable, indeclarable, indescribable, exquisite, perfect. (*common, trivial, superficial, vulgar, conversational, colloquial, obvious, commonplace*)

ineffectual fruitless, useless, vain, idle, unavailing, abortive, inoperative, ineffective. (*effective, effectual, successful*)

inexcusable unmitigated, unpardonable, indefensible, unjustifiable. (*mitigable, pliable, justifiable, vindicable, defensible, pardonable*)

inexhaustible incessant, unwearied, indefatigable, perennial, illimitable. (*limited, scant, poor*)

inexpedient undesirable, inadvisable, disadvantageous. (*advisable, profitable, expedient*)

infamy despair, degradation, disgrace, ignominy, obloquy, extreme vileness, dishonor. (*honor*)

infatuation fatuity, hallucination, madness, self-deception. (*clear-sightedness, sagacity, wisdom*)

inference deduction, corollary, conclusion, consequence. (*statement, proposition, enunciation*)

inferiority subordination, minority, poverty, mediocrity, subjection, servitude, depression. (*superiority, majority, excellence, eminence, independence, mastery, exaltation, elevation*)

infidel skeptic, disbeliever, heretic, freethinker. (*believer, devotee, pietist*)

inflame fire, kindle, excite, rouse, fan, incense, madden, infuriate, exasperate, irritate, embitter, anger, enrage. (*quench, extinguish, allay, cool*)

influence effect, control, causation, affection, impulse, power, credit, character, sway, weight, ascendancy, prestige, authority. (*inefficiency, ineffectiveness, inoperativeness, nullity, neutrality*)

influential potent, powerful, efficacious, forcible, persuasive, controlling, guiding, considerable. (*weak, ineffective, inoperative, unpersuasive*)

information instruction, advice, counsel, notice, notification, knowledge. (*concealment, hiding, occultation, mystification, ignorance*)

infringe break, violate, transgress, contravene. (*observe, conserve, preserve, keep within bounds*)

ingenious skillful, adept, clever, inventive, ready, frank, sincere. (*unskillful, slow, uninventive, unready*)

ingenuous noble, candid, generous, frank, sincere, straightforward, honorable, open, artless, honest. (*mean, reserved, sly, disingenuous*)

ingredient element, component, constituent. (*noningredient, refuse, residuum, counteragent*)

inherent innate, congenial, immanent, ingrained, inborn, intrinsic, natural, inbred. (*foreign, ascititious, temporary, separable, extraneous*)

initiative start, leadership, commencement, example. (*wake, rear, prosecution, termination*)

injunction mandate, order, command, exhortation, precept. (*disobedience, insubordination*)

injurious hurtful, deleterious, prejudicial, noxious, detrimental, baleful, pernicious, wrongful, mischievous, damaging, baneful. (*helpful, beneficial, advantageous*)

innocence innocuousness, inoffensiveness, guilelessness, guiltlessness, simplicity, purity, sinlessness. (*hurtfulness, offensiveness, guile, guilt, contamination, corruption, impurity, sinfulness*)

innocuous inoffensive, harmless, wholesome. (*obnoxious, hurtful, deleterious, insidious*)

inquiry interrogation, question, asking, investigation, search, examination, research, scrutiny, exploration. (*conjecture, guess, intuition, hypothesis, assumption, supposition*)

insatiable voracious, unappeasable, ravenous, rapacious, greedy. (*moderate, delicate, fastidious, dainty, squeamish*)

insidious wily, treacherous, designing, dangerous, deceitful, sly, crafty, artful. (*straightforward*)

insinuate introduce, insert, worm, ingratiate, intimate, suggest, infuse, hint. (*withdraw, retract*)

insipid tasteless, vapid, uninteresting, characterless, flavorless, flat, insulse, lifeless, prosy, stupid. (*tasty, sapid, relishing, racy, interesting*)

insist stand, demand, maintain, contend, persist, persevere, urge. (*abandon, waive, concede*)

insolent haughty, overbearing, contemptuous, abusive, saucy, impertinent, opprobrious, offensive. (*meek, polite, well-mannered*)

insolvent bankrupt, ruined, penniless, beggared. (*flush, flourishing, monied, thriving*)

inspire animate, inspirit, inflame, imbue, impel, encourage, inhale, enliven, cheer, breathe in, infuse, exhilarate. (*depress, dispirit, discourage, deter*)

instance entreaty, request, prompting, persuasion, example, solicitation, case, illustration, exemplification, occurrence, point, precedence. (*dissuasion, depreciation, warning, rule, statement*)

instill pour, infuse, introduce, import, implant, insinuate, inculcate. (*drain, strain, extract, eradicate, eliminate, remove, extirpate*)

instinctive natural, voluntary, spontaneous, intuitive, impulsive. (*cultivated, forced, reasoning*)

instruction teaching, education, information, counsel, advice, direction, order, command. (*misteaching, misinformation, misguidance*)

insufferable intolerable, unpermissible, unallowable, unendurable, unbearable. (*tolerable, allowable, endurable, supportable*)

insupportable unbearable, intolerable, insufferable, unendurable. (*endurable, comfortable*)

integrity uprightness, honor, honesty, probity, truthfulness, candor, single-mindedness, conscientiousness, entireness, rectitude, completeness, parity. (*unfairness, sleight, underhandedness, meanness, chicanery, duplicity, fraud, roguery, rascality*)

intellectual mental, metaphysical, psychological, inventive, learned, cultured. (*unintellectual*)

intelligence understanding, apprehension, comprehension, conception, announcement, report, rumor, tidings, news, information, publication, intellectual capacity, mind, knowledge, advice, notice, instruction, intellect. (*misunderstanding, misinformation, misconception, stupidity, dullness*)

intensity tension, force, concentration, strain, attention, eagerness, ardor, energy. (*laxity, debility, relaxation, languor, indifference, coolness, hebetude, diminution*)

intentional purposed, designed, deliberate, intended, done on purpose, contemplated, premeditated, studied. (*undesigned, casual, unintentional*)

intercourse correspondence, dealing, intercommunication, intimacy, connection, commerce. (*reticence, suspension, cessation, disconnection, interception, interpellation*)

interest concern, business advantage, profit, attention, curiosity, behalf, cause, share. (*unconcern, disconnection, repudiation, disadvantage, loss*)

intermediate intervening, included, interposed, comprised, middle, moderate, interjacent. (*circumjacent, surrounding, enclosing, embracing, outside, extreme, excluded, exclusive*)

interpret translate, render, construe, explain, expound, expone, represent, declare, understand, elucidate, decipher, solve. (*misinterpret, misunderstand, mistake, misconceive, falsify, distort, misdeclare, misrepresent*)

interrupt break, disconnect, discontinue, intersect, disturb, stop, hinder. (*continue, prosecute*)

interval interim, meantime, period, gap, intermission, interspace, cessation, space between, season. (*continuity, simultaneousness, uninterruptedness*)

intimate impart, communicate, announce, declare, tell, suggest, hint, insinuate, mention briefly. (*reserve, repress, withhold, conceal*)

intoxication venom, poison, obfuscation, bewilderment, delirium, hallucination, ravishment, ecstasy, inebriation, drunkenness, inebriety. (*antidote, clarification, sobriety, sanity, ebriety, melancholy, depression*)

intricate complicated, involved, mazy, labyrinthine, entangled, tortuous. (*simple, uninvolved*)

introduction induction, importation, leading, taking, presentation, insertion, commencement, preliminary, preface, initiative, portico, vestibule, entrance, gate, preamble, prelude. (*eduction, extraction, exportation, elimination, ejection, estrangement, conclusion, completion, end, egress*)

introductory prefatory, initiatory, commendatory, precursory, preliminary, preparatory. (*completive, final, conclusive, alienative, supplemental*)

intuition instinct, apprehension, recognition, insight. (*information, learning, instruction, elaboration, acquirement, induction, experience*)

invalid infirm, sick, weak, frail, feeble. (*strong, rigorous, healthy, well*)

invent discover, contrive, concoct, imagine, elaborate, conceive, design, devise, fabricate, originate, find out, frame, forge, feign. (*imitate*)

invincible impregnable, immovable, inexpugnable, unsubduable, irresistible, indomitable, unconquerable, insuperable, insurmountable. (*weak, spiritless, powerless, puny, effortless*)

involve implicate, confound, mingle, envelop, compromise, include, complicate, entangle. (*separate, extricate, disconnect*)

irreligious undevout, ungodly, godless, profane, impious. (*religious, godly, reverent, reverential, pious, devout*)

irrepressible unrepressible, ungovernable, uncontrollable, insuppressible, free, unconfined, excitable. (*repressible, governable, controllable, calm*)

irresponsible unbound, unencumbered, unaccountable, not answerable, excusable, lawless.

jealous envious, self-anxious, covetous, invidious, suspicious. (*unenvious, liberal, genial*)

jingle rhyme, chime, tinkle, tingle. (*euphony*)

join unite, adhere, adjoin, add, couple, connect, associate, annex, append, combine, link, accompany, confederate. (*separate, disjoin, subtract, disconnect*)

jollification revelry, festivity, conviviality, fun, carnival, merrymaking. (*weariness, tediousness*)

jolly gay, joyful, gladsome, mirthful, genial, jovial, jubilant, robust, lively, plump, merry. (*sad*)

jostle hustle, push, thrust, jog, jolt, incommode. (*clear, lead, extricate, convoy, escort, precede, pilot, attend*)

joy gladness, pleasure, delight, happiness, exultation, transport, felicity, ecstasy, rapture, bliss, gaiety, mirth, merriment, festivity, hilarity, charm, blessedness. (*sorrow, pain, trouble, misery*)

jubilant joyous, triumphant, festive, congratulatory, exultant. (*doleful, mournful, sorrowful, wailing, penitent, penitential, lugubrious, remorseful*)

judgment decision, determination, adjudication, sagacity, penetration, judiciousness, sense, intellect, belief, estimation, opinion, verdict, sentence, discernment, discrimination, intelligence, prudence, award, condemnation. (*argument, consideration, inquiry, speculation, proposition*)

judicious wise, sagacious, expedient, sensible, prudent, discreet, well-judged, well-advised, polite, discerning, thoughtful. (*foolish, unwise, silly*)

juggle conjure, cheat, bamboozle, shuffle, trick, beguile, circumvent, swindle, overreach, mystify, mislead. (*expose, correct, enlighten, guide, lead, undeceive, disillusion, detect*)

just exact, fitting, true, fair, proportioned, harmonious, honest, reasonable, sound, honorable, normal, impartial, equitable, upright, regular, orderly, lawful, right, righteous, proper. (*inexact*)

justice equity, impartiality, fairness, right, reasonableness, propriety, uprightness, desert, integrity. (*injustice, wrong, partiality, unfairness*)

juvenile youthful, young, infantile, boyish, girlish, early, immature, adolescent, pubescent, childish, puerile. (*mature, later, manly, womanly*)

keen eager, vehement, sharp, piercing, penetrating, acute, cutting, biting, severe, sarcastic, satirical, ardent, prompt, shrewd. (*indifferent*)

keep hold, restrain, retain, detain, guard, preserve, suppress, repress, conceal, tend, support, maintain, conduct, continue, obey, haunt, observe, frequent, celebrate, protect, adhere to, practice, hinder, sustain. (*release, acquit, liberate, send, dismiss*)

kind *n.* style, character, description, designation, denomination, genus, species, sort, class, nature, set, breed. (*dissimilarity*)

kind *a.* benevolent, benign, tender, indulgent, humane, clement, lenient, compassionate, gentle, good, gracious, forbearing, kindhearted. (*unkind, harsh, severe, cruel, hard, illiberal*)

knot tie, bond, intricacy, difficulty, perplexity, cluster, collection, band, group, protuberance, joint. (*loosening, unfastening, dissolution, solution, explication, unraveling, dispersion, multitude*)

knowing shrewd, astute, discerning, sharp, acute, sagacious, penetrating, proficient, skillful, intelligent, experienced, well-informed, accomplished. (*simple, dull, innocent, gullible, undiscerning, stolid, silly*)

knowledge apprehension, comprehension, recognition, understanding, conversance, experience, acquaintance, familiarity, cognizance, notice, information, instruction, learning, enlightenment, scholarship, attainments, acquirements. (*misapprehension, inobservance, incomprehension, misunderstanding, misconception, inconversance, inexperience, ignorance, unfamiliarity, incognizance*)

l

laborious assiduous, diligent, painstaking, indefatigable, arduous, burdensome, toilsome, wearisome, industrious, hardworking, active, difficult, tedious. (*idle, indiligent, lazy, indolent, easy*)

laconic terse, curt, epigrammatic. (*prolix*)

lame weak, faltering, hobbling, hesitating, ineffective, impotent, crippled, halt, defective, imperfect. (*robust, agile, potent, efficient, satisfactory*)

language speech, talk, conversation, dialect, discourse, tongue, diction, phraseology, articulation, accents, vernacular, expression. (*jargon, jabber, gibberish, babble, gabble, cry, whine, bark, howl*)

languid faint, weary, feeble, unnerved, unbraced, pining, drooping, enervated, exhausted, flagging, spiritless. (*strong, healthy, robust, vigorous, active, braced*)

large big, bulky, extensive, abundant, capacious, ample, liberal, comprehensive, enlightened, catholic, great, vast, wide. (*small, mean, narrow*)

last *v.* continue, remain, hold, endure, abide, live. (*cease, fail, fade, fly, wane, depart, disappear*)

last *a.* latest, ending, final, concluding, hindmost, past, extreme, lowest, remotest, ultimate. (*first, introductory, initiatory, opening, foremost*)

laughter merriment, glee, derision, ridicule, cachinnation, contempt. (*weeping, tears, mourning, sorrow, admiration, veneration, respect*)

law rule, edict, regulation, decree, command, order, statute, enactment, mode, method, sequence, principle, code, legislation, adjudication, jurisdiction, jurisprudence. (*misrule, disorder, anarchy*)

lawful legal, permissible, orderly, right, allowable, fair, constitutional, rightful, legitimate. (*illegal, impermissible, unlawful, wrong, lawless, unfair*)

lay place, establish, deposit, allay, prostrate, arrange, dispose, put, spread, set down. (*erect*)

lead *v.* conduct, guide, precede, induce, spend, pass, commence, inaugurate, convoy, persuade, direct, influence. (*misconduct, mislead, follow*)

lead *n.* priority, preeminence, initiative, guidance, control. (*subordination, inferiority, submission*)

lean *a.* meager, lank, tabid, emaciated, shriveled, bony, thin, scraggy, skinny, slender, scanty. (*fat, brawny, plump, well-conditioned*)

lean *v.* incline, rest, support, tend, bend, depend, hang, repose, confide, slope. (*stabilize*)

learned conversant, erudite, read, skilled, scholarly, literary, knowing, well-informed, versed. (*illiterate, ignorant, unlearned, unscholarly*)

learning knowledge, erudition, literature, lore, letters, acquirements, attainments, scholarship, education, tuition, culture. (*ignorance, boorishnees, illiterateness, emptiness, sciolism, intuition*)

leave liberty, permission, license, concession. (*restriction, prohibition, prevention, inhibition, refusal*)

legend myth, fable, marvelous story, fiction. (*history, fact, actual occurrence*)

lengthy diffuse, prolix, tedious, long-drawn, verbose. (*concise, compendious, curt, short, brief*)

lesson precept, warning, instruction, lecture, homily, information. (*misinstruction, misguidance, misinformation*)

level *n.* plane, surface, floor, equality, aim, platform, ground, coordinateness, horizontalness. (*unevenness, acclivity, declivity, inequality, incoordinateness, verticality*)

level *v.* plane, smooth, roll, flatten, equalize, raze. (*roughen, furrow, disequalize, graduate*)

level *a.* horizontal, plain, flat, even, smooth. (*rough, uneven, broken, rolling*)

libel defamation, detraction, traducement, calumny, slander, defamatory publication, lampoon. (*retraction, vindication, apology, eulogy, panegyric*)

liberal free, gentle, refined, polished, generous, bountiful, catholic, enlarged, copious, ample, profuse, large, handsome, munificent, abundant, nobleminded, bounteous, tolerant, plentiful. (*churlish*)

liberty freedom, leave, independence, permission, privilege, license, franchise, immunity, insult, impropriety, volition, voluntariness, exemption. (*slavery, servitude, restraint, constraint, submission*)

licentious voluptuous, dissolute, rakish, debauched, self-indulgent, lax, profligate, loose, unbridled. (*temperate, strict, sober, self-controlled*)

lie *n.* falsehood, untruth, fabrication, subterfuge, evasion, fib, fiction, falsity. (*truth, fact, veracity*).

lie *v.* rest, repose, be, remain. (*rise, move, stir*)

life vitality, duration, existence, condition, conduct, animation, vivacity, personality, state, society, morals, spirit, activity, history, career. (*mortality, decease, death, nonexistence, dullness*)

lift raise, elevate, upraise, upheave, exalt, hoist, elate, erect. (*lower, sink, depress, crush, overwhelm*)

light *n.* luminosity, radiance, beam, gleam, phosphorescence, scintillation, coruscation, flash, brightness, brilliancy, effulgence, splendor, blaze, candle, lamp, lantern, explanation, instruction, illumination, understanding, interpretation, day, life. (*darkness, dimness, obscurity, shade, duskiness, gloom, extinction, misinterpretation, ignorance*)

light *a.* imponderous, portable, unweighted, buoyant, volatile, easy, digestible, scanty, active, unencumbered, empty, slight, gentle, unsteady, capricious, vain, frivolous, characterless, thoughtless, unthoughtful, unconsidered, inadequate, unsubstantial, inconsiderable, not difficult, bright, whitish, trifling. (*heavy, ponderous*)

likeness similarity, resemblance, correspondence, similitude, parity, copy, imitation, portrait, representation, image, effigy, carte de visite, picture. (*dissimilarity, dissimilitude, disparity, inequality, unlikeness, original*)

line cord, thread, length, outline, row, direction, verse, course, method, succession, sequence, continuity. (*breadth, contents, space, divergency*)

liquid fluid, liquescent, melting, running, watery, fluent, soft, mellifluous, limpid, flowing, clear, smooth. (*solid, solidified, concrète, congealed*)

listen hear, attend, hearken, incline, give ear, heed. (*disregard, ignore, refuse, repudiate*)

literal exact, grammatical, verbal, close, real, positive, actual, plain. (*general, substantial, metaphorical, free, spiritual*)

literary erudite, scholarly, studious. (*illiterate*)

literature lore, erudition, reading, study, learning, attainment, scholarship, literary works. (*genius, intuition, inspiration*)

little small, tiny, pygmy, diminutive, short, brief, scanty, unimportant, insignificant, slight, weak, inconsiderable, trivial, illiberal, mean, petty, paltry, dirty, shabby, dwarf. (*big, bulky, large*)

live *v.* vegetate, grow, survive, continue, abide, dwell, last, subsist, behave, act, breathe, exist. (*die, perish, wither, demise, migrate, vanish, fade*)

live *a.* animate. (*inanimate, defunct*)

load *n.* weight, lading, cargo, oppression, incubus, drag, burden. (*refreshment, support, solace*)

load *v.* burden, charge, lade, cargo, cumber, oppress. (*disburden, unload, disencumber, lighten*)

loan advance, mortgage, hypothecation. (*recall, resumption, foreclosure*)

locate place, establish, settle, fix, dispose, lodge. (*displace, disestablish, dislodge, remove*)

lofty elevated, towering, high, dignified, eminent, stately, haughty, majestic, airy, tall. (*depressed, low, stunted, undignified, ordinary, unstately, mean, unimposing, unassuming, affable*)

logical close, argumentative, sound. (*inconclusive, illogical, fallacious*)

lonesome forlorn, dreary, forsaken, wild, solitary, desolate, lonely. (*cheerful, befriended, festive*)

long protracted, produced, dilatory, lengthy, tedious, prolix, extensive, diffuse, far-reaching. (*short, curt, curtailed, brief, speedy, quick, concise*)

loose *v.* untie, unfasten, let go. (*tie, fasten, hold*)

loose *a.* unbound, detached, flowing, scattered, sparse, vague, inexact, rambling, dissoluted, licentious. (*bound, tied, fastened, tight*)

lose miss, drop, mislay, forfeit. (*keep, retain*)

loss mislaying, dropping, forfeiture, missing, privation, waste, detriment, damage. (*preservation, recovery, earning, satisfaction, restoration, economy, augmentation, advantage, gain*)

lot chance, fortune, fate, hazard, ballot, doom. (*law, provision, arrangement, disposal, design, purpose, plan, portion, allotment*)

loud sounding, sonorous, resonant, noisy, audible, vociferous, clamorous, obstreperous. (*soft*)

love affection, attachment, passion, devotion, benevolence, charity, kindness. (*hatred, dislike*)

lovely amiable, lovable, enchanting, beautiful, pleasing, delightful, charming. (*unamiable, unlovable, hateful, hideous, plain, homely, unattractive*)

lover suitor, wooer, sweetheart, swain, beau. (*husband, wife, mate*)

low abated, sunk, depressed, stunted, declining, deep, subsided, inaudible, cheap, gentle, dejected, degraded, mean, abject, base, unworthy, lowly, feeble, moderate, frugal, repressed, subdued, reduced, poor, humble. (*elevated, lofty, tall*)

lower *v.* depress, decrease, reduce, bate, abate, drop, humiliate, sink, debase, humble, diminish. (*hoist, raise, heighten, exalt, increase, aggrandize*)

lower *a.* inferior. (*higher, superior*)

loyal submissive, obedient, faithful, allegiant, true, constant. (*insubmissive, insurgent, malcontent, rebellious, disobedient, unfaithful, unallegiant*)

lucky fortunate, auspicious, prosperous, successful, favorable. (*unlucky, unfortunate, inauspicious*)

ludicrous ridiculous, farcical, laughable, comic, droll, funny, comical. (*serious, momentous, grave*)

lunatic mad, maniacal, crazy, wild, unthinking. (*sane, levelheaded, intelligent*)

lurid murky, lowering, wan, dismal, gloomy. (*bright, luminous*)

luscious sweet, delicious, sugary, honied, delightful, toothsome, delightsome. (*sour, sharp*)

luxurious voluptuous, self-indulgent, pleasurable, sensual, pampered. (*hard, painful, self-denying, ascetic, hardy*)

luxury effeminacy, epicurism, voluptuousness, wantonness, self-indulgence, softness, animalism, delicacy, dainty, profuseness. (*hardness, asceticism, stoicism, self-denial, hardship*)

lying mendacious, false, untrue, untruthful. (*true, veracious*)

mad insane, demented, furious, lunatic, infuriated, crazy, maniacal, frantic, rabid, wild, distracted. (*sane, sound, sensible, quiet, composed*)

madden infuriate, enrage, exasperate, inflame. (*calm, pacify, assuage, mesmerize, lay*)

magnanimous noble, high-minded, exalted, high-souled, great-souled, lofty, honorable. (*mean*)

magnificent grand, magnanimous, noble, splendid, superb, august, imposing, gorgeous, stately, majestic, dignified, sublime, pompous. (*petty*)

maid maiden, girl, damsel, lass, virgin. (*matron, married woman*)

main bulk, majority, body, principal, trunk, chief, leading, most important, first. (*portion, section, minority, branch, limb, tributary, member*)

majority superiority, eldership, priority, bulk, preponderance, seniority. (*inferiority, juniority*)

make create, produce, fashion, frame, fabricate, construct, effect, do, perform, execute, find, gain, compel, establish, constitute, reach, mold, shape, form, bring about. (*annihilate, unmake, undo, dismember, disintegrate, destroy, defeat, miss, lose, mar*)

manage handle, manipulate, control, conduct, administer, mold, regulate, contrive, train, husband, direct, wield. (*mismanage, misconduct, upset, derange, misuse*)

manageable easy, feasible, possible, docile, tractable, practicable. (*difficult, impracticable, impossible, unmanageable, intractable, refractory*)

management treatment, conduct, administration, government, address, skill, superintendence, skillful treatment. (*maltreatment, misconduct, maladministration, misgovernment, maladroitness*)

manifest visible, obvious, distinct, conspicuous, indubitable, clear, plain, patent, apparent, evident, open. (*invisible, dubious, inconspicuous, indistinct*)

manner mode, method, style, form, fashion, carriage, behavior, deportment, habit, sort, kind. (*work, project, design, performance, life, action, proceeding, appearance, being*)

manners deportment, behavior, carriage, courtesy, politeness, intercourse, demeanor. (*misdemeanor, misbehavior, unmannerliness*)

manufacture make, production, fabrication, composition, construction, manipulation, molding. (*use, employment, consumption, wear*)

many numerous, abundant, frequent, manifold, divers, sundry, multifarious. (*few, scarce, rare*)

mark *n.* trace, token, sign, symptom, impression, vestige, indication, note. (*erasure, obliteration, effacement, unindicativeness, plainness*)

mark *v.* stamp, label, sign, indicate, decorate, brand, stigmatize, signalize, note, observe, regard, heed, specify, specialize. (*ignore, overlook, omit*)

martial military, brave, warlike. (*unmartial, unmilitary, peaceful*)

marvel wonder, prodigy, admiration, portent, miracle, astonishment, amazement, phenomenon. (*incuriosity, unconcern, joke, trifle, farce, bagatelle*)

masculine male, manly, manful. (*female, feminine, womanish, womanly*)

mask *n.* pretext, screen, pretense, ruse, cover, hypocrisy. (*truth, nakedness, detection, exposure*)

mask *v.* hide, screen, blink, cloak, disguise. (*expose, unmask, detect*)

master *n.* lord, ruler, governor, owner, possessor, proprietor, teacher, professor, adept, chief. (*servant, slave, subject, property, learner, pupil, tyro*)

master *v.* conquer, overcome, subdue, overpower. (*yield, fail, surrender, succumb*)

masterly finished, artistic, consummate, skillful, clear, dexterous, expert. (*clumsy, rude, bungling, unskilled, botchy, maladroit*)

match *n.* equal, mate, companion, contest, competition, tally, equality, pair. (*superior, inferior*)

match *v.* equal, compare, oppose, pit, adapt, sort, suit, mate. (*fail, exceed, predominate, surpass, mismatch, dissociate, separate, misfit, misadapt, missort*)

matchless consummate, incomparable, peerless, surpassing, inimitable. (*common, ordinary*)

matter substance, stuff, subject, body, importance, the visible, tangible, substantial, corporeal, physical, ponderable. (*immateriality, spirituality, mind, intellect*)

meager thin, lean, lank, scanty, barren, dry, tame. (*stout, fat, brawny, abundant, fertile, copious*)

mean *a.* common, low, base, spiritless, dishonorable, contemptible, despicable, beggarly, sordid, vulgar, niggardly, vile, middle, intermediate, average. (*high, exalted, eminent, spirited, honorable*)

mean *n.* medium, moderation, balance, average. (*extreme, excess, preponderance, disproportion*)

mean *v.* intend, purpose, design, signify, denote, indicate, hint, suggest. (*say, state, enunciate*)

meanness penuriousness, littleness, selfishness, baseness, smallness, illiberality, ungenerousness, sordidness. (*nobleness, unselfishness, liberality*)

means resources, instrument, media. (*end, purpose, object*)

mechanical habitual, automatic, unreflective, spontaneous, effortless, unimpassioned. (*labored, self-conscious, feeling, forced, spirited, appreciative*)

meddlesome officious, obtrusive, intrusive, interfering. (*unofficious, inobtrusive, unmeddlesome*)

mediocrity mean, commonplace, medium, average, sufficiency. (*excellence, superiority, rarity*)

meek mild, gentle, submissive, modest, yielding, unassuming. (*bold, arrogant, self-asserting*)

melancholy gloomy, sad, dejected, disconsolate, dismal, moody, hypochondriacal, cast down. (*lively, sprightly, gladsome, gleesome, blithesome*)

mellow ripe, rich, full-flavored, jovial, mature, soft. (*unripe, harsh, sour, acid, acrid, crabbed*)

memorable great, striking, remarkable, conspicuous, prominent, noticeable, illustrious, extraordinary, famous, distinguished. (*petty, trifling*)

memory remembrance, reminiscence, perpetuation, recollection, retention, retrospect, fame. (*forgetfulness, oblivion*)

mend repair, restore, correct, promote, improve, rectify, reform, amend, ameliorate, better. (*damage, impair, pervert, retard, deteriorate, falsify*)

menial domestic, attendant, dependent, servile, drudge. (*paramount, sovereign, supreme, lordly*)

mental intellectual, subjective, metaphysical, psychical, psychological. (*corporeal, objective, physical, bodily*)

mention declaration, notice, announcement, observation, remark, hint, communication. (*silence, suppression, forgetfulness, omission*)

mercantile commercial, interchangeable, wholesale, retail, marketable. (*stagnant, unmarketable*)

merchant trader, dealer, importer, tradesman. (*shopman, salesman, hawker, huckster*)

merciful compassionate, kindhearted, element, gracious, kind. (*pitiless, unrelenting, remorseless*)

mere pure, unmixed, absolute, uninfluenced, unadulterated, unaffected, simple. (*mixed, compound, impure, biased*)

merit goodness, worth, worthiness, desert, excellence. (*badness, demerit, unworthiness, worthlessness, weakness, imperfection, error, defect, fault*)

meteoric momentary, flashing, displosive, phosphorescent, pyrotechnic, coruscant, volcanic. (*permanent, beaming, burning, steady, persistent, enduring*)

method order, system, rule, way, manner, mode, course, process, regularity, arrangement. (*disorder, conjecture, quackery, empiricism, experimentation, assumption, guesswork*)

methodical methodic, orderly, systematical, systematic, regular. (*disorderly, unmethodical, unsystematical, irregular*)

middling ordinary, average, pretty well, not bad, well enough.

midst middle, center, thick, throng, heart. (*outskirt, confine, edge, limit, extreme, purlieu, margin*)

might strength, force, power, ability. (*weakness, infirmity, feebleness*)

mild moderate, lenient, calm, gentle, genial, tempered, soft, meek, tender, placid. (*violent, wild, fierce, savage, strong, severe, merciless, harsh*)

mind soul, spirit, intellect, understanding, opinion, sentiment, judgment, belief, choice, inclination, desire, will, liking, purpose, spirit, impetus, memory, remembrance, recollection. (*body, limbs, organization, action, proceeding, conduct*)

mindful regardful, attentive, thoughtful, careful, recollective. (*regardless, inattentive, mindless*)

mingle mix, compound, blend, confound, confuse, intermingle, associate, amalgamate. (*separate, segregate, sift, sort, analyze, discompound, eliminate, classify, unravel, avoid*)

minister servant, officer, delegate, official, ambassador, subordinate, ecclesiastic, clergyman, priest, parson, divine, preacher, pastor, shepherd, reverend, curate, vicar. (*monarch, government, master, superior, principal, head, layman, fold, flock*)

minute diminutive, microscopic, tiny, exact, searching, specific, detailed. (*monstrous, enormous, huge, inexact, superficial, general, broad, comprehensive*)

mischief damage, hurt, detriment, disservice, annoyance, injury, ill turn, damage, harm. (*compensation, good turn, benefit, gratification*)

mischievous detrimental, injurious, spiteful, wanton. (*beneficial, advantageous, reparatory, conservative, careful, protective*)

miser niggard, churl, skinflint, curmudgeon, screw, scrimp, hunks. (*prodigal, spendthrift, rake*)

miserable abject, forlorn, pitiable, wretched, worthless, despicable, disconsolate. (*respectable, worthy, happy, contented, comfortable*)

misery wretchedness, heartache, woe, unhappiness. (*happiness, glee*)

mock jeer, ridicule, flout, mimic, insult, ape, deride, deceive, imitate. (*salute, welcome, respect, admire, compliment*)

model standard, pattern, example, type, mold, design, kind. (*imitation, copy, production, execution, work*)

moderate *v.* control, soften, allay, regulate, repress, govern, temper. (*disturb, disorganize, excite, misconduct*)

moderate *a.* limited, temperate, calm, dispassionate, sober, abstinent, sparing, steady, ordinary. (*extravagant, intemperate, rigorous, excessive, violent, extraordinary*)

modern present, existent, new, newfangled, new-fashioned, recent, late, novel, later. (*past, bygone, former, older, ancient, old-fashioned, antiquated, obsolete*)

modesty sobriety, diffidence, bashfulness, humility, pure-mindedness. (*vanity, conceit, self-sufficiency, self-admiration, foppery, coxcombry, wantonness, shamelessness, effrontery*)

moment instant, second, importance, twinkling, trice, weight, force, gravity, consequence, avail. (*age, period, century, generation, triviality, insignificance, worthlessness, unimportance, inefficacy*)

monopoly privilege, engrossment, appropriation, exclusiveness, preoccupancy, impropriation. (*participation, partnership, community, competition*)

monotonous uniform, unvaried, dull, humdrum, undiversified, tedious. (*varying, changing*)

monstrous prodigious, portentous, marvelous, deformed, abnormal, hideous, preposterous, intolerable. (*ordinary, familiar, unnoticeable, fair, comely, shapely, regular, natural, reasonable, just*)

moral mental, ideal, intellectual, spiritual, ethical, probable, inferential, presumptive, analogous, virtuous, well-conducted. (*physical, material, practical, demonstrative, mathematical, immoral, vicious*)

mortal human, ephemeral, sublunary, short-lived, deadly, fatal, perishable, destructive. (*immortal, divine, celestial, life-giving, venial, superficial*)

motive inducement, purpose, design, prompting, stimulus, reason, impulse, incitement. (*execution, action, effort, deed, attempt, project, preventive*)

move change, go, progress, stir, affect, agitate, actuate, impel, propose, advance, propel, instigate, provoke. (*stand, stop, lie, rest, stay, allay, deter*)

movement motion, move, change of place. (*stop, rest, pause, stillness, quietness*)

much abundant, plenteous, greatly, abundantly, far, considerable, ample. (*little, scant, slightly, shortly, short, near*)

muddle fail, waste, fritter away, confuse, derange, misarrange. (*clarify, manage, economize*)

muggy foggy, misty, dank, damp, murky, dim, vaporous, cloudy. (*clear, bright, vaporless*)

multitude crowd, swarm, accumulation, throng, concourse, number, host, mob, rabble. (*paucity, scantiness, sprinkling*)

munificent liberal, princely, bounteous, generous. (*niggardly, beggarly*)

murmur undertone, whisper, mutter, grumble, complaint, repining. (*clamor, vociferation, bawling*)

muscular powerful, brawny, robust, sinewy, strong, stalwart, athletic, lusty, sturdy. (*debile, flabby, feeble, lanky*)

musical melodious, harmonious, dulcet, concordant, rhythmical, tuneful, mellifluous. (*unmelodious, inharmonious, harsh, discordant*)

musty fusty, rank, moldy, frowzy, stale, sour, fetid, mildewed. (*fragrant, fresh, balmy, aromatic*)

mutter murmur, mumble. (*enunciate, exclaim, pronounce, vociferate*)

mysterious dim, obscure, unrevealed, unexplained, unaccountable, reserved, veiled, hidden, secret, incomprehensible, mystic, inexplicable. (*clear, plain, obvious, explained, understood, easy*)

mystery enigma, puzzle, obscurity, secrecy, veil, shroud, arcanum. (*publication, solution, commonplace, truism, matter of fact*)

mystify confuse, bamboozle, hoodwink, puzzle, confound, mislead, obfuscate. (*illumine, enlighten, inform, guide*)

naked nude, bare, unclothed, denuded, undraped, defenseless, destitute, unqualified, uncolored, unvarnished, mere, simple. (*dressed, robed, draped, muffled, protected, qualified, veiled, shrouded*)

name *n.* designation, cognomenation, appellation, title, fame, reputation, authority, appointment, stead, representation. (*namelessness, anonymity, misnomer, pseudonym, obscurity, ingloriousness, disrepute, individuality, person*)

name *v.* specify, designate, call, indicate. (*misname, miscall, misdesignate, misindicate, hint, suggest, shadow, adumbrate*)

narrow straight, straightened, slender, thin, spare, contracted, limited, cramped, pinched, scant, close, scrutinizing, near, bigoted, niggardly, tight. (*wide, broad, ample, thick, expanded, easy, liberal*)

nasty foul, offensive, odious, disagreeable, indelicate, impure, gross, unclean, obscene. (*nice, pleasant, sweet, savory, agreeable, pure*)

natural intrinsic, essential, regular, normal, cosmical, true, probable, consistent, spontaneous, artless, original. (*ascititious, adventitious, abnormal*)

nature essence, creation, constitution, structure, disposition, truth, regularity, kind, sort, character, species, affection, naturalness. (*thing, object, subject, man, being, creature, monstrosity, unnaturalness, art, fiction, romance, invention*)

near nigh, close, adjacent, neighboring. (*far away, distant, remote*)

necessary certain, inevitable, indispensable, requisite, essential, compulsory, needful, expedient. (*contingent, casual, optional, discretional, unnecessary, unessential, free*)

necessity indispensableness, inevitableness, need, indigence, requirement, want, fate, destiny. (*dispensability, uncertainty, superfluity, uselessness, competence, affluence, casualty, contingency*)

neglect *v.* slight, overlook, omit, disregard, disesteem, despise, contemn. (*consider, respect, notice, observe, regard, esteem, tend, attend, foster, study*)

neglect *n.* negligence, disregard, omission, failure, default, slight, carelessness, remissness. (*attention, consideration, respect, notice, regard, esteem*)

nerve strength, firmness, resolution. (*nerveless, forceless, feeble, weak, enfeebled, impotent, palsied*)

new novel, recent, fresh, modern. (*old, ancient, antique, antiquated, obsolete*)

nice fastidious, scrupulous, accurate, neat, discerning, dainty, pleasant, agreeable, exact, fine, finished, particular. (*coarse, unscrupulous, inaccurate, rude, rough, undiscriminating, nasty, nauseous, disagreeable*)

nobility distinction, dignity, rank, peerage, lordship, loftiness, generosity, rank, aristocracy. (*obscurity, meanness, commonalty, serfdom, paltriness, contemptibleness, plebeianism*)

noble grand, aristocratic, generous, illustrious, exalted, worthy, magnanimous, dignified, excellent, lofty-minded, honorable, fine. (*mean, plebeian, ignoble, paltry*)

noisome hurtful, harmful, nocuous, pestilential. (*wholesome, salutary, salubrious, beneficial*)

noisy loud, clamorous, stunning. (*still, soft, inaudible, whispering, soothing, musical, melodious*)

nominal trifling, suppositious, ostensible, professed, pretended, formal. (*real, deep, serious, important, grave, substantial, actual, intrinsic, veritable*)

nonsense absurdity, trash, folly, pretense, jest, balderdash. (*sense, wisdom, truth, fact, gravity*)

notice observation, cognizance, heed, advice, news, consideration, visitation, mark, note. (*oversight, disregard, misinformation, mistidings, neglect*)

notion apprehension, idea, conception, judgment, opinion, belief, expectation, sentiment. (*misapprehension, falsification, misbelief, misjudgment, frustration, misconception*)

notorious known, undisputed, recognized, allowed. (*suspected, reported, reputed*)

nuisance offense, annoyance, plague, pest, trouble. (*gratification, blessing, pleasure, delight*)

obedience submission, compliance, subservience. (*resistance, rebellion, violation, transgression*)

obesity fatness, fleshiness, corpulence, plumpness, corpulency, embonpoint. (*leanness, thinness*)

obey submit, comply, yield. (*resist, disobey*)

object appearance, sight, design, end, aim, motive, intent, view, goal. (*idea, notion, conception, fancy, subject, proposal, purpose, effect*)

object to oppose, contravene, obstruct, demur to, except to, gainsay, disapprove. (*approve, approve of*)

oblige compel, coerce, necessitate, force, benefit, favor, accommodate, gratify, bind, constrain. (*release, acquit, induce, persuade, annoy, disoblige*)

obliging kind, considerate, compliant, complaisant, accommodating. (*discourteous, rude, crossgrained, perverse, unaccommodating, disobliging*)

obscene impure, immodest, indecent, lewd, foul, indelicate, filthy, disgusting, foulmouthed. (*pure, modest, decent*)

obscure dark, dim, lowering, indistinct, enigmatical, uncertain, doubtful, unascertained, humble, unintelligible, mean. (*bright, luminous, distinct, lucid, plain, plainspoken, intelligible, unambiguous, ascertained, eminent, prominent*)

observance attention, fulfillment, respect, celebration, performance, ceremony, custom, form, rule, practice. (*inobservance, inattention, breach, disrespect, disregard, desuetude, disuse, nonperformance, informality, unceremoniousness, omission*)

observant regardful, attentive, mindful, obedient, watchful, heedful. (*disregardful, neglectful*)

observation contemplation, study, remark, attention, notice, comment. (*disregard, oversight*)

obstacle impediment, obstruction, hindrance, objection, bar, difficulty, check. (*course, proceeding, career, advancement*)

obstinate headstrong, stubborn, refractory, self-willed, pertinacious, obdurate, perverse, intractable. (*amenable, complaisant, yielding, docile, ductile, characterless, irresolute, wavering*)

obvious plain, self-evident, manifest, explicit, apparent, open, patent. (*remote, obscure, far-fetched, involved, latent*)

occasion conjuncture, opportunity, occurrence, cause, need, event, reason, necessity, opening, ground. (*untimeliness, unseasonableness, frustration*)

occult latent, hidden, unrevealed, mysterious, secret, dark, unknown. (*developed, plain, patent*)

occupation employment, avocation, possession, usurpation, encroachment, tenure, calling, pursuit, trade, business, holding. (*idleness, vacancy, leisure*)

odd alone, sole, unmatched, remaining, over, fragmentary, uneven, singular, peculiar, queer, quaint, fantastical, uncommon, nondescript. (*aggregate, consociate, matched, balanced, squared, integrant, even, common, usual, regular, normal*)

odious hateful, offensive, detestable, abominable, hated. (*delectable, grateful, acceptable*)

offense attack, sin, crime, umbrage, transgression, misdeed, injury, wrong, affront, outrage, insult, trespass, indignity, misdemeanor. (*defense, innocence, guiltlessness*)

offensive aggressive, obnoxious, distasteful, displeasing, foul, fetid, unsavory. (*defensive, grateful, pleasant, savory*)

offer propose, exhibit, proffer, present, tender, extend, adduce, volunteer. (*withhold, withdraw*)

office service, duty, appointment, function, employment, station, business, post. (*leisure, vacancy*)

officious meddling, interfering, pushing, forward, intrusive, intermeddling. (*backward, negligent, remiss, unofficious, retiring, modest, backward*)

often frequently, repeatedly. (*infrequently*)

old aged, pristine, long-standing, ancient, preceding, antiquated, obsolete, senile, antique. (*youthful, young, recent, fresh, modern, subsequent*)

ominous portentous, suggestive, threatening, foreboding, premonitory, unpropitious. (*auspicious, propitious, encouraging*)

open *v.* unclose, lay open, lay bare, expose, explain, disclose, initiate, begin, commence. (*close, shut up, conceal, enclose, mystify, misinterpret, conclude, cover*)

open *a.* accessible, free, available, unshut, unfolded, public, free, unrestricted, unreserved, unaffected, genuine, barefaced, undisguised, aboveboard, liberal, unclosed, candid, frank, ingenuous, unsettled, undetermined. (*inaccessible, closed, barred, unavailable, shut, close, secretive, reserved*)

opening aperture, gap, opportunity, space, commencement, initiation, start, inauguration, hole, fissure, chink, beginning. (*occlusion, obstruction, stopgap, unreasonableness, contretemps, inopportuneness, enclosure, termination, close, end, conclusion*)

operation agency, action, exercise, production, influence, performance. (*cessation, inaction, rest*)

opinion conviction, view, judgment, notion, idea, impression, estimation, theory.

opportunity occasion, turn, opening, convenience. (*inopportuneness, unseasonableness, lapse*)

opposite facing, adverse, repugnant, inconsistent, irreconcilable, contrary, antagonistic, counter, contradictory. (*agreeing, coincident, consentaneous*)

opposition resistance, hostility, obstacle, obstruction.

oppressive heavy, overpowering, unjust, galling, extortionate, grinding. (*light, just, compassionate*)

order *n.* arrangement, condition, sequence, direction, rank, grade, class, decree, succession, series, method, injunction, precept, command. (*disarrangement, confusion, disorder*)

order *v.* arrange, dispose, regulate, adjust, direct, command, classify, ordain, enjoin, prescribe, appoint, manage. (*disarrange, confuse, unsettle, disorganize*)

ordinary settled, wonted, conventional, plain, inferior, commonplace, humdrum, matter of fact. (*extraordinary, unusual, uncommon, superior*)

organization structure, form, construction. (*disorganization*)

origin source, commencement, spring, cause, derivation, rise, beginning. (*termination, conclusion, extinction*)

original primary, initiatory, primordial, peculiar, pristine, ancient, former, first. (*subsequent, terminal, modern, later, derivative*)

oust eject, dispossess, deprive, evict, eject, dislodge, remove. (*install, reinstate, readmit, restore*)

outcast castaway, reprobate, vagrant, vagabond, exiled.

outlandish strange, queer, grotesque, foreign, rustic, barbarous, rude. (*fashionable, modish*)

outline delineation, sketch, contour, draft, plan. (*form, substance, figure, object, subject, field*)

outrage outbreak, offense, wantonness, mischief, abuse, ebullition, violence, indignity, affront, insult. (*moderation, self-control, self-restraint, subsidence, coolness, calmness*)

outrageous excessive, unwarrantable, unjustifiable, wanton, flagrant, nefarious, atrocious, violent. (*moderate, justifiable, reasonable*)

outset opening, start, commencement, exordium, beginning, inauguration, preface. (*close, termination, conclusion, peroration*)

outward external, apparent, visible, sensible, superficial, ostensible, forthcoming, extrinsic, extraneous. (*internal, intrinsic, withdrawn, inapparent, inward*)

overcome vanquish, conquer, surmount, exhaust, defeat.

overflow redundancy, exuberance, superabundance, deluge, inundation. (*deficiency, exhaustion*)

overlook condone, connive, disregard, oversee, supervise, inspect, survey, review, excuse, pardon, forgive, neglect. (*visit, scrutinize, investigate, mark*)

oversight error, omission, mistake, neglect, slip, inadvertence, inspection, superintendence. (*scrutiny, correction, emendation, attention, mark*)

overthrow destroy, subvert, upset, overturn, ruin, demolish, defeat, rout, overcome, discomfit, invert, overset, reverse. (*restore, reinstate, construct, regenerate, redintegrate, revive, re-edify*)

overwhelm crush, quell, extinguish, drown, subdue, swamp. (*raise, reinvigorate, reinstate*)

owing due, imputable, ascribable, attributable. (*casualty, perchance, by chance, by accident*)

own possess, hold, have, acknowledge, avow, admit, confess. (*alienate, forfeit, lose, disclaim*)

pacify appease, conciliate, calm, still, soothe, quiet, tranquilize. (*exasperate, agitate, excite, irritate, rouse, provoke*)

pack *n.* burden, bundle, package, lot, parcel, load.

pack *v.* stow, compact, compress, cook. (*unpack, unsettle, jumble, displace, misarrange, dissipate, neutralize*)

pain *n.* penalty, suffering, distress, uneasiness, grief, labor, effort, anguish, torture, agony. (*reward, remuneration, ease, gratification, joy, pleasure*)

pain *v.* hurt, grieve, afflict, torment, rack, agonize, trouble, torture, aggrieve, annoy, distress. (*gratify, please, delight, rejoice, charm, relieve, ease*)

painful afflicting, distressful, grieving, grievous, excruciating, hurting.

painstaking careful, attentive, diligent, laborious. (*careless, negligent*)

palatable tasteful, savory, appetizing, delicious, toothsome.

pale pallid, wan, faint, dim, undefined, etiolated, sallow, cadaverous. (*ruddy, high-colored*)

palmy prosperous, glorious, distinguished, victorious, flourishing. (*depressed, inglorious, undistinguished, unflourishing*)

paltry mean, shabby, shuffling, trifling, prevaricating, shifty, contemptible, pitiable, vile, worthless, beggarly, trashy. (*noble, honorable, candid, conscientious, determined, straightforward*)

pang paroxysm, throe, agony, convulsion, smart, anguish, pain, twinge. (*pleasure, enjoyment, gratification, delight, delectation, fascination*)

paradox contradiction, enigma, mystery, absurdity, ambiguity. (*precept, proposition, axiom*)

parallel correspondent, congruous, correlative, analogous, concurrent, equidistant. (*different, opposed, incongruous, irrelative, divergent*)

paralyze deaden, benumb, prostrate, enervate, debilitate, enfeeble. (*give life, strengthen, nerve*)

pardon forgive, condone, absolve, acquit, remit, excuse, overlook. (*condemn, punish, visit*)

pardonable venial, excusable. (*inexcusable, unpardonable*)

parsimonious sparing, close, penurious, frugal, niggardly, illiberal, stingy. (*liberal, unsparing, profuse, extravagant*)

part portion, piece, fragment, fraction, division, member, constituent, element, ingredient, share, lot, concern, interest, participation, side, party, interest, faction, behalf, duty. (*whole, completeness, entirety, integrity, totality, mass, bulk, body*)

partake share, participate, accept, derive. (*forfeit, relinquish, forego, cede, yield, afford*)

partial restricted, local, peculiar, specific, favoring, inequitable, unfair, biased, particular. (*unrestricted, total, universal, general, impartial, equitable, just, fair, unbiased*)

particular local, specific, subordinate, detailed, partial, special, fastidious, minute, scrupulous, careful, accurate, exact, circumstantial, precise, delicate, nice. (*universal, general, unspecial, comprehensive, unscrupulous, uncareful, inaccurate, inexact, rough, coarse, indiscriminate, undiscriminating*)

partisan adherent, follower, party man, henchman, clansman, supporter, disciple.

partition barrier, division, enclosure, compartment, interspace, separation, distribution, allotment, screen. (*nonpartition, nondistinction, nonseparation, inclusion, comprehension, combination*)

partner associate, sharer, participator, colleague, coadjutor, confederate, accomplice, partaker, companion, spouse. (*rival, alien, competitor*)

passable traversable, navigable, penetrable, admissible, tolerable, ordinary. (*impassable, impervious, impenetrable, inadmissible, excellent*)

passage journey, thoroughfare, road, course, avenue, route, channel, clause, phrase, sentence, paragraph.

passive inactive, inert, quiescent, unresisting, unquestioning, negative, enduring, patient. (*active, alert, resistant, positive, unsubmissive, malcontent, vehement, impatient*)

pastime recreation, entertainment, amusement, diversion, play, sport. (*business, study, labor, task*)

patent obvious, evident, indisputable, plain. (*dubious, ambiguous, questionable*)

pathetic affecting, moving, emotional, tender, melting. (*ludicrous, farcical, unaffecting*)

patience endurance, resignation, submission, perseverance. (*resistance, unsubmissiveness, repining, rebellion, inconsistency, impatience*)

pattern model, sample, archetype, exemplar, specimen, shape, precedent, mold, design, shape. (*monstrosity, caricature, perversion, misrepresentation*)

pause *n.* stop, cessation, suspension, halt, intermission, rest. (*continuance, advancement, perseverance*)

pause *v.* cease, suspend, intermit, forbear, stay, wait, hesitate, demur, stop, desist. (*continue, proceed, advance, persist, persevere*)

peace quiet, tranquility, calm, repose, pacification, order, calmness, reconciliation, harmony, concord. (*noise, disturbance, tumult, agitation, hostility*)

peaceable unwarlike, inoffensive, quiet, peaceful, innocuous, mild, unquarrelsome, serene, placid. (*pugnacious, warlike, litigious, quarrelsome, savage*)

peculiar private, personal, characteristic, exceptional, exclusive, special, specific, particular, unusual, singular, uncommon, strange, rare, odd. (*public, common, general, universal, unspecial, ordinary*)

peculiarity speciality, individuality, distinctiveness, idiosyncrasy. (*generality, universality, community, uniformity, homology, homogeneity*)

people nation, community, populace, mob, crowd, vulgar, herd, mass, persons, inhabitants, commonalty, fellow creatures, tribe, race, group. (*aristocracy, nobility, government, ruler, oligarchy*)

perceive discern, distinguish, descry, observe, feel, touch, see, recognize, understand, know. (*miss, overlook, misunderstand, misconceive, misperceive*)

perception cognizance, apprehension, sight, understanding, discernment. (*incognizance, ignorance, imperception, misapprehension, misunderstanding*)

peremptory decisive, express, absolute, authoritative, dictatorial, dogmatic, imperious, despotic, positive. (*suggestive, entreative, mild, postulatory*)

perfect consummate, complete, full, indeficient, immaculate, absolute, faultless, impeccable, infallible, unblemished, blameless, unexceptionable, mature, ripe, pure. (*incomplete, meager, faulty, scant, short, deficient, defective, imperfect, peccable*)

perfectly fully, wholly, entirely, completely, totally, exactly, accurately. (*imperfectly, incompletely, partially, inaccurately*)

perform accomplish, do, act, transact, achieve, execute, discharge, fulfill, effect, complete, consummate, enact. (*miss, mar, misperform, misexecute*)

perhaps possibly, peradventure, perchance, maybe. (*certainly, inevitably*)

perilous hazardous, dangerous. (*safe, secure*)

period time, date, epoch, era, age, duration, continuance, limit, bound, end, conclusion, determination. (*eternity, datelessness, immemoriality, infinity, perpetuity, illimitability, endlessness, indefiniteness, indeterminateness*)

periodic stated, recurrent, regular, systematic, calculable. (*indeterminate, eccentric, irregular, incalculable, spasmodic, fitful*)

permeable penetrating, pervading. (*impenetrable, ineffective*)

perpetual constant, unceasing, endless, eternal, everlasting, unfailing, perennial, continual, enduring, incessant, uninterrupted. (*inconstant, periodic, recurrent, temporary, transient, falling, exhaustible*)

perplex embarrass, puzzle, entangle, involve, encumber, complicate, confuse, bewilder, mystify, harass, entangle. (*clear, enlighten, explicate, untangle, simplify, elucidate, disencumber*)

perseverance persistence, steadfastness, constancy, indefatigability, resolution, tenacity. (*inconstancy, unsteadfastness, fitfulness, caprice, irresoluteness, vacillation, wavering, indecision, variableness, levity, volatility*)

persuade induce, influence, incline, convince, dispose, urge, allure, incite. (*deter, disincline, indispose, mispersuade, misinduce, coerce, compel*)

perverse forward, untoward, stubborn, fractious, wayward, unmanageable, intractable, crotchety. (*docile, ductile, amenable, governable, complacent, accommodating, pleasant, obliging*)

pet darling, fondling, favorite, cosset, jewel, minion, idol. (*bugbear, aversion, scarecrow*)

petition supplication, entreaty, craving, application, appeal, salutation, prayer, request, instance. (*deprecation, expostulation, protest, command, injunction, claim, demand, requirement*)

petty small, mean, paltry, ignoble, trifling, narrow, trivial, contemptible. (*large, bighearted, noble, generous, chivalrous, magnificent, liberal*)

philanthropy humanity, love of mankind, generosity, charity, benevolence. (*misanthropy, hatred of men, selfishness, stinginess*)

philosopher doctor, savant, teacher, master, schoolman. (*ignoramus, sciolist, freshman, tyro, greenhorn, fool, dunce*)

philosophical wise, sound, conclusive, scientific, accurate, enlightened, rational, calm, unprejudiced. (*unsound, crude, vague, loose, inaccurate, popular*)

physical natural, material, visible, tangible, substantial, corporeal. (*mental, moral, intellectual, spiritual, immaterial, invisible, intangible, unsubstantial, supernatural, hyperphysical*)

picture likeness, resemblance, drawing, painting, representation, image, engraving. (*original*)

picturesque comely, seemly, graceful, scenic, artistic, pictorial, graphic. (*unseemly, uncouth, rude, unpicturesque, ugly, flat, tame, monotonous*)

pinch squeeze, grip, press, compress, nip, distress.

piquant pungent, sharp, lively, racy, severe, biting, cutting, smart, stimulating, keen, stinging, tart. (*tame, dull, flat, characterless, insipid*)

pithy terse, forceful, laconic, expressive, concise, spongy. (*weak, characterless, diluted, pointless*)

pity mercy, compassion, tenderness, commiseration, ruth, sympathy, condolence. (*cruelty, hardheartedness, relentlessness, pitilessness, ruthlessness*)

place locate, assign, fix, establish, settle, attribute, situate, put, set. (*disturb, remove, unsettle, disarrange, disestablish, misplace, misattribute, misassign, uproot, transplant, extirpate, eradicate, transport*)

plain level, even, flat, smooth, open, clear, unencumbered, unobstructed, uninterrupted, manifest, evident, obvious, unmistakable, simple, easy, natural, unaffected, homely, unsophisticated, open, unvarnished, unembellished, unreserved, artless. (*uneven, undulating, rugged, rough, abrupt, broken, confused, encumbered, obstructed, interrupted, questionable, uncertain, dubious, ambiguous, enigmatical*)

plan *n.* design, drawing, sketch, draft, scheme, project, contrivance, stratagem, device.

plan *v.* contrive, devise, sketch out, design, hatch

platonic cold, intellectual, unsensual, mental, philosophical. (*ardent, animal, sensual, passionate*)

plausible specious, superficial, passable, unctuous, fair-spoken, pretentious, ostensible, right, apparent, colorable, feasible, probable. (*genuine, sterling, unmistakable, profound*)

playful lively, sportive, jocund, frolicsome, gay, vivacious, sprightly. (*somber, dull*)

plea excuse, vindication, justification, ground, defense, apology, entreaty, request. (*charge, accusation, impeachment, action*)

pleasant grateful, agreeable, acceptable, pleasurable, desirable, gratifying, cheerful, enlivening, sportive, delicious, delectable, jocular, satisfactory, exquisite, merry. (*unpleasant, ungrateful, disagreeable, obnoxious, unacceptable, offensive, unlively*)

pleasure enjoyment, gratification, sensuality, self-indulgence, voluptuousness, choice, preference, will, inclination, purpose, determination, favor, satisfaction, indulgence. (*pain, suffering, affliction, trouble, asceticism, self-denial, abstinence, disinclination, aversion, indisposition, denial, refusal*)

plebeian low, vulgar, low-born, low-bred, coarse, ignoble. (*patrician, noble, aristocratic, refined, high-born, high-bred*)

plodding painstaking, industrious, persevering, laborious, studious. (*indiligent, unindustrious, distracted, inattentive, impatient, unpersevering, flighty, fitful*)

plot *n.* scheme, plan, stratagem, conspiracy, machination.

plot *v.* devise, concoct, conspire, contrive, frame, hatch, plan, scheme.

plump well-conditioned, well-rounded, chubby, strapping, bouncing, fleshy, brawny, full, fat, round, massive, portly. (*ill-conditioned, lean, emaciated, scraggy, weazen, macilent, lank, rawboned, shriveled, flaccid, tabid*)

plunge dip, dive, douse, duck, submerge, immerse, precipitate, sink, overwhelm, thrust under, pitch headlong. (*emerge, issue, soar, raise, extricate*)

poetical metrical, rhythmic, versified, lyric, rhyming, imaginative, creative, romantic, fictitious, dreamy, flighty. (*unmetrical, unrhythmical, prosaic, unpoetical, unversified, unimaginative, commonplace, historical, mathematical, logical, matter-of-fact, veracious, sober*)

poisonous venomous, infectant, vicious, corruptive, vitiative, noxious, baneful, malignant, morbific, virulent, pestiferous, deleterious. (*wholesome, genial, beneficial, sanative, invigorative, healthful, innoxious, restorative, remedial, hygienic*)

polite elegant, refined, well-bred, courteous, obliging, complaisant, civil, courtly, polished, genteel, accomplished. (*awkward, rude, uncouth, ill-bred, discourteous, boorish, clownish, disobliging*)

politic prudent, wise, sagacious, provident, diplomatic, judicious, cunning, wary, well-devised, discreet. (*imprudent, unwise, improvident, undiplomatic, impolitic*)

pompous magnificent, gorgeous, splendid, showy, sumptuous, ostentatious, stately, lofty, grand, bombastic, turgid, stiff, inflated, pretentious, coxcombical, assuming. (*unpretending, unobtrusive, modest, unassuming, plain-mannered, humbleminded*)

ponder think over, meditate on, weigh, consider, cogitate, deliberate, ruminate, reflect, amuse, study, resolve.

poor indigent, moneyless, impecunious, penniless, weak, meager, insufficient, deficient, faulty, unsatisfactory, inconsiderable, thin, scanty, bald. (*rich, wealthy, copious, affluent, abundant, liberal*)

popular common, current, vulgar, public, general, received, favorite, beloved, prevailing, approved, widespread, liked. (*exclusive, restricted, scientific, esoteric, unpopular, odious, detested*)

positive real, actual, substantial, absolute, independent, unconditional, unequivocal, explicit, fixed, settled, definitive, indisputable, decisive, express, enacted, assured, confident, direct, dogmatic, overbearing, dogmatical. (*negative, insubstantial, unreal, fictitious, imaginary, relative, contingent, dependent, conditional, implied, dubious, questionable*)

possess occupy, enjoy, have, hold, entertain, own. (*abandon, renounce, abjure, surrender, lose, forfeit, resign*)

possible practicable, feasible, likely, potential. (*impracticable, impossible*)

postpone defer, delay, prorogue, procrastinate. (*expedite, dispatch, accelerate*)

poverty want, need, indigence, destitution. (*abundance, wealth, affluence*)

power faculty, capacity, capability, potentiality, ability, strength, force, might, energy, susceptibility, influence, dominion, sway, command, government, agency, authority, rule, jurisdiction, effectiveness. (*incapacity, incapability, impotence, inability, weakness, imbecility, inertness, insusceptibility, subjection, powerlessness, obedience, subservience, ineffectiveness*)

powerful strong, potent, puissant, masterful, mighty. (*weak, poor*)

practice *n.* usage, habit, exercise, experience, exercitation, action, custom, manner, performance. (*disuse, dishabituation, inexperience, theory, speculation, nonperformance*)

practice *v.* perform, exercise, deal in, carry on.

praise eulogize, laud, commend, honor, glorify, compliment, celebrate, puff, extol, applaud, panegyrize. (*blame, censure, discommend, reprove*)

pray beg, beseech, entreat, implore, solicit, supplicate, adjure, invoke, crave.

prayer petition, supplication, entreaty, orison, benediction, suit, request.

precaution forethought, provision, premonition, anticipation, prearrangement, care, providence. (*carelessness, thoughtlessness, improvidence*)

preceding precedent, former, forgoing, prior, previous, antecedent, anterior. (*following, subsequent, posterior*)

precious dear, valuable, costly, cherished, treasured, beloved, estimable, of great value. (*cheap, valueless, worthless, unvalued, disesteemed*)

precise definite, exact, nice, pointed, accurate, correct, particular, formal, explicit, scrupulous, terse, punctilious, ceremonious, formal. (*indefinite, vague, inexact, rough, inaccurate, loose, circumlocutory, ambagious, tortuous, informal, unceremonious*)

predict prophesy, foretell, forecast, prognosticate, forebode, foreshadow.

prediction prophecy, prognostication, vaticination, foreannouncement, premonstration, foretelling, forebodement, presage, augury, foreshowing. (*narration, relation, history, account, report*)

preface introduction, proem, prelude, prologue, preamble, premiss. (*peroration, sequel, appendix, epilogue, postscript*)

prefer choose, elect, select, fancy, promote, advance, further. (*reject, postpone, defer, withhold*)

prejudice prepossession, prejudgment, predisposition, bias, unfairness, injury, harm, impairment, detriment, partiality, disadvantage, damage. (*judgment, fairness, impartiality, advantage*)

premature hasty, crude, unauthenticated, untimely, precocious, precipitate, too early, rash, unseasonable. (*ripe, timely, seasonable, opportune*)

premium reward, guerdon, encouragement, douceur, enhancement, bribe, recompense, bonus, prize, bounty. (*penalty, fine, amercement, mulct, forfeit, depreciation*)

preparation provision, readiness. (*unpreparedness, without provision*)

prepare fit, adapt, qualify, adjust, provide, arrange, order, lay, plan, equip, furnish, ready. (*misfit, misadapt, misprovide, derange, disarrange*)

prepossessing attractive, alluring, charming, winning, taking, engaging. (*repulsive, unattractive*)

preposterous monstrous, exorbitant, unreasonable, absurd, irrational, foolish, ridiculous. (*just, due, fair, reasonable, moderate, right, judicious*)

presence nearness, influence, intercourse, closeness. (*remoteness, absence, separation, distance*)

preserve defend, guard, save, keep safe, uphold, protect, maintain, rescue, spare. (*ruin, destroy*)

president chairman, moderator, principal, superintendent. (*member, subordinate, constituent, corporation, society, ward, institution*)

press urge, crowd, compel, force, squeeze, crush, compress, express, constrain, hurry, instigate, inculcate, impress, throng, encroach, lean, weigh, harass. (*relax, inhibit, persuade, entice, allure, solicit, touch, skim, graze, free, liberate, ease*)

presume suppose, anticipate, apprehend, venture, take for granted, conjecture, believe, deem, assume. (*infer, deduce, prove, argue, retire, withdraw, hesitate, distrust*)

pretend feign, simulate, offer, allege, exhibit, propound, affect, profess. (*verify, unmask, detect*)

pretense excuse, pretext, fabrication, simulation, cloak, mask, color, show, garb, plea, assumption, make-believe, outside show, pretension. (*verity, reality, truth, simplicity, candor, guilelessness, openness, veritableness, actuality, fact*)

pretty handsome, attractive, neat, trim, tasteful, pleasing, beautiful, fine, comely. (*ugly, grotesque*)

prevailing controlling, ruling, influential, operative, predominant, prevalent, rife, ascendant, most general, most common. (*mitigated, diminishing, subordinate, powerless*)

prevent hinder, obstruct, bar, neutralize, nullify, thwart, intercept, anticipate, forefend, frustrate, obviate, checkmate. (*promote, aid, facilitate, expedite, encourage, advance, accelerate, induce*)

price cost, figure, charge, expense, compensation, value, appraisement, worth. (*donation, discount, allowance, remittance, abatement*)

pride loftiness, haughtiness, lordliness, self-exaltation, arrogance, conceit, vainglory. (*lowliness, meekness, modesty, self-distrust*)

priggish coxcombical, dandified, foppish, affected, prim, conceited. (*plain, sensible, unaffected, simpleminded, simple-mannered*)

prim formal, precise, demure, starched, stiff, self-conscious, unbending, priggish. (*unformal, easy, genial, unaffected, natural, free, naive*)

primary first, original, earliest, elementary, main, chief, principal, important, leading, primitive, pristine. (*secondary, subordinate, posterior, unimportant, inferior, subsequent, later*)

primitive old-fashioned, primeval, quaint, simple, unsophisticated, archaic, pristine. (*modern, newfangled, sophisticated, modish*)

princely imperial, munificent, magnificent, superb, august, regal, royal, supreme. (*beggarly, mean, niggardly, poverty-stricken*)

principal highest, first, main, leading, chief, primary, foremost, preeminent, prominent. (*inferior, subordinate, secondary, supplemental, subject, auxiliary, minor*)

principle source, origin, motive, cause, energy, substance, element, power, faculty, truth, tenet, law, doctrine, axiom, maxim, postulate, rule. (*exhibition, manifestation, application, development*)

private special, peculiar, individual, secret, not public, retired, privy. (*general, public, open, unconcealed*)

privilege prerogative, immunity, franchise, right, liberty, advantage, claim, exemption. (*disfranchisement, disqualification, exclusion, prohibition, inhibition*)

prize booty, spoil, plunder, prey, forage, trophy, laurels, guerdon, premium, honors, ovation, palm. (*loss, forfeiture, fine, penalty, amercement, sacrifice, disappointment, failure, brand, stigma*)

probability likelihood, presumption, verisimilitude, chance, appearance. (*unlikelihood, improbability, impossibility, inconceivableness*)

probable likely, presumable, credible, reasonable. (*unlikely, unreasonable, incredible*)

proceed move, pass, advance, progress, continue, issue, emanate, flow, arise. (*recede, deviate, retreat, stand, stop, stay, desist, discontinue, ebb, retire*)

procession train, march, caravan, file, cortege, cavalcade, retinue. (*rabble, herd, rush, disorder, mob, confusion, rout*)

prodigal lavish, profuse, extravagant, reckless, wasteful, squandering, improvident. (*frugal, saving, hoarding, economical, niggardly, miserly, close*)

prodigious marvelous, portentous, wonderful, astounding, enormous, monstrous, amazing, surprising, remarkable, extraordinary, huge, vast. (*ordinary, commonplace, everyday, usual, familiar, moderate*)

produce *v.* exhibit, bear, furbish, afford, cause, create, originate, yield, extend, prolong, lengthen. (*withdraw, retain, stifle, withhold, neutralize, destroy, annihilate, curtail, shorten, contract, reduce*)

produce *n.* product, yield, fruit, profit, effect, consequence, result, amount.

product fruit, result, issue, consequence, effect, emanation, work. (*cause, principle, power, motive, energy, operation, action, tendency, law*)

production origination, evolution, formation, genesis, manufacture.

profane unconsecrated, secular, temporal, unsanctified, unholy, irreligious, irreverent, ungodly, wicked, godless, impious, blasphemous. (*holy, consecrated, sacred, spiritual, sanctified, reverent*)

profess declare, avow, acknowledge, own, confess, pretend, proclaim, lay claim to. (*conceal, suppress, disown, disavow, repudiate, renounce, abjure*)

profit gain, emolument, advantage, avail, acquisition, benefit, service, use, improvement. (*loss, detriment, damage, disadvantage, waste*)

profitable gainful, advantageous, desirable, beneficial, useful, productive, remunerative, lucrative. (*unprofitable, disadvantageous, undesirable, detrimental, unbeneficial, unprofitable, useless, vain, fruitless, unproductive, unremunerative*)

program advertisement, notice, plan, catalogue, schedule, performance. (*review, rehearsal, repetition, resume, analysis, précis*)

progress advancement, advance, movement, proceeding, way, journey, proficiency, speed, growth. (*delay, stoppage, retreat, stay, regression, failure, relapse*)

project plan, purpose, design, scheme, contrivance, device, venture. (*hazard, chance*)

prominent jutting out, protuberant, embossed, extended, manifest, conspicuous, eminent, distinguished, main, important, leading, characteristic, distinctive. (*receding, concave, rebated, indented, hollowed, engraved, entailed, withdrawn*)

promiscuous mingled, confused, undistinguished, unselected, unarranged, undistributed, unassorted, common, unreserved, casual, disorderly, unordered. (*sorted, select, orderly, arranged, distributed, reserved, assorted, exclusive, nice*)

promise *v.* pledge, engage, assure, covenant, pledge, stipulate.

promise *n.* engagement, assurance, word, pledge, oath, covenant.

promote aid, further, advance, excite, exalt, raise, elevate, prefer. (*discourage, repress, hinder, check, allay, depress, degrade, dishonor*)

prompt ready, alert, responsive, active, quick, brisk, apt, unhesitating. (*unready, sluggish, irresponsive, inactive*)

pronounce articulate, utter, declare, propound, deliver, assert, affirm, enunciate, express. (*mispronounce, mispropound, misaffirm, suppress, stifle, silence, choke, swallow, gabble, mumble*)

proof test, trial, examination, criterion, essay, establishment, comprobation, demonstration, evidence, testimony, scrutiny. (*disproof, failure, invalidity, shortcoming, fallacy, undemonstrativeness, reprobation*)

proper peculiar, appertinent, personal, own, constitutional, special, befitting, adapted, suited, suitable, appropriate, just, fair, equitable, right, decent, becoming, fit. (*common, inappertinent, alien, universal, nonspecial, unbefitting, unadapted*)

property quality, attribute, peculiarity, nature, characteristic, possessions, goods, wealth, estate, gear, resources, ownership.

proportion adaptation, relation, rate, distribution, adjustment, symmetry, interrelationship, uniformity, correlation. (*misproportion, misadjustment, incongruity, disparity, disharmony, disorder, irrelation, disproportion*)

propose offer, tender, proffer, bring forward, purpose, intend, mean, propound, move, design.

prosaic dull, matter-of-fact, tedious, prolix. (*poetic, animated, interesting, lively, fervid, eloquent*)

prospect view, vision, field, landscape, hope, anticipation, probability. (*viewlessness, dimness, obscurity, darkness, cloud, veiling, occultation, hopelessness, improbability*)

prospectus program, plan, catalogue, announcement, bill, scheme, compendium, brochure. (*subject, transaction, proceeding*)

prosperity success, wealth, welfare, good fortune, well-being, good luck. (*unsuccess, woe, adversity, failure, reverse*)

protect defend, fortify, guard, shield, preserve, cover, secure, save, vindicate. (*betray, endanger, imperil, abandon, expose*)

proud arrogant, haughty, imperious, supercilious, presumptuous, boastful, vainglorious, vain, ostentatious, elated, self-satisfied, lofty, imposing, magnificent, self-conscious. (*deferential, humble, affable, unpresuming, meek, lowly, ashamed, unimposing, mean*)

prove try, assay, test, establish, demonstrate, ascertain, argue, show, confirm, examine, substantiate, make trial of, verify, ascertain. (*pass, pretermit, refute, disprove, contradict, disestablish, neutralize*)

proverbial notorious, current, acknowledged, unquestioned. (*dubious, unfounded, suspicious, suspected, questionable*)

provide prepare, arrange, procure, afford, supply, contribute, yield, cater, furnish, get, agree, produce, collect, stipulate. (*neglect, overlook, withhold, retain, appropriate, refuse, deny*)

province tract, region, department, section, sphere, domain, territory. (*metropolis, center, capital*)

provision, provisions preparation, arrangement, produce, supply, anticipation, food, supplies, victuals, edibles, eatables. (*neglect, forgetfulness, thoughtlessness, oversight, destitution*)

provoke educe, summon, rouse, irritate, excite, challenge, vex, impel, offend, exasperate, anger, tantalize. (*allay, relegate, pacify, soothe, conciliate*)

proxy agency, substitution, representation, agent, substitute, representative, deputy, commissioner, lieutenant, delegate. (*principalship, personality, principal, person, authority*)

prudent wise, wary, cautious, circumspect, discreet, careful, judicious. (*foolish, unwary, incautious, indiscreet, rash, imprudent*)

prudish coy, overmodest, overnice, squeamish, reserved, demure. (*promiscuous*)

public open, notorious, common, social, national, exoteric, general, generally known. (*close, secret, private, domestic, secluded, solitary, personal*)

pull draw, drag, adduce, extract, tug, haul, pluck. (*push, eject, extrude, propel*)

punch perforate, poke, pierce, puncture, terebrate, bore. (*stop, plug, seal, bung*)

punish chastise, castigate, chasten, correct, whip, scourge, discipline. (*reward, recompense, remunerate, indemnify*)

pupil scholar, learner, student, tyro, novice, ward. (*teacher, master, proficient, adept, guardian*)

puppy youth, fop, coxcomb, prig. (*boor, clown, lout*)

pure clear, unmixed, simple, genuine, sheer, mere, absolute, unadulterated, uncorrupted, unsullied, unblemished, chaste, real, clean, spotless, immaculate, undefiled, unspotted, guileless, innocent, guiltless. (*foul, turbid, impure, adulterated, corrupt, sullied, stained, tarnished, defiled, mixed*)

purpose *v.* intend, determine, design, resolve, mean, propose. (*chance, risk, hazard, revoke, miscalculate, venture, stake*)

purpose *n.* intention, design, mind, meaning, view, object, aim, end, scope, point, resolve. (*chance, fortune, fate, accident, hazard, lot, casualty, lottery, hit*)

push press, drive, impel, shove, press against, propel, butt, thrust, urge, expedite, accelerate, reduce. (*pull, draw, drag, adduce*)

put place, lay, set, propose. (*remove, raise, displace, transfer, withdraw*)

puzzle *v.* pose, perplex, embarrass, bewilder, confound, mystify, confuse. (*enlighten, instruct*)

puzzle *n.* embarrassment, bewilderment, enigma, confusion, conundrum, intricacy, labyrinth. (*disentanglement, solution, explanation, extrication*)

quack empiric, mountebank, charlatan, impostor, pretender, humbug. (*dupe, gull, victim*)

quaint curious, recondite, abstruse, elegant, nice, affected, whimsical, odd, antique, archaic, fanciful, singular, old-fashioned. (*commonplace, ordinary, usual, coarse, common, modern, modish, fashionable, dowdy*)

qualified fitted, adapted, competent, suitable. (*unsuited, inappropriate, ineligible*)

quality condition, character, property, attribute, peculiarity, disposition, temper, sort, kind, description, capacity, power, virtue, nature, tendency. (*anomalousness, heterogeneousness, nondescript, incapacity, weakness, indistinctiveness, ineffectiveness, disqualification, negation, disability*)

quantity measure, amount, bulk, size, sum, portion, aggregate, muchness, part, share, division. (*margin, deficiency, deduction, want, inadequacy, scantiness, insufficiency, loss, deterioration, diminution, waste, wear, leakage*)

quarrel brawl, altercation, affray, squabble, feud, tumult, dispute, wrangle, variance, disagreement, misunderstanding, hostility, quarreling, embroilment, bickering, broil. (*confabulation, conversation, pleasantry, conciliation, friendliness*)

quarrelsome choleric, irascible, petulant, litigious, pugnacious, brawling, fiery, hot-tempered, contentious, irritable. (*peaceable, amenable, genial, unquarrelsome, inoffensive, mild, meek, conciliatory*)

quarter region, district, locality, territory, mercy, forbearance, pity. (*extermination, mercilessness, unsparingness, pitilessness, ruthlessness*)

queer odd, whimsical, quaint, cross, strange, crotchety, singular, eccentric. (*ordinary, common, usual, familiar, customary*)

question *v.* ask, inquire, interrogate, doubt, investigate, dubitate, controvert, dispute. (*dictate, state, assert, pronounce, enunciate, concede, endorse*)

question *n.* inquiry, interrogation, doubt, scrutiny, investigation, topic. (*reply, response, solution, answer, explanation, admission, concession*)

questionable doubtful, dubious, problematical, disputable, debatable, uncertain, suspicious. (*certain, evident, self-evident, obvious, indisputable*)

quick fast, rapid, speedy, expeditious, swift, hasty, prompt, ready, clever, sharp, shrewd, adroit, keen, fleet, active, brisk, nimble, lively, agile, alert, sprightly, transient, intelligent, irascible. (*slow, tardy, sluggish, inert, inactive, dull, insensitive*)

quiet *n.* rest, repose, stillness, calm, appeasement, pacification, silence, peace. (*unrest, motion, noise, agitation, excitement, disturbance, turmoil*)

quiet *v.* allay, appease, still, pacify, hush, lull, tranquilize, soothe, calm. (*rouse, excite, disturb, agitate, stir, urge, goad*)

quit leave, resign, abandon, relinquish, discharge, release, surrender, give up, depart from, forsake. (*seek, occupy, invade, bind, enforce, haunt*)

quite perfectly, entirely, completely, wholly, truly, altogether, totally. (*partially, imperfectly, barely, insufficiently, hardly*)

quote cite, name, adduce, plead, allege, note, repeat. (*disprove, refute, retort, oppose, contradict*)

racy fine-flavored, fresh, rich, pungent, piquant, spirited, smart, lively, vivacious, spicy. (*flavorless, dull, stupid*)

radical original, fundamental, thoroughgoing, unsparing, extreme, entire, innate, natural, essential, immanent, ingrained, underived, deep-seated. (*derived, ascititious, adventitious, superficial, extraneous, partial, moderate, conservative, acquired*)

rage *n.* fury, rabidity, choler, indignation, frenzy, anger, ire, dudgeon, mania, passion, madness, ferocity. (*reason, moderation, gentleness, temperateness, calmness, quiescence, mitigation, assuagement, tranquillity, mildness, softness*)

rage *v.* rave, storm, fume, be furious, be violent. (*be calm, be composed, be peaceful*)

raise lift, heave, elevate, exalt, advance, promote, heighten, enhance, awaken, rouse, excite, call forth, cultivate, rear, produce, collect, summon, erect, originate, propagate. (*lay, cast, depress, degrade, retard, dishonor, lower, depreciate, lull, compose, quiet, calm, blight, destroy, disperse, disband*)

range rank, dispose, class, place, order, collocate, file, concatenate, ramble, stroll, rove. (*disturb, disconnect, disorder, derange, intermit, disconnect, remain, be stationary*)

rank *a.* luxuriant, exuberant, extreme, excessive, rampant. (*meager, sparse, thin*)

rank *n.* row, line, tier, order, degree, grade, dignity. (*disconnection, disorder, incontinuity, intermission, hiatus, plebeianism, meanness*)

rankle fester, smolder, burn, irritate, gall, disquiet. (*heal, cool, close, calm, quiet, compose*)

rapid quick, swift, speedy, accelerated, flying. (*slow, tardy, retarded, cumbrous, lazy*)

rare scarce, choice, infrequent, excellent, few, exceptional, sparse, unusual, singular, uncommon, incomparable, extraordinary, unique, dispersed, valuable, precious, thin, volatile. (*common, frequent, abundant, numerous, mean, ordinary, usual, regular, crowded, dense, vulgar, worthless, cheap*)

rash headstrong, audacious, hasty, precipitate, reckless, foolhardy, careless, adventurous, thoughtless, indiscreet, venturesome, overventuresome, incautious, unwary, heedless. (*wary, cautious, calculating, discreet, unventuresome, dubitating, hesitating, reluctant, timid*)

rashness hastiness, precipitancy, recklessness, venturesomeness, temerity, indiscretion. (*slowness, carefulness, cautiousness, discretion*)

rate *n.* tax, impost, assessment, duty, standard, allowance, ratio, quota, worth, price, value.

rate *v.* compute, calculate, estimate, value, scold, abuse, appraise.

rational sane, sound, intelligent, reasoning, reasonable, judicious, sober, sensible, probable, equitable, moderate, fair. (*insane, unsound, weak, silly, unintelligent, absurd, injudicious, fanciful, extravagant, preposterous, unreasoning, unreasonable*)

ravel separate, undo, untwist, unwind, disentangle. (*entangle, complicate, confuse*)

ravish entrance, transport, enchant, enrapture, charm, violate, outrage, debauch.

raw uncooked, unprepared, unfinished, unripe, crude, unseasoned, inexperienced, fresh, green, unpracticed, untried, bare, bald, exposed, galled, chill, bleak, piercing. (*cooked, dressed, prepared, finished, ripe, mature, mellow, seasoned, experienced, expert, adept, habituated, familiar, practiced, trained, tried*)

reach extend, thrust, stretch, obtain, arrive at, attain, gain, grasp, penetrate, strain, aim. (*fail, stop, cease, revert, rebate, miss, drop*)

read peruse, interpret, decipher, unravel, discover, recognize, learn. (*misread, misinterpret, overlook, misobserve*)

ready prompt, alert, expeditious, speedy, unhesitating, dexterous, apt, skillful, handy, expert, facile, easy, opportune, fitted, prepared, disposed, willing, free, cheerful, compliant, responsive, quick. (*unready, tardy, slow, hesitating, reluctant, dubitating, awkward, unhandy, clumsy, remote, inaccessible, unavailable, inopportune, unsuited, unfitted, unprepared, indisposed, unwilling, constrained, grudging*)

real actual, veritable, existent, authentic, legitimate, true, genuine, developed. (*fictitious, imaginary, unreal, nonexistent, untrue, false, artificial, adulterated, assumed, pretended, potential, possible*)

really veritably, truly, indeed, unquestionably. (*questionably, possibly, perhaps, falsely, untruly*)

reason *n.* ground, account, cause, explanation, motive, proof, apology, understanding, reasoning, rationality, right, propriety, justice, order, object, sake, purpose. (*pretext, pretense, misinterpretation, falsification, misconception, disproof, unreasonableness, absurdity, fallacy, irrationality, wrong, unreason, impropriety, unfairness, folly, aimlessness*)

reason *v.* debate, discuss, argue, infer, deduce, conclude.

reassure rally, restore, encourage, inspirit, animate, countenance. (*discourage, cow, browbeat, intimidate, discountenance*)

rebuff *n.* rebuke, discouragement, repulsion, check. (*welcome, acceptance, encouragement*)

rebuff *v.* rebuke, repel, repulse, check, snub, oppose.

rebuke reprove, chide, rebuff, reprimand, censure. (*approve, encourage, eulogize, applaud, incite*)

receipt acknowledgment, reception, voucher.

receive take, accept, admit, hold, entertain, assent to. (*give, impart, afford, reject, discharge*)

reception admission, admittance, acceptance, acceptation, entertainment. (*denial, protest, repudiation, rejection, nonacceptance, dismissal, discardment, renunciation, abjuration*)

recess cavity, nook, withdrawal, retirement, retreat, seclusion, privacy, vacation, holiday. (*promontory, protrusion, projection, publicity, worktime*)

reckless careless, heedless, incautious, foolhardy, thoughtless, rash, overventuresome, regardless, inconsiderate, improvident. (*careful, heedful, cautious, timid, chary, thoughtful, calculating, provident, considerate, wary, circumspect*)

reckon compute, calculate, count, regard, estimate, value, account, consider, argue, infer, judge. (*miscompute, miscalculate, misestimate, misreckon*)

recognize identify, acknowledge, concede, know again, avow, own, allow. (*ignore, overlook, misobserve, repudiate, disavow, disown, disallow*)

recollect recover, recall, remember, bethink, bring to mind, call up, think of. (*forget, lose*)

recommend commend, confide, praise, applaud, approve, advise. (*discommend, disapprove, warn*)

recompense *n.* reward, indemnification, satisfaction, remuneration, amends.

recompense *v.* requite, remunerate, reward, indemnify, satisfy, repay, reimburse, compensate. (*damnify, injure, misrequite, dissatisfy*)

reconcile unite, conciliate, propitiate, pacify, harmonize, adjust, adapt, suit, reunite. (*separate, sever, dissever, estrange, disharmonize, derange*)

record registry, entry, enrollment, list, index, catalogue, register, schedule, roll, scroll, enumeration, inventory, muniment, instrument, archive, memorandum, rememberance. (*obliteration, oblivion, nonregistration, desuetude, obsolescence*)

recover regain, repossess, resume, retrieve, recruit, heal, cure, revive, restore, reanimate, save. (*lose, forfeit, miss, sacrifice, deteriorate, impair, decay, decline, relapse*)

recovery repossession, regaining, reinstatement, vindication, renovation, restitution, re-establishment, retrieval, rectification, replacement, reanimation, resuscitation, revival, redemption. (*loss, forfeiture, privation, deprival, sacrifice, abandonment, relapse, retrogression, decay, declension, incurableness, ruin*)

recreation refreshment, cheer, reanimation, amusement, diversion, revival, holiday, sport, pastime, relaxation. (*weariness, toil, lassitude, labor, fatigue, employment, assiduity, work*)

redeem repurchase, regain, retrieve, make amends for, recompense, ransom, liberate, rescue, recover, satisfy, fulfill, discharge. (*pledge, lose, forfeit, abandon, betray, surrender, sacrifice*)

reduce lessen, diminish, curtail, attenuate, impoverish, narrow, contract, weaken, impair, subdue, subjugate, bring, refer, subject, classify, convert. (*enlarge, magnify, increase, augment, produce, extend, amplify, broaden, expand, renovate, invigorate, restore, repair, liberate, free, except, dissociate, transform*)

refer attribute, associate, assign, advert, connect, relate, point, belong, allude, apply, appeal. (*disconnect, dissociate, misapply, misappertain, alienate, misbeseem, disresemble*)

reference relation, regard, intimation, allusion.

refinement clarification, purification, filtration, sublimation, polish, elegance, cultivation, civilization, subtility, finesse, sophistry. (*turbidity, grossness, foulness, coarseness, impurity, unrefinement, rudeness, inelegance, boorishness, broadness, bluntness, unsophistication*)

reflect return, image, mirror, exhibit, consider, think, cogitate, meditate, contemplate, ponder, muse, ruminate, heed, advert, animadvert. (*divert, dissipate, idle, dream, wander, rove, stargaze, woolgather, connive, disregard, overlook*)

reform amend, ameliorate, correct, rectify, better, reclaim, regenerate, remodel, reconstitute, reorganize, improve. (*corrupt, vitiate, worsen, deteriorate, perpetuate, stabilitate, confirm, impair, deform*)

refresh cool, refrigerate, invigorate, revive, reanimate, renovate, recreate, renew, restore, cheer, freshen, brace. (*heat, oppress, weary, burden, afflict, annoy, tire, fatigue, exhaust, debilitate, enervate*)

refuse *v.* deny, withhold, reject, decline, repudiate. (*grant, afford, yield, concede, acquiesce*)

refuse *n.* offal, scum, dregs, sediment, recrement, sweepings, trash, offscourings, debris, remains, dross. (*cream, pickings, first fruits, flower*)

regard behold, view, contemplate, esteem, consider, deem, affect, respect, reverence, revere, value, conceive, heed, notice, mind. (*miss, overlook, disregard, despise, dislike, contemn, hate, loathe, misconsider, misconceive, misestimate, misjudge*)

regardless heedless, inconsiderate, careless, unmindful, inattentive, unobservant, disregarding, indifferent, despising. (*careful, considerate, regardful, attentive, prudent, cautious, circumspect, scrupulous*)

regret *n.* sorrow, grief, concern, remorse, lamentation, repentance.

regret *v.* grieve, lament, repent, miss, desiderate, deplore. (*welcome, hail, approve, abandon, abjure, forget, disregard*)

regular customary, normal, ordinary, orderly, stated, recurrent, periodical, systematic, methodic, established, recognized, formal, symmetrical, certain. (*unusual, exceptional, abnormal, capricious, rare, irregular, disordered, fitful, unsymmetrical, variable, eccentric, erratic, uncertain*)

regulation rule, law, adjustment, disposal, method, government, order, control, arrangement. (*misrule, disorder, anarchy, misgovernment, maladministration, disarrangement, nonregulation, caprice, license, insubjection, uncontrol*)

reject repel, renounce, throw by, cast away, repudiate, decline, discard, refuse, exclude. (*hail, welcome, accept, appropriate, choose, select, admit*)

rejoice delight, glory, exult, joy, triumph, gladden, delight, revel, be glad, cheer, please, enliven, gratify. (*mourn, grieve, lament, weep, sorrow, repent, trouble, afflict, oppress, weary, depress, disappoint, burden, darken, distress, pain, sadden, vex, annoy*)

relation reference, aspect, connection, narration, proportion, bearing, affinity, homogeneity, association, relevancy, pertinency, fitness, harmony, ratio, relative, agreement, kinsman, kindred, appurtenancy. (*irrelation, disconnection, dissociation, irrelevancy, impertinency, disproportion, misproportion, unfitness, unsuitableness, heterogeneity, disharmony, disagreement, alien*)

release free, loose, liberate, discharge, quit, acquit, exempt, extricate, disengage, indemnify. (*bind, constrain, confine, shackle, fetter, yoke*)

reliance confidence, trust, dependence, assurance. (*distrust, misgiving, suspicion, diffidence*)

relief succor, support, release, extrication, alleviation, mitigation, aid, help, assistance, remedy, redress, exemption, deliverance, refreshment, comfort. (*oppression, aggravation, intensification, burdensomeness, trouble, exhaustion, weariness, discomfort*)

religion faith, creed, theology, belief, profession, piety, sanctity, godliness, holiness. (*unbelief, irreligion, godlessness, atheism, impiety, sacrilege, scoffing, blasphemy, skepticism, profanity, hypocrisy, sanctimoniousness, pharisaism*)

religious pious, godly, devout, devotional, divine, holy, sacred. (*impious, ungodly, not devout, sacrilegious, blasphemous, skeptical, profane*)

relish zest, recommendation, enhancement, flavor, savor, gusto, taste, appetite, piquancy, sapidity. (*drawback, disflavor, disrecommendation, nauseousness, disrelish, insipidity, unsavoriness*)

remain stay, continue, wait, stop, tarry, halt, sojourn, rest, dwell, abide, last, endure, accrue, survive. (*fly, vanish, remove, depart, speed, hasten, press, flit, disappear, pass*)

remarkable observable, noticeable, extraordinary, unusual, rare, striking, noteworthy, notable, distinguished, famous, peculiar, prominent, singular. (*unremarkable, unnoticeable, ordinary, mean, commonplace, everyday, undistinguished*)

remedy cure, restorative, counteraction, reparation, redress, relief, help, specific. (*evil, disease, hurt, infection, plague, ill, impairment, deterioration, aggravation, provocation*)

remember recollect, recall, retain, bear in mind, mind. (*forget, obliviate, disregard, overlook*)

remembrance recollection, memory, memorial, token, souvenir, memento, reminiscence, (*forgetfulness, oblivion*)

remiss stack, careless, negligent, inattentive, wanting, slow, slothful, idle, lax, dilatory, tardy, remissful. (*energetic, careful, attentive, active, assiduous, alert, painstaking, diligent, strict*)

remit relax, pardon, absolve, forgo, discontinue, surrender, forgive, resign. (*increase, intensity, enforce, exact*)

remorse compunction, anguish, self-condemnation, penitence, sting of conscience. (*complacency, self-approval, self-congratulation*)

remote distant, indirect, unconnected, unrelated, foreign, alien, heterogeneous, separate, contingent. (*near, close, direct, connected, related, homogeneous, immediate, proximate, essential, present, pressing, urgent, actual*)

remove displace, separate, abstract, transport, carry, transfer, eject, oust, dislodge, suppress, migrate, depart. (*restore, conserve, stabilize, perpetuate, establish, reinstate, reinstall, install, fix*)

reader give, present, return, restore, give up, apportion, assign, surrender, pay, requite, deliver. (*keep, retain, withhold, appropriate, alienate, misapportion, misappropriate, misrequite*)

renew recreate, restore, refresh, renovate, rejuvenate, furbish, recommence, repeat, reiterate, reissue, regenerate, reform, transform. (*impair, wear, deteriorate, vitiate, exhaust, discontinue, corrupt, weaken, defile, deprave*)

renounce reject, abjure, disclaim, disown, forgo, disavow, deny, quit, resign, abandon, recant, relinquish, repudiate. (*acknowledge, recognize, claim, maintain, assert, propound, own, vindicate, avow, profess, hold, retain, defend*)

renowned famous, celebrated, wonderful, illustrious.

repay remunerate, reimburse, recompense, reward, retaliate, requite, refund. (*defraud, misappropriate, embezzle, waste, alienate, extort, confiscate*)

repeal *v.* abolish, revoke, rescind, cancel, annul, recall, abrogate, reverse, discontinue, make void. (*continue, establish, pass, institute, sanction, enact, perpetuate, confirm*)

repeal *n.* abrogation, rescisson, revocation, annulment. (*continuance, establishment, perpetuation*)

repeat reiterate, iterate, renew, cite, quote, relate, rehearse, recapitulate, reproduce. (*discontinue, drop, discard, abandon, ignore, suppress, misrepeat, misquote, misrecite, misrepresent, misinterpret, misconvey*)

repeatedly frequently, again and again, often. (*seldom, rarely*)

repentance penitence, contrition, compunction, regret, remorse, sorrow, self-reproach, self-condemnation. (*impenitence, obduracy, recusancy, hardness, reprobation, self-approval*)

repetition iteration, reiteration, dwelling upon, diffuseness, verbosity, relation.

replace restore, supply, substitute, reinstate, rearrange, reestablish. (*move, abstract, withdraw, remove, damage, deprive*)

reply *n.* answer, rejoinder, response, replication. (*passing by, ignoring*)

reply *v.* replicate, answer, respond, rejoin. (*ignore, drop, pretermit, pass, disregard*)

report *v.* announce, relate, tell, circulate, notify, narrate, recite, describe, detail, communicate, declare. (*silence, hush, suppress, misreport, misrepresent, misrelate, falsify*)

report *n.* tidings, announcement, relation, narration, recital, description, communication, declaration, news, rumor, fame, repute, noise, reverberation. (*silence, suppression, misannouncement, fabrication, noiselessness*)

represent portray, delineate, reproduce, exhibit, personate, state, describe, indicate, embody, enact, illustrate, denote, play, dramatize, resemble. (*misportray, misdelineate, distort, falsify, caricature*)

representative agent, commissioner, proxy, deputy, substitute, embodiment, personation, delegate, vicar, vicegerent, principal, sovereign. (*autocrat, dictator*)

reproach blame, censure, taunt, rebuke, upbraid, reprobate, reprove. (*laud, praise, approve, commend*)

reprobate castaway, villain, ruffian, miscreant, scapegrace, scalawag. (*example, pattern, mirror, model, paragon*)

repudiate disavow, disown, discard, cast off, abjure, renounce, disclaim, divorce. (*avow, own, vindicate, assert, retain, vaunt, claim, profess, recognize, acknowledge, accept*)

repulsive forbidding, deterrent, ungenial, odious, ugly, unattractive, disagreeable, revolting. (*charming, agreeable, attractive, winning, captivating, fascinating, alluring, seductive, pleasant*)

reputable respectable, creditable, honorable, estimate. (*unrespectable, discreditable, dishonorable, disgraceful, disreputable*)

rescue retake, recover, recapture, liberate, extricate, save, deliver, preserve. (*endanger, imperil, betray, surrender, abandon, expose*)

resemblance likeness, similarity, similitude, semblance, representation, portrait, reflection, image. (*unlikeness, dissimilarity, disresemblance, difference, contrariety*)

resent repel, resist, rebel, recalcitrate, take ill. (*acquiesce, submit, condone, pardon, overlook*)

reserve reservation, retention, limitation, backwardness, coldness, shyness, coyness, modesty. (*boldness, rashness, recklessness, immodesty*)

residence sojourn, stay, abode, home, habitation, domicile, mansion.

resist withstand, oppose, hinder, check, thwart, baffle, disappoint. (*weaken, yield, give up, surrender*)

resolute determined, decided, fixed, steadfast, steady, constant, persevering, bold, firm, unshaken. (*weak, infirm, shy, cowardly, inconstant*)

resource material, means, supplies, expedients, wealth, riches. (*destitution, exhaustion, lack, drain, nonplus, poverty*)

respect regard, esteem, honor, revere, venerate. (*mock, scorn, ridicule, disparage, deride*)

respond answer, reply, rejoin.

rest remainder, surplus, remnant, residue, others.

restless unquiet, uneasy, disturbed, disquieted, sleepless, agitated, anxious, unsettled, roving, wandering. (*steady, quiet, settled*)

restrain check, hinder, stop, withhold, repress, curb, suppress, coerce, restrict, abridge, limit, confine. (*give full rein to, let go, release, free*)

result effect, consequence, conclusion, inference, issue, event.

retain keep, hold, restrain. (*yield, give up*)

retire withdraw, leave, depart, secede, recede. (*join, participate*)

retort repartee, answer.

retreat retirement, departure, withdrawment, seclusion, solitude, privacy, asylum, shelter, refuge. (*advance, forward march*)

return restore, requite, repay, recompense, render, remit, report.

reveal communicate, disclose, divulge, unveil, uncover, open, discover, impart, show. (*keep secret, withhold, cover, conceal, hide*)

revengeful vindictive, resentful, spiteful, malicious. (*open, ingenuous, frank, hearty, generous, kind, cordial*)

revenue receipts, returns, income, proceeds, wealth, result. (*expense, outgo*)

reverence awe, honor, veneration, adoration.

review re-examination, resurvey, retrospect, survey, reconsideration, revise, revision.

reward recompense, compensation, remuneration, pay, requital, retribution, punishment.

rich wealthy, affluent, opulent, ample, copious, abundant, fruitful, costly, sumptuous, precious, generous, luscious. (*poor, weak, straitened, cheap, scanty, sordid*)

ridicule derision, twit, banter, raillery, burlesque, mockery, sarcasm, gibe, jeer, sneer.

ripe mature, mellow, complete, finished. (*green, young, incomplete, unfinished*)

rise arise, mount, ascend, climb, scale. (*descend*)

risk danger, hazard, peril, jeopardy, exposure.

rival competitor, emulator, antagonist. (*friend, partner*)

road way, highway, street, lane, pathway, route, passage, course.

robbery theft, depredation, spoliation, despoilation, despoilment, plunder, pillage, freebooting, piracy.

romance fable, novel, fiction, tale.

romantic sentimental, fanciful, fictitious, extravagant, wild, chimerical.

room space, compass, scope, latitude.

round circular, spherical, globular, globose, orbicular, orbed, cylindrical, full, plump, rotund. (*square, oblong, angular, lean, thin*)

rout defeat, smite, conquer. (*victory*)

route roadway, path, track.

royal kingly, regal, monarchical, imperial, kinglike, princely, august, majestic, superb, splendid, illustrious, noble, magnanimous.

ruin destruction, downfall, perdition, fan, overthrow, subversion, defeat, bane, peat, mischief.

rule regulation, law, precept, maxim, guide, canon, order, method, direction, control, government, sway, empire.

rustic rural, rude, unpolished, inelegant, untaught, awkward, rough, coarse, plain, unadorned, simple, artless, honest.

sacred holy, divine, hallowed, consecrated, dedicated, devoted, religious, venerable, reverend.

sad sorrowful, mournful, gloomy, dejected, depressed, cheerless, downcast, sedate, serious, grave, grievous, afflictive, calamitous. (*gay, lively, happy, spirited, sprightly, jolly, fortunate, seductive*)

safe secure, unendangered, sure. (*in danger, dangerous, exposed, risky*)

sagacity penetration, shrewdness, judiciousness. (*stupidity, thick-headedness, dullness, foolishness*)

salutary wholesome, healthful, salubrious, beneficial, useful, advantageous, profitable. (*unhealthy, infectious, tainted*)

sample specimen, example, illustration.

sanction ratify, support, endorse.

satire lampoon, sarcasm, irony, ridicule, burlesque, wit, humor.

satisfaction contentment, content, gratification, pleasure, recompense, compensation, amends, remuneration, indemnification, atonement.

satisfy satiate, content, please, gratify, recompense, compensate, remunerate, indemnify.

saucy impertinent, insolent, rude, impudent.

savage ferocious, wild, uncultivated, untaught, uncivilized, unpolished, rude, brutish, brutal, heathenish, barbarous, cruel, inhuman, fierce, pitiless, merciless, unmerciful, murderous. (*cultured, refined, kind, gentle, merciful, humane, human, tame*)

save preserve, rescue, deliver, protect, spare, reserve, prevent. (*abandon, expose, give up, throw away*)

saying declaration, speech, adage, maxim, aphorism, apothegm, saw, proverb, byword.

scandal defamation, detraction, slander, calumny, opprobrium, reproach, shame, disgrace. (*honor, glory, respect*)

scanty deficient, gaunt, meager, scarce. (*full, ample, plenty*)

scarce rare, infrequent, deficient, uncommon. (*common, general, usual, frequent*)

scatter disperse, dissipate, spread, strew, sprinkle. (*gather, keep together, collect, preserve*)

scheme plan, project, design, contrivance, purpose, device, plot.

scholar pupil, learner, disciple, learned man, sage.

science knowledge, discipline, information.

scorn contempt, disdain, derision, contumely, despite, slight, dishonor, contempt. (*love, respect, honor, admiration, flattery*)

scrupulous cautious, careful, conscientious, hesitating. (*unscrupulous, careless, scatterbrained, reckless, daring, dishonest*)

scurrilous opprobrious, abusive, reproachful, insulting, insolent, offensive, gross, vile, vulgar, low, foul, foul-mouthed, indecent, mean.

seasonable opportune, timely, fit, convenient.

secret hidden, concealed, secluded, unseen, unknown, private, obscure, recondite, latent, covert, clandestine, privy. (*open, free, known, public*)

sectarian heretic, partisan, schismatic.

section part, division, portion.

security protection, defense, guard, shelter, safety, certainty, ease, assurance, carelessness, confidence, surety, pledge. (*danger, exposure, doubt, uncertainty*)

sedate sober, demure, serious, calm, grave, settled, serene, passive, quiet. (*flighty, frolicsome, indiscreet, ruffled, agitated, disturbed*)

seem appear, look.

seemly becomingly, fit, suitable, proper, appropriate, congruous, meet, decent, decorous. (*improper, immodest, unconventional, gross, rude*)

seize catch, grasp, clutch, snatch, append, arrest, take, capture.

sense understanding, reason, perception, sensation, feeling, meaning, import, significance, notion, opinion, judgment.

sensible intelligent, wise, cognizant, satisfied, persuaded. (*scatter-brained, foolish, ignorant of*)

sentiment thought, opinion, sensibility, feeling.

serious grave, solemn, important, weighty. (*gay, lively, happy, light, unimportant*)

serve obey, minister to, subserve, promote, aid, help, assist, benefit, succor.

set *v.* sink, settle, subside, decline, compose, consolidate, harden. (*rise, ascend, soar, mount, stir, agitate, loosen, run, soften, melt, mollify, fuse, flow*)

set *a.* fixed, established, firm, determined, regular, formal.

settle fix, establish, regulate, arrange, compose, adjust, determine, decide, adjudicate, quiet, allay, still, sink, fall, subside, lower, calm, acquiesce, abate, agree. (*remove, disestablish, misregulate, derange, discompose, aggravate, disorder, disturb, confuse, misdetermine, mis-arrange, misplace, unsettle, rise, ascend, move, disagree, increase, heighten*)

settlement subsidence, dregs, residuum, precipitation, colonization, location, colony. (*excitement, perturbation, turbidity, fluctuation*)

several separate, distinct, diverse, sundry, divers, various, different. (*one, same, identical, indistinguishable, inseparable, united, total, integral*)

severe serious, austere, stern, grave, strict, harsh, rigid, rigorous, sharp, afflictive, distressing, violent, extreme, exact, critical, censorious, caustic, sarcastic, cutting, keen, better, cruel. (*smiling, cheerful, relaxed, joyous, mild, genial, indulgent, light, trivial, trifling, inconsiderable, inexact, loose, uncritical, lenient, inextreme, moderate, gentle*)

shabby ragged, threadbare, contemptible, beggarly, paltry.

shadowy dim, cloudy, obscure, dark, murky, gloomy, mysterious.

shallow shoal, slight, flimsy, trifling, simple, superficial, unprofound. (*deep, profound*)

sham phantom, ghost, delusion, illusion, mockery, shadow, pretense, counterfeit, unreality. (*substance, reality, verity, substantiality, truth*)

shame abashment, humiliation, modesty, shamefacedness, decency, decorum, reproach, dishonor, ignominy, contempt, degradation, discredit, dispraise. (*shamelessness, barefacedness, immodesty, impudence, indecency, indecorum, impropriety, honor, glory, exaltation, renown, credit*)

shameful disgraceful, degrading, scandalous, outrageous, dishonorable, indecent, unbecoming.

shape *v.* form, mold, figure, adapt, delineate, adjust, contrive, create, execute, make. (*pervert, distort, misadapt, misdelineate, derange, discompose, miscontrive, misproduce, caricature*)

shape *n.* figure, form, outline, mold, fashion, pattern, cast, model.

share portion, apportionment, lot, division, participation, allowance, quota, contingent, allotment. (*whole, mass, aggregate, entirety*)

sharp thin, fine, keen, shrewd, discerning, clever, sarcastic, acute, pointed, aculeated, penetrating, pungent, acid, shrill, piercing, afflictive, distressing, harsh, severe, cutting, eager, active, ardent, sore, hard, animated, spirited. (*thick, blunt, dull, obtuse, knobbed, rounded, bluff, mellow, bass, hollow, deep, light, trifling, trivial, mild, gentle, soft, tender, lenient, sluggish, inactive, indifferent, careless, spiritless, tame*)

shatter split, dissipate, disrupt, derange, break in pieces, rend, demolish, shiver, dismember, disintegrate. (*construct, organize, collocate, fabricate, compose, rear, constitute*)

sheer pure, mere, unmixed, unqualified, unmitigated, absolute, simple, unadulterated. (*mixed, qualified, adulterated, modified, partial*)

shelve dismiss, discard, swamp, stifle, shift. (*start, prosecute, pursue, revive, agitate*)

shift *v.* change, alter, transfer, shelve, displace, remove. (*fix, fasten, locate, insert, pitch, plant, place*)

shift *n.* contrivance, expedient, substitute, pretext, motive, change, evasion, device, artifice, resource, transference. (*fixity, steadiness, retention, location, permanence*)

shocking sad, horrible, disgraceful, hateful, revolting, abominable, loathsome, foul. (*pleasing, honorable, charming, delightful, creditable, edifying, exemplary, attractive, alluring, enticing*)

short brief, limited, scanty, inadequate, insufficient, lacking, deficient, defective, imperfect, incomplete, soon, near, narrow, weak, incomprehensive, inextensive, less, abrupt, blunt, concise, condensed. (*long, protracted, extended, unlimited, plentiful, ample, abundant, adequate, sufficient, exuberant, liberal, large, copious, complete, distant, deferred, wide, strong, comprehensive, extensive, exceeding, courteous, inabrupt, expanded, diffuse*)

show *n.* appearance, exhibition, demonstration, parade, pomp, semblance, likeness, pretext, profession, pretense, illusion. (*nonappearance, disappearance, concealment, suppression, secrecy, disguise, dissimilarity, unlikeness, ungenuineness, reality, sincerity, substance*)

show *v.* exhibit, present, demonstrate, unfold, reveal, teach, inform, conduct, manifest, evince, evidence, prove, explain. (*conceal, suppress, hide, withhold, obscure, mystify, wrap, misdemonstrate, misdeclare, contradict, refute, deny, disprove, misinterpret, falsify, misexplain*)

showy gay, gaudy, high-colored, gorgeous, flashy, tinsel. (*inconspicuous, unnoticeable, quiet, subdued*)

shrewd sagacious, penetrating, astute, discriminating, intelligent, discerning, acute. (*stolid, undiscerning, unsagacious, stupid, dull*)

shrink contract, shrivel, withdraw, retire, recoil, revolt. (*stretch, expand, dilate, venture, dare*)

shrivel contract, dry up, wither, wrinkle, corrugate, decrease. (*expand, flatten, develop, unfold, spread, dilate*)

shuffle confuse, interchange, shift, intershift, intermix, derange, agitate, evade, prevaricate, equivocate, quibble, cavil, sophisticate, mystify, palter, dissemble. (*deal, distribute, order, arrange, compose, confess, propound, declare, explain, elucidate, reveal*)

shy timid, reserved, modest, bashful, suspicious, shrinking, chary. (*bold, brazenfaced, impudent, audacious, reckless*)

sick diseased, ill, disordered, distempered, indisposed, weak ailing, feeble, morbid, nauseated, disgusted, corrupt, impaired, valetudinarian. (*whole, well, healthy, sound, robust, strong, well-conditioned, salubrious*)

sickly weak, diseased, disordered, ailing, feeble, pining, drooping, morbid, unhealthy, vitiated, delicate, tainted, valetudinary. (*strong, healthy, vigorous, flourishing, salubrious, sound, robust*)

side margin, edge, verge, border, laterality, face, aspect, plane, party, interest, cause, policy, behalf. (*center, body, core, interior, essence, neutrality, disconnection, severance, secession, opposition*)

sight seeing, perception, view, vision, visibility, spectacle, show, inspection, examination, representation, appearance. (*nonperception, invisibility, blindness, obscuration, disappearance, oversight, nonappearance, undiscernment*)

sign token, indication, proof, memorial, expression, symbol, emblem, prefiguration, badge, type, premonition, symptom, prognostic, mark, wonder, presage, signal. (*misindication, misrepresentation, misleader*)

signal eminent, conspicuous, remarkable, extraordinary, notable, memorable, illustrious, important, salient, distinguished. (*ordinary, common, unnoticeable, mediocre, unmemorable, unimportant*)

signify portend, purport, prognosticate, mean, represent, indicate, communicate, denote, betoken, declare, utter, forebode, presage. (*conceal, suppress, misindicate, misdenote, nullify, refute, neutralize, preclude*)

silence taciturnity, stillness, calm, peace, hush, muteness, secrecy, oblivion. (*garrulity, loquacity, talkativeness, chatter, noise, brawl, clamor, clatter, din, babel, tumult, agitation, restlessness, storm, unrest, roar, bruit, reverberation, resonance, commotion, cackling, proclamation, publicity, fame, rumor, remembrance, repute, celebrity*)

silly simple, foolish, weak, shallow, witless, unwise, indiscreet, imprudent, absurd. (*sagacious, intelligent, astute, wise, deep, discreet, prudent, sound, rational*)

similar correspondent, resembling, alike, common, homogeneous, concordant, harmonious, congruous. (*different, unlike, dissimilar, alien, heterogeneous, discordant, incongruous*)

simple single, incomplex, uncompounded, unblended, isolated, pure, unmixed, mere, absolute, plain, unadorned, unartificial, artless, sincere, undesigning, single-minded, unaffected, silly, weak, unsophisticated, humble, homely, lowly, elementary, ultimate, primal, rudimentary. (*double, complex, compounded, blended, mixed, fused, multiform, multigenerous, various, compound, articulated, subdivided, organized, connected, modified, complicated, elaborate, artificial, artful, designing, insincere, double-minded, affected, self-conscious, sagacious, sophisticated, great, eminent, illustrious, complete, developed, perfect*)

simultaneous synchronous, concomitant, concurrent. (*separate, apart, intermittent, periodic*)

sin transgression, iniquity, unrighteousness, ungodliness, wickedness, evil, impurity, crime, wrongdoing. (*sinlessness, obedience, holiness, righteousness, purity, godliness, goodness*)

sincere pure, unmixed, genuine, unadulterated, hearty, honest, unaffected, unvarnished, candid, cordial, frank, unfeigned, true. (*impure, adulterated, dishonest, insincere, hypocritical, feigned, false*)

single one, unique, only, individual, sole, solitary, separate, uncombined, unmarried, uncompounded. (*plural, many, collective, united, numerous, frequent, married*)

singular single, individual, unique, eminent, extraordinary, conspicuous, consummate, unusual, uncommon, odd, whimsical quaint, peculiar, unexampled, unprecedented, solitary, sole, eccentric, fantastic, exceptional, particular, remarkable, curious, queer. (*common, frequent, numerous, ordinary, usual, unnoticeable, everyday, customary, general, regular*)

situation locality, position, topography, state, seat, post, place, condition, residence, aspect, footing, office, birth, plight, predicament, standing. (*nonsituation, nonlocation, absence, nonassignment, unfixedness, displacement, dislodgement*)

slender thin, narrow, slight, slim, small, trivial, spare, inadequate, fragile, feeble, flimsy, meager, inconsiderable, superficial. (*stout, thick, broad, robust, massive, considerable, ample, deep*)

slow sluggish, inactive, inert, lazy, unready, tardy, late, gradual, tedious, dull, dilatory, lingering, slack. (*active, quick, fast, rapid, alert, ready, prompt, early, sudden, immediate*)

sly cunning, subtle, crafty, artful, wily, underhanded, astute, stealthy. (*open, frank, artless, undesigning*)

small little, diminutive, slight, minute, feeble, trivial, insignificant, paltry, narrow, mean, weak, slender, fine, inferior. (*great, large, big, considerable, bulky, extensive, ample, spacious, stout, strong, important, broad, liberal*)

smart keen, pungent, piercing, quick, vigorous, sharp, severe, active, clever, brilliant, vivacious, witty, ready, spruce, brisk, fresh, dressy, showy. (*dull, heavy, aching, slow, inactive, stupid, sluggish, unready, slow-minded, unwitty, dowdy, shabby, clownish*)

smooth even, plain, level, flat, polished, glossy, sleek, soft, unruffled, unobstructed, bland, oily, suave. (*uneven, rough, rugged, abrupt, precipitous, unpolished, harsh, blunt*)

smother suffocate, stifle, repress, gag, conceal, suppress, choke, strangle, allay, swallow. (*fan, ventilate, foster, cherish, nurture, publish, promulgate, divulge, spread, excite, vent*)

sneer scoff, gibe, jeer, taunt, disparagement, contempt, scorn, superciliousness, disdain. (*compliment, eulogy, commendation, deference*)

snub mortify, check, rebuke, reprimand.

snug close, housed, compressed, compact, comfortable, sheltered. (*exposed, loose, disordered, incompact, uncomfortable, bare, shivering*)

sober temperate, unintoxicated, cool, dispassionate, reasonable, calm, self-possessed, sound, unexcited, serious, grave, sedate, steady, abstemious, moderate (*intemperate, drunk, intoxicated, heated, excited, impassioned, unreasonable, agitated, furious, passionate, extravagant, extreme, exorbitant, immoderate, flighty, erratic, eccentric*)

society community, polity, association, collection, companionship, fellowship, connection, participation, company, sociality, communion, intercourse, sodality. (*individuality, personality, segregation, separation, solitariness, unsociality, privacy, dissociation, disconnection*)

soft yielding, pressible, impressible, smooth, delicate, fine, sleek, glossy, mild, gentle, balmy, kind, feeling, flexible, effeminate, luxurious, unmanly, tender, irresolute, undecided. (*hard, tough, stubborn, unyielding, rigid, unimpressible, rough, coarse, harsh, abrupt, ungentle, rigorous, cutting, severe, unkind, unfeeling, sharp, inflexible, stern, austere, ascetic, self-denying, resolute, determined*)

soften mollify, palliate, compose, mitigate, assuage, dulcify, lenify, yield, macerate, humanize, abate, moderate. (*harden, indurate, aggravate, excite, infuriate, consolidate*)

solemn sacred, formal, devotional, reverential, ritual, ceremonial, impressive, religious, grave, serious. (*profane, undevotional, secular, light, gay, trivial, unceremonial, informal, unsolemn*)

solid hard, firm, compact, resistant, dense, substantial, weighty, strong, valid, just, sound, impenetrable, stable, cubic. (*soft, hollow, yielding, frail, brittle, flimsy, elastic, resilient, malleable, impressible, fluid, liquid, frivolous, light, trifling, weak, invalid, unsound, fallacious, weakly*)

solitude loneliness, remoteness, seclusion, retirement, isolation, wildness, desertion, barrenness, wilderness, privacy. (*publicity, populousness, society, frequency, intercourse, resort, meeting, reunion, throng, crowd*)

solution separation, discerption, disruption, breach, discontinuance, disconnection, disentanglement, elucidation, explanation, key, answer, resolution, disintegration. (*union, combination, amalgamation, continuity, connection, conjunction, entanglement, complication, confusion, mystification, obscurity, integration*)

sore painful, irritated, susceptible, excoriated, raw, scarified, ulcerous, grievous, afflictive, heavy, burdensome. (*painless, sound, whole, healthful, healed, unbroken, unscarified, light, trivial, unburdensome, pleasant, untroublesome, grateful*)

sorry grieved, pained, hurt, afflicted, woebegone, doleful, downhearted, mortified, vexed, dejected, poor, mean, vile, shabby, worthless. (*glad, rejoiced, delighted, pleased, gratified, fine, choice, handsome*)

sort kind, species, nature, class, order, character, rank, manner, quality, condition, description, designation, genus. (*nondescription, solitariness, uniqueness, nonclassification, heterogeneity*)

sound entire, unbroken, whole, perfect, unhurt, well-grounded, uninjured, unimpaired, healthy, firm, strong, vigorous, weighty, solid, irrefragable, irrefutable, thorough, valid, wholesome, correct, substantial. (*partial, broken, injured, impaired, unhealthy, unsound, weak, frail, fragile, light, trivial, unfounded, hollow, fallacious, imperfect, unwholesome, incorrect, unsubstantial, invalid*)

sour tart, rancid, coagulated, turned, harsh, crabbed, austere, morose, pungent, crusty, acid, churlish, bitter, acetous, acrimonious, peevish. (*sweet, wholesome, untainted, mellow, genial, kindly*)

spacious ample, extensive, broad, vast, capacious, large, wide, roomy, expansive. (*narrow, restricted, limited, cramped, confined, inextensive*)

spare *a.* scanty, unplentiful, inabundant, meager, economical, frugal, stinted, restricted, parsimonious, niggardly, chary, superfluous, disposable, available, lean, thin, ill-conditioned. (*ample, plentiful, abundant, profuse, liberal, unrestricted, generous, bountiful, unsparing, unstinted, unbounded, available, well-conditioned*)

spare *v.* save, afford, grant, reserve, do without, husband, economize, retain, store, grudge, discard, omit, forbear, withhold, refrain, abstain. (*spend, squander, waste, lavish, scatter, expend, indulge, vent*)

special particular, specific, peculiar, appropriate, proper, distinctive, extraordinary, especial, exceptional. (*general, universal, common, generic*)

speculation contemplation, consideration, view, weighing, thought, theory, scheme, hypothesis, conjecture. (*realization, proof, fact, verification, certainty*)

speed dispatch, expedite, accelerate, urge, hasten, hurry, press. (*retard, delay, postpone, obstruct, drag, loiter, dawdle, linger, tag, stay*)

spend bestow, waste, exhaust, squander, expend, lay out, consume, disburse, lavish. (*retain, save, hoard, accumulate, husband, economize*)

spirit air, breath, life, soul, vital, force, essential quality, essence, immateriality, intelligence, disembodiment, specter, apparition, ghost, energy, ardor, enthusiasm, activity, earnestness, courage, zeal, disposition, temper, principle, motive, distillation. (*substance, body, corporeity, materiality, flesh, organization, frame, embodiment, spiritlessness, listlessness, soullessness, lifelessness, torpor, deadness, timidity, dejection, slowness, sluggishness*)

spirited animated, lively, vivacious, ardent, buoyant, sprightly, courageous. (*dull, dispirited, depressed, cowardly*)

spiritual divine, religious, holy, ghostly, ethical, immaterial, incorporeal, intellectual. (*carnal, fleshy, unspiritual, gross, material, sensuous*)

spite malice, malevolence, grudge, pique, hatred, ill will, vindictiveness, rancor, spleen. (*goodwill, benevolence, kindness*)

splendid brilliant, showy, magnificent, sumptuous, gorgeous, glorious, pompous, imposing, illustrious, superb, famous, heroic, grand, signal. (*dull, obscure, tame, somber, poor, beggarly, unimposing, ordinary, ineffective, inglorious*)

split divide, separate, rive, cleave, crack, splinter, burst, rend, sunder, disagree, secede, disunite. (*cohere, unite, amalgamate, coalesce, conform, agree, splice, consolidate, integrate*)

spoil plunder, strip, rob, devastate, pillage, denude, corrupt, vitiate, mar, deteriorate. (*invest, enrich, endow, replenish, renovate, improve, better, ameliorate, rectify, preserve*)

spontaneous voluntary, self-generated, self-originated, willing, unbidden, gratuitous. (*involuntary, imposed, compulsory, unwilling, necessitated*)

sport play, frolic, wantonness, joke, diversion, merriment, gaiety, fun, amusement, recreation, game, pastime. (*work, seriousness, business, earnestness*)

spread extend, stretch, expand, open, unfurl, divulge, propagate, publish, disperse, diffuse, overlay, distribute, scatter, circulate, disseminate, ramify. (*contract, furl, gather, fold, close, shut, secrete, suppress, confine, restrict, repress, hush, conceal, recall, collect, stagnate, concentrate, localize*)

spring leap, bound, jump, start, emerge, issue, proceed, originate, rise, emanate, germinate, burst, flow. (*settle, alight, land, drop, arrive, issue, eventuate, end, terminate, debouch, disembogue*)

staid grave, demure, steady, sober, sedate. (*unsteady, flighty, indiscreet, wanton, insedate, erratic, eccentric, agitated, discomposed, ruffled*)

stammer stutter, hesitate, falter. (*speak clearly, speak unhesitatingly*)

stamp genus, kind, description, make, mark, impression, imprint, print, brand, cast, mold, character, type. (*heterogeneity, nondescription, formlessness*)

stand rest, remain, stop, be, exist, keep one's ground, insist, depend, await, consist, hold, continue, endure, pause, halt. (*progress, move, proceed, advance, fall, fail, yield, succumb, drop, lie, vanish, fade, run, depart*)

standard measure, gauge, criterion, test, rule, exemplar, banner, flag, type, model, scale, plummet, touchstone. (*mismeasurement, misrule, misadjustment, miscomparison, inconformity, misfit, incommensurateness, noncriterion*)

state *n.* position, condition, situation, circumstances, plight, predicament, case, province.

state *v.* say, declare, propound, aver, set forth, narrate, specify, avow, recite. (*suppress, repress, suppose, imply, deny, contradict, retract*)

stately dignified, imposing, lofty, elevated, lordly, proud, majestic, pompous, magnificent, grand. (*undignified, unimposing, unstately, commonplace, mean*)

stay hold, stop, restrain, withhold, arrest, hinder, delay, obstruct, support, rest, repose, remain, continue, dwell, await, halt, abide, wait, tarry, confide, trust, lean. (*loose, liberate, send, expedite, speed, free, accelerate, hasten, oppress, depress, burden, fail, fall, proceed, move, depart, overthrow, mistrust*)

steady firm, fixed, constant, uniform, consistent, equable, regular, undeviating, well-regulated. (*infirm, variable, unsteady, inconstant, changeable, wavering, ill-regulated*)

step advance, pace, space, grade, remove, degree, gradation, progression, track, trace, vestige, walk, gait, proceeding, action, measure. (*retreat, recession, halting, station, standing, nongraduation, nonprogression, standstill, stop, tracklessness, untraceableness, nonimpression, desinence, desistance, inaction*)

stern severe, austere, rigid, harsh, strict, rigorous, unrelenting, unyielding, forbidding. (*lenient, genial, kindly, easy, flexible, encouraging*)

stiff unbending, inflexible, rigid, unyielding, unpliant, strong, stubborn, obstinate, pertinacious, constrained, affected, starched, formal, ceremonious, difficult. (*pliant, flexible, flaccid, yielding, easy, unaffected, genial, affable, unceremonious*)

still quiet, calm, noiseless, hushed, silent, pacific, serene, motionless, stagnant, peaceful, quiescent, tranquil, stationary. (*unquiet, disturbed, agitated, moved, noisy, resonant, turbulent, moving, transitional*)

stingy close, avaricious, mean, niggardly, closefisted, hidebound, parsimonious, sparing, sordid, penurious. (*liberal, generous, large, handsome, lavish, bountiful, unsparing*)

stop close, obstruct, plug, cork, bar, seat, arrest, suspend, end, rest, halt, hinder, suppress, delay, cease, terminate. (*open, expedite, clear, broach, unseal, promote, advance, further, continue, proceed, speed, hasten*)

stout strong, lusty, vigorous, robust, sturdy, brawny, corpulent, resolute, brave, valiant, redoubtable. (*weak, debile, frail, attenuated, thin, slender, lean, irresolute, feeble, cowardly, timid*)

straight direct, rectilinear, undeviating, unswerving, right, nearest. (*indirect, winding, incurved, tortuous, sinuous, serpentine, circuitous, waving, crooked*)

strange foreign, alien, exotic, unfamiliar, unusual, odd, irregular, abnormal, exceptional, surprising, wonderful, marvelous, astonishing, uncommon, peculiar. (*home, domestic, familiar, usual, ordinary, common, regular, customary, commonplace, unsurprising, universal, general*)

strength force, vigor, power, security, validity, vehemence, intensity, hardness, soundness, nerve, fiber, sinew. (*weakness, imbecility, feebleness, insolidity, insecurity, invalidity, frailty, delicacy, softness, flimsiness, hollowness*)

strenuous strong, resolute, determined, earnest, vigorous, ardent, bold, energetic, vehement. (*weak, irresolute, undetermined, unearnest, debile, feeble, emasculate*)

strict close, exact, accurate, rigorous, severe, stringent, nice, precise. (*loose, inexact, inaccurate, lenient, mild, indulgent, lax*)

striking impressive, affecting, admirable, wonderful, surprising.

strong powerful, vigorous, solid, secure, fortified, forcible, impetuous, hale, hearty, brawny, sinewy, sound, robust, cogent, influential, zealous, potent, pungent, muscular, hardy, stanch, tenacious. (*powerless, weak, frail, insecure, defenseless, feeble, mild, calm, gentle, delicate, sickly, inefficacious, unsatisfactory, unconvincing, unimpressive, vapid, impotent, unavailing, lukewarm, debile, flaccid, nerveless, tender, moderate, indifferent*)

stubborn tough, unbending, unyielding, hard, obstinate, intractable, obdurate, stiff, harsh, inflexible, headstrong, refractory, heady, contumacious, pigheaded. (*docile, tractable, manageable, pliant, pliable, malleable, flexible*)

studious literary, diligent, desirous, attentive, careful, thoughtful, assiduous, reflective. (*unliterary, illiterate, idle, indulgent, careless, regardless, indifferent, inattentive, negligent, thoughtless*)

stupid dull, senseless, stolid, doltish, besotted, insensate, obtuse, prosy, addlepated, dull-witted. (*quick, sharp, bright, sensible, sagacious, penetrating, clever*)

subdue conquer, reduce, overpower, break, tame, quell, vanquish, master, subjugate. (*aggrandize, exalt, fortify, strengthen, empower, liberate, enfranchise*)

subject subordinate, subservient, exposed, liable, prone, disposed, obnoxious, amenable. (*superior, independent, exempt, indisposed, unliable, unamenable*)

submissive obedient, compliant, yielding, obsequious, humble, docile, modest, passive, acquiescent, subservient. (*disobedient, incompliant, unyielding, inobsequious, recalcitrant, refractory, proud, resistant, renitent, malcontent, recusant*)

substantial existing, real, solid, true, corporeal, material, strong, stout, massive, bulky, tangible. (*imaginary, unreal, insubstantial, fictitious, suppositious, incorporeal, chimerical, visionary, inmaterial, weak, frail, airy, disembodied, spiritual*)

subtle sly, artful, cunning, insinuating, wily, astute, nice, discriminating, crafty, fine, shrewd, sophistical, jesuitical. (*open, frank, honest, artless, undiscriminating, rough, blunt, undiscerning, unsophisticated, simple*)

success achievement, luck, consummation, prosperity, victory, good fortune. (*failure, defeat, disaster, ruin*)

succession following, supervention, consecutive, sequence, order, series, rotation, continuity, supply, suite. (*precedence, anticipation, prevention, antecedence, irregularity, disorder, nonsequence, solution, failure, intermission, break, gap, inconsecutiveness*)

suffer bear, endure, sustain, undergo, let, permit, allow, admit, tolerate, experience, support. (*resist, repel, expel, reject, disallow, repudiate, forbid, ignore*)

sufficient adequate, equal, competent, satisfactory, fit, qualified, adapted, suited, enough, ample. (*inadequate, unequal, incompetent, unqualified, unadapted, insufficient, unsuited, meager, bare, scanty, short, deficient*)

suit fit, adapt, match, adjust, harmonize, apportion, befit, beseem, tally, correspond, answer, comport, please, serve, agree, become, accord. (*misfit, misadapt, mismatch, misapportion, unbeseem, vary, differ, disagree, miscomport*)

summary analysis, tabulation, abridgment, résumé, compendium, digest, epitome, abstract. (*dilatation, expansion, dilution*)

superb grand, magnificent, elegant, princely, splendid, showy, proud, august, stately, gorgeous. (*mean, common, commonplace, unimposing, shabby*)

supercilious haughty, contemptuous, disdainful, arrogant, insolent. (*affable, courteous, respectful, modest, bashful*)

superficial light, slight, imperfect, showy, external, flimsy, surface, shallow, smattering, skin-deep. (*deep, profound, abstruse, recondite, accurate, exact, deep-seated*)

superior higher, upper, better, preferable, surpassing, loftier, excellent, remarkable, eminent, conspicuous. (*inferior, lower, worse, subordinate, ordinary, common, unremarkable, average, mean, mediocre*)

supple pliant, bending, yielding, flexible, elastic, servile, fawning, cringing, adulatory, sycophantic, lithe, limber, compliant. (*firm, unbending, unyielding, stiff, stubborn, inflexible, inelastic, independent, self-assertive, supercilious*)

supply furnish, afford, provide, accouter, give, minister, yield, contribute. (*expend, use, consume, waste, exhaust, absorb, demand, withhold, withdraw, retain*)

support *n.* prop, stay, foundation, buttress, help, aid, assistance, influence, maintenance, living, patronage, subsistence, livelihood, food.

support *v.* bear, uphold, sustain, underlie, befriend, assist, second, promote, further, suffer, defend, foster, nurture, nourish, cherish, endorse, maintain, continue, countenance, patronize, subsidize, help, back, stay, favor, prop. (*drop, betray, surrender, abandon, discontinue, oppose, discourage, weaken, exhaust, thwart, discountenance, disfavor, subvert, suppress*)

suppose assume, presume, believe, divine, deem, fancy, think, regard, conceive, imagine, imply, presuppose, conjecture, guess, conclude, judge, consider. (*prove, demonstrate, substantiate, realize, disbelieve, negative, deny*)

sure certain, secure, safe, assured, unmistakable, stable, firm, knowing, believing, confident, trusting, unquestioning, positive, unfailing, strong, permanent, abiding, enduring, infallible, indisputable, fast. (*uncertain, ignorant, dubious, doubtful, hesitating, distrustful, questioning, vacillating, weak, untrustworthy, precarious, insecure, impermanent, transient, evanescent, fallible, disputable, loose*)

susceptible capable, impressible, tender, sensitive. (*incapable, unimpressible, insensitive, insusceptible, impassible*)

suspense protraction, uncertainty, doubt, solicitude, cessation, pause, waiting, intermission, discontinuance, abeyance, stoppage, indetermination, incertitude, indecision. (*determination, settlement, execution, continuance, uninterruption, revival, decision, finality*)

sway *n.* wield, influence, rule, authority, government, superiority, bias, dominion, control, preponderance, domination, supremacy, mastery, ascendancy, weight, force, power. (*weakness, inferiority, subordination, irresistance, obedience, subservience, subjection*)

sway *v.* influence, govern, rule, bias, wave, swing, wield

sweet saccharine, luscious, fragrant, dulcet, melodious, harmonious, musical, beautiful, lovely, wholesome, pleasing, pure, mild, winning, agreeable, fresh, gentle, amiable. (*sour, bitter, unsweet, fetid, offensive, nauseous, olid, stinking, nasty, inharmonious, discordant, unlovely, repulsive, unwholesome, putrid, fainted, ungentle, unamiable*)

swell dilate, extend, enlarge, heighten, heave, enhance, rise, expand, increase, augment, protuberate, aggravate, amplify, distend. (*contract, curtail, shrivel, diminish, lessen, retrench, reduce, collapse, fold, narrow, condense, concentrate*)

sympathy fellow feeling, congeniality, commiseration, compassion, pity, concert, tenderness, agreement, condolence. (*antipathy, antagonism, incongeniality, pitilessness, mercilessness, compassionlessness, unkindness, harshness, unkindliness*)

system method, scheme, order, regularity, classification, arrangement, rule, plan. (*disorder, derangement, confusion, fortuity, chance, medley, haphazard, incongruity, nonarrangement, nonclassification*)

take seize, grasp, catch, capture, siege, use, obtain, pursue, employ, follow, assume, procure, captivate, engage, interest, charm, choose, select, admit, accept, receive, conduct, transfer. (*drop, reject, abandon, surrender, lose, miss, repel*)

tall high, lofty, towering, elevated. (*low*)

tame domesticated, reclaimed, tamed, subjugated, broken, gentle, mild, docile, meek, spiritless, tedious, dull, flat. (*undomesticated, unreclaimed, untamed, unbroken, savage, wild, fierce, spirited, animated, ferine, interesting, exciting, stirring, lively*)

task work, function, labor, job, operation, business, undertaking, drudgery, toil, lesson. (*relaxation, leisure, amusement, hobby*)

taste gustation, savor, flavor, sapidity, relish, perception, judgment, discernment, nicety, critique, sensibility, choice, zest, predilection, delicacy, elegancy, refinement. (*nongustation, insipidity, disrelish, nonpreception, indiscrimination, indiscernment, indelicacy, coarseness, inelegancy*)

tasteful sapid, relishing, savory, agreeable, tasty, toothsome, palatable, elegant, refined. (*insipid, unrelishing, unsavory, unpalatable, nauseous, inelegant, tasteless, unrefined, vapid*)

teach impart, tell, direct, instruct, inform, counsel, admonish, educate, inculcate, enlighten, advise, indoctrinate, train. (*withhold, misteach, misdirect, misinstruct, misinform, misguide, mislead*)

teacher instructor, schoolmaster, preceptor, tutor, professor, pedagogue, educationist, educator, schoolmistress. (*pupil, scholar, disciple, learner*)

tedious wearisome, tiresome, monotonous, dilatory, dreary, sluggish, irksome, dull, flat, prolix. (*interesting, exciting, stirring, charming, fascinating, delightful, amusing*)

tell mention, number, enumerate, count, recount, utter, recite, state, narrate, disclose, publish, betray, divulge, promulgate, acquaint, teach, inform, explain, communicate, report, rehearse, discern, judge, discriminate, ascertain, decide, describe. (*repress, suppress, misrecount, misnarrate, miscommunicate, misdeclare, misrecite, misjudge, misdescribe*)

temporary present, immediate, partial, limited, transient, impermanent. (*perpetual, lasting, confirmed, complete, final, perfect, permanent, entire*)

tendency vergency, proneness, bias, gravitation, drift, scope, aim, disposition, predisposition, proclivity, leaning, inclination, attraction, conduciveness, course. (*disinclination, aversion, repulsion, contravention, deviation, divergency, tangency, divarication, opposition, renitency, reluctance, prevention, neutralization, termination*)

tender *v.* offer, proffer, propose, bid, produce, present. (*withhold, withdraw, retain, appropriate*)

tender *a.* delicate, frail, impressible, susceptible, yielding, soft, effeminate, weak, feeble, compassionate, affectionate, careful, jealous, gentle, mild, meek, pitiful, merciful, pathetic. (*strong, sturdy, hardy, robust, tough, iron, pitiless, unmerciful, cruel, hard-hearted, careless, liberal, lavish, unchary, ungentle, rough, rude, coarse, unsentimental, unmoving, unfeeling, unimpressive, unimpassioned, unimpressed, vigorous, tenacious*)

term limit, boundary, condition, time, season, period, expression, designation, word, name, article, proviso, stipulation.

terrible awful, fearful, dreadful, formidable, terrific, frightful, tremendous, horrible, shocking. (*unimpressive, not startling or astonishing*)

terror fear, dread, alarm, fright, consternation, horror, dismay. (*confidence, fearlessness, boldness, reassurance*)

test cupel, trial, examination, proof, criterion, standard, experiment, touchstone, experience, ordeal. (*misindication, misjudgment, misproof*)

testimony witness, evidence, attestation, affirmation, corroboration, confirmation, proof. (*refutation, contradiction, disproof, confutation, contravention, invalidation*)

theatrical dramatic, scenic, melodramatic, showy, ceremonious, gesticulatory, pompous, meretricious, tinsel. (*chaste, genuine, simple, unaffected, quiet, subdued, mannerless, plain*)

thick dense, condensed, inspissated, close, compact, turbid, luteous, coagulated, muddy, dull, misty, foggy, vaporous, crowded, numerous, solid, bulky, deep, confused, inarticulate. (*race, fine, thin, sparse, strained, pure, percolated, limpid, crystalline, scanty, incompact, slight, shallow, laminated, clear, articulate, distinct*)

thicken condense, inspissate, incrassate, compact, solidify, befoul, obscure, bemire, becloud, increase, coagulate, amalgamate, commingle, intermix, crowd, multiply, enlarge, expand, extend, broaden, deepen, obstruct, confuse. (*rarify, dissipate, refine, attenuate, clear, purify, strain, percolate, clarify, defecate, depurate, brighten, lighten, open, filtrate, diminish, separate, reduce, narrow, contract, liberate, free, extricate, unravel, disentangle, loosen*)

thin slim, slender, flimsy, attenuated, diluted, watery, meager, unsubstantial, lean.

think ponder, meditate, consider, reflect, contemplate, conceive, imagine, apprehend, fancy, hold, regard, believe, deem, opine, purpose, judge, reckon.

thought reflection, reasoning, cogitation, supposition, view, sentiment, meditation, conception, idea, opinion, judgment, conceit, fancy, design, purpose, intention, deliberation, care, provision. (*vacuity, incogitation, thoughtlessness, dream, hallucination, aberration, misconception, incogitancy, carelessness, improvidence, unreflectiveness*)

threatening menacing, intimidating, minatory, comminatory, minacious, foreboding, unpromising, imminent, impending. (*encouraging, promising, reassuring, enticing, passed, overpast, withdrawn*)

tide flow, course, current, rush, inundation, influx, stream, movement, flood. (*stagnation, arrestation, stoppage, cessation, motionlessness, subsidence*)

tight firm, compact, fast, close, tidy, neat, smart, natty, tense, stretched. (*loose, incompact, open, flowing, loose-fitting, large, untidy, lax, relaxed*)

time period, duration, season, interval, date, opportunity, age, era, occasion, term, space, span, spell. (*neverness, eternity, nonduration, indetermination, indeterminableness*)

timid fearful, pusillanimous, shy, diffident, coy, timorous, afraid, cowardly, fainthearted, inadventurous. (*bold, confident, venturesome, courageous, overventuresome, rash, audacious*)

tint color, hue, tinge, dye, complexion. (*achromatism, decoloration, paleness, pallor, bleaching, etiolation, colorlessness, sallowness, wanness, cadaverousness, exsanguineousness*)

title inscription, heading, denomination, style, designation, appellation, distinction, address, epithet, name. (*nondesignation, indistinction, nondescript, namelessness, indenomination*)

together unitedly, conjointly, contemporaneously, concertedly, simultaneously, coincidently, concomitantly, concurrently. (*separately, disconnectedly, independently, variously, incoincidently, inconcurrently*)

tolerable endurable, bearable, supportable, sufferable, allowable, permissible, sufficient, passable. (*unendurable, unbearable, insupportable, insufferable, unallowable, impermissible, insufficient, intolerable*)

tongue discourse, speech, language, dialect, idiom.

tool utensil, implement, machine, instrument, dupe, cat's-paw, hireling.

topic question, theme, subject, subject matter.

tough resistant, stubborn, lentous, fibrous, difficult, refractory, hard, unmanageable, tenacious, firm, strong. (*yielding, tender, soft, brittle, fragile, frangible, friable*)

tragedy disaster, calamity, affliction, adversity, catastrophe, grief. (*joy, delight, boon, prosperity, comedy*)

train *n.* suite, procession, retinue, cortege, course, series.

train *v.* lead, rear, accustom, habituate, inure, drill, exercise, practice, discipline, instruct, bend, educate. (*force, break, trail, disaccustom, dishabituate, miseducate, disqualify*)

transfer convey, transport, remove, sell, assign, remand, make over, transplant, give, alienate, translate, transmit, forward, exchange. (*retain, withhold, fix, appropriate, keep*)

transient fleeting, fugitive, transitory, temporary, passing, evanescent, ephemeral, momentary, brief. (*abiding, permanent, perpetual, persistent, lasting, enduring*)

transparent pellucid, crystalline, translucent, limpid, diaphanous, obvious, clear, indisputable, self-evident. (*thick, turbid, opaque, intransparent, mysterious, dubious, questionable*)

travel journey, wandering, migration, pilgrimage, excursion, tramp, expedition, trip, ramble, voyage, tour, peregrination. (*rest, settlement, domestication*)

treatise tract, essay, paper, pamphlet, disquisition, brochure, dissertation, monograph, article. (*jottings, notes, adversaria, memoranda, effusion, ephemera*)

treaty contract, agreement, league, covenant, alliance, negotiation, convention. (*neutrality, noninterference, nonalliance, nonagreement, nonconvention*)

tremble shake, quake, quiver, totter, shiver, shudder, vibrate, jar. (*stand, steady, settle, still, calm*)

tremendous terrible, dreadful, awful, fearful, appalling. (*unimposing, unappalling, inconsiderable*)

trial test, gauge, experiment, temptation, trouble, affliction, grief, burden, suffering, attempt, endeavor, proof, essay, criterion, ordeal, tribulation, verification. (*nontrial, nonprobation, mismeasurement, miscalculation, misestimate, trifle, triviality, alleviation, relief, disburdenment, refreshment, nonattempt, pretermission, oversight, disregard, nonverification*)

trick artifice, contrivance, machination, guile, stratagem, wile, fraud, cheat, juggle, antic, vagary, finesse, sleight, deception, imposition, delusion, legerdemain. (*blunder, exposure, bungling, mishap, botch, fumbling, inexpertness, maladroitness, genuineness, openhandedness, artlessness*)

trifle bauble, bagatelle, toy, straw, nothing, triviality, levity, joke, cipher, bubble, gewgaw, kickshaw, rush. (*treasure, portent, phenomenon, crisis, conjuncture, importance, urgency, weight, necessity, seriousness*)

triumph victory, success, ovation, achievement, conquest, exultation, trophy. (*defeat, discomfiture, failure, unsuccess, abortion, baffling, disappointment*)

trivial trifling, trite, common, unimportant, useless, nugatory, paltry, inconsiderable. (*important, weighty, critical, original, novel*)

trouble *v.* disturb, vex, agitate, confuse, perplex, distress, annoy, harass, tease, molest, grieve, mortify, oppress. (*compose, calm, allay, appease, please, soothe, delight, gratify, recreate, entertain, relieve, refresh*)

trouble *n.* affliction, disturbance, annoyance, perplexity, molestation, vexation, inconvenience, calamity, distress, uneasiness, tribulation, disaster, torment, misfortune, adversity, anxiety, embarrassment, sorrow, misery, grief, depression, difficulty, labor, toil, effort. (*alleviation, composure, pleasure, appeasement, delight, assuagement, happiness, gratification, boon, blessing, exultation, joy, gladness, ease, facility, luck, recreation, amusement, carelessness, indifference, indolence, inertia, indiligence*)

troublesome tiresome, irksome, difficult, tedious, arduous, laborious, grievous, importunate, vexatious. (*easy, pleasant, amusing, facile, light, unlaborious, untroublesome*)

true veritable, veracious, exact, precise, accurate, faithful, actual, loyal, genuine, pure, real. (*fictitious, unreliable, unhistorical, untrustworthy, inveracious, false, inaccurate, unfaithful, faithless, fickle, treacherous, erroneous, spurious, perfidious, counterfeit, adulterated*)

trust *v.* confide, rely, credit, believe, charge, deposit, entrust, repose, hope. (*distrust, suspect, discredit, doubt, disbelieve, withdraw, despair*)

trust *n.* faith, confidence, reliance, belief, hope, expectation, credit, duty, commission, charge.

try attempt, endeavor, strive, aim, examine, test, sound, gauge, probe, fathom. (*ignore, pretermit, reject, abandon, discard, misexamine, misinvestigate*)

turn *n.* revolution, rotation, recurrence, change, alteration, vicissitude, winding, bend, deflection, curve, alternation, opportunity, occasion, time, deed, office, act, treatment, purpose, requirement, convenience, talent, gift, tendency, character, exigence, crisis, form, cast, shape, manner, mold, fashion, cut. (*stability, fixity, immobility, stationariness, unchangeableness, uniformity, rectilinearity, indeflection, continuity, untimeliness, incognizance, oversight, independence, nonrequirement, malformation, shapelessness*)

turn *v.* round, shape, mold, adapt, spin, reverse, deflect, alter, transform, convert, metamorphose, revolve, rotate, hinge, depend, deviate, incline, diverge, decline, change. (*misshape, perpetuate, stabilize, stereotype, fix, arrest, continue, proceed*)

turncoat trimmer, deserter, renegade.

tutor guardian, governor, instructor, teacher, preceptor, professor, master, savant. (*ward, pupil, scholar, student, disciple, learner, tyro*)

twine twist, wind, embrace, entwine, wreath, bind, unite, braid, bend, meander. (*untwist, unwind, separate, disunite, detach, unwreath, unravel, disentwine, continue, straighten*)

twist contort, convolve, complicate, pervert, distort, wrest, wreath, wind, encircle, form, weave, insinuate, unite, interpenetrate. (*straighten, untwist, rectify, verify, represent, reflect, render, preserve, express, substantiate, unwreath, unwind, detach, disengage, separate, disunite, disentangle, disincorporate, unravel*)

type mark, stamp, emblem, kind, character, sign, symbol, pattern, archetype, form, model, idea, image, likeness, expression, cast, mold, fashion. (*nondescription, nonclassification, inexpression, misrepresentation, misindication, falsification, abnormity, deviation, caricature, monstrosity*)

ugly loathesome, hideous, hateful, frightful, uncouth, ill-favored, unsightly, in-looking, plain, homely, deformed, monstrous, ungainly. (*attractive, fair, seemly, shapely, beautiful, handsome*)

ultimate last, final, extreme, conclusive, remotest, farthest. (*prior, intermediate, proximate, preliminary*)

unanimous of one mind, agreeing, like-minded. (*discordant, disagreeing*)

unanswerable unquestionable, indisputable, undeniable, incontrovertible.

uncertain doubtful, dubious, questionable, fitful, equivocal, ambiguous, indistinct, variable, fluctuating.

undeniable incontestable, indisputable, unquestionable, incontrovertible.

undergo bear, suffer, endure, sustain, experience. (*evade, shun, elude*)

underhand clandestine, furtive, dishonest, unfair, fraudulent, surreptitious. (*openhanded, straightforward, fair, honest, undisguised*)

understand apprehend, comprehend, know, perceive, discern, conceive, learn, recognize, interpret, imply. (*misapprehend, miscomprehend, ignore, misinterpret, declare, state, enunciate, express*)

understanding knowledge, discernment, interpretation, construction, agreement, intellect, intelligence, mind, sense, conception, reason, brains. (*ignorance, misapprehension, misunderstanding, misinterpretation, misconstruction, mindlessness, irrationality*)

unfit *a.* improper, unsuitable, inconsistent, untimely, incompetent.

unfit *v.* disable, incapacitate, disqualify, render unfit.

unfortunate calamitous, ill-fated, unlucky, wretched, unhappy, miserable. (*fortunate, lucky, fortuitous*)

uniform unvarying, invariable, conformable, homogeneous, consistent, equal, even, alike, unvaried, regular, symmetrical, equable. (*varying, variable, inconformable, incongruous, diverse, heterogeneous, inconsistent, irregular, unsymmetrical, multifarious, multigenous, polymorphic, bizarre, eccentric, erratic*)

union junction, coalition, combination, agreement, harmony, conjunction, concert, league, connection, alliance, confederacy, concord, confederation, consolidation. (*disjunction, separation, severance, divorce, disagreement, discord, disharmony, secession, disruption, multiplication, diversification, division*)

unit ace, item, part, individual. (*total, aggregate, collection, sum, mass*)

unite join, combine, link, attach, amalgamate, associate, coalesce, embody, merge, be mixed, conjoin, connect, couple, add, incorporate with, cohere, concatenate, integrate, converge. (*disjoin, sever, dissociate, separate, disamalgamate, resolve, disconnect, disintegrate, disunite, disrupt, divide, multiply, part, sunder, diverge*)

unity oneness, singleness, individuality, concord, conjunction, agreement, uniformity, indivisibility. (*plurality, multitude, complexity, multiplicity, discord, disjunction, separation, severance, variety, heterogeneity, diversity, incongruity, divisibility*)

universal all-embracing, total, unlimited, boundless, comprehensive, entire, general, whole, exhaustive, complete. (*partial, local, limited, incomplete, exclusive, particular, inexhaustive, exceptional, narrow, special, only*)

unreasonable foolish, silly, absurd, preposterous, immoderate, exorbitant, ridiculous.

upright vertical, erect, perpendicular, honest, honorable, pure, principled, conscientious, just, fair, equitable. (*inverted, inclined, dishonest, dishonorable, corrupt, unprincipled, unconscientious*)

urge press, push, drive, impel, propel, force, importune, solicit, animate, incite, instigate, stimulate, hasten, expedite, accelerate, dispatch. (*repress, hold, retain, inhibit, coerce, restrain, cohibit, hinder, retard, discourage, damp, obstruct*)

urgent pressing, imperative, immediate, importunate, forcible, strenuous, serious, grave, momentous, indeferrable. (*unimportant, insignificant, trifling, trivial, deferrable*)

use *n.* advantage, custom, habit, practice, service, utility, usage.

use *v.* employ, exercise, treat, practice, accustom, habituate, inure. (*discard, suspend, ignore, avoid, dishabituate*)

useful advantageous, profitable, helpful, serviceable, beneficial, available, adapted, suited, conducive. (*disadvantageous, unprofitable, obstructive, retardative, preventative, antagonistic, hostile, cumbersome, burdensome, unbeneficial, unavailable, inconducive, useless, fruitless, ineffectual*)

usual common, customary, ordinary, normal, regular, habitual, wonted, accustomed, general. (*uncommon, rare, exceptional, uncustomary, extraordinary, abnormal, irregular, unusual*)

utter *a.* extreme, perfect, complete, unqualified, absolute, thorough, consummate, entire, sheer, pure. (*imperfect, incomplete, impure*)

utter *v.* circulate, issue, promulgate, express, articulate, pronounce, speak. (*recall, suppress, repress, hush, stifle, check, swallow*)

utterly totally, completely, wholly, quite, altogether, entirely.

vacant empty, leisure, unemployed, unencumbered, unoccupied, void, unfilled, mindless, exhausted. (*full, replenished, business, employed, engaged, occupied, filled, thoughtful*)

vague general, lax, indefinite, undetermined, popular, intangible, equivocal, unsettled, uncertain, ill-defined, pointless. (*strict, definite, determined, limited, scientific, pointed, specific*)

vain empty, worthless, fruitless, unsatisfying, unavailing, idle, ineffectual, egotistic, showy, unreal, conceited, arrogant. (*solid, substantial, sound, worthy, efficient, effectual, cogent, potent, unconceited, modest, real*)

valid strong, powerful, cogent, weighty, sound, substantial, available, efficient, sufficient, operative, conclusive. (*weak, invalid, powerless, unsound, unsubstantial, unavailable, inefficient, insufficient, inoperative, obsolete, effete, superseded, inconclusive*)

value appreciate, compute, rate, estimate, esteem, treasure, appraise, prize. (*miscompute, misestimate, disesteem, disregard, vilipend, underrate*)

vanity emptiness, unsubstantiality, unreality, falsity, conceit, self-sufficiency, ostentation, pride, worthlessness, triviality. (*substance, solidity, substantiality, reality, truth, modesty, self-distrust, simplicity, unostentatiousness, humility*)

variable changeable, mutable, fickle, capricious, wavering, unsteady, inconstant, shifting. (*unchanging, unchangeable, immutable, constant, firm*)

variation deviation, alteration, mutation, diversity, departure, change, abnormity, exception, discrepancy. (*continuance, fixity, indivergency*)

variety difference, diversity, medley, miscellany, multiplicity, multiformity, abnormity. (*uniformity, species, type, specimen*)

various different, diverse, multiform, multitudinous, several, sundry, uncertain, manifold, diversified. (*one, same, identical, uniform, few*)

vast waste, wild, desolate, extensive, spacious, widespread, gigantic, wide, boundless, measureless, enormous, mighty, huge, immense, colossal, prodigious, far-reaching. (*narrow, close, confined, frequented, populated, cultivated, tended, filled, limited*)

vehement violent, impetuous, ardent, burning, fervent, raging, furious, passionate, fervid, urgent, forcible, eager. (*mild, feeble, inanimate, subdued*)

vengeance retribution, retaliation, revenge. (*forgiveness, pardon, condonation, amnesty, grace, remission, absolution, oblivion, indulgence, reprieve*)

venture speculation, risk, chance, hazard, stake, undertaking, luck experiment, throw. (*nonspeculation, caution, reservation, calculation, certainty, law*)

veracity truth, truthfulness, credibility, exactness, accuracy.

verdict finding, judgment, answer, opinion, decision, sentence. (*nondeclaration, indecision, indetermination*)

verge tend, bend, slope, incline, approach, approximate, trend, bear. (*decline, deviate, revert, depart, recede, return, back, retrocede*)

verify establish, confirm, fulfill, authenticate, substantiate, identify, realize, test, warrant, demonstrate. (*disestablish, subvert, fail, falsify, mistake*)

versed skilled, practiced, conversant, acquainted, initiated, indoctrinated, clever, familiar, thoroughly acquainted, proficient. (*unskilled, ill-versed, unpracticed, inconversant, unfamiliar, uninitiated, ignorant, awkward, strange, unversed, untaught*)

vex tease, irritate, provoke, plague, torment, tantalize, bother, worry, pester, trouble, disquiet, afflict, harass, annoy. (*soothe, appease, gratify, quiet*)

vice corruption, fault, defect, evil, crime, immorality, sin, badness. (*purity, faultlessness, perfection, virtue, immaculateness, goodness, soundness*)

vicious corrupt, faulty, defective, bad, morbid, peccant, debased, profligate, unruly, impure, depraved. (*pure, sound, perfect, virtuous, healthy*)

victory conquest, triumph, ovation, success. (*failure, defeat, frustration, disappointment, abortion*)

view *v.* behold, examine, inspect, explore, survey, consider, contemplate, reconnoiter, observe, regard, estimate, judge. (*ignore, overlook, disregard*)

view *n.* sight, vision, survey, examination, inspection, judgment, estimate, scene, representation, apprehension, sentiment, conception, opinion, object, aim, intention, purpose, design, end, light, aspect. (*blindness, occultation, obscuration, darkness*)

vile cheap, worthless, valueless, low, base, mean, despicable, hateful, bad, impure, vicious, abandoned, abject, sinful, sordid, ignoble, wicked, villainous, degraded, wretched. (*costly, rare, precious, valuable, high, exalted, noble, honorable, lofty*)

villain scoundrel, ruffian, wretch.

villainous base, knavish, depraved, infamous.

vindicate assert, maintain, uphold, clear, support, defend, claim, substantiate, justify, establish. (*waive, abandon, surrender, forgo, disprove, disestablish, neutralize, nullify, destroy, subvert, annul*)

violate ravish, injure, abuse, disturb, hurt, rape, outrage, debauch, break, infringe, profane, transgress, disobey. (*respect, foster, observe, regard*)

violence vehemence, impetuosity, force, rape, outrage, rage, profanation, injustice, fury, infringement, fierceness, oppression. (*lenity, mildness, self-restraint, feebleness, gentleness, respect, forbearance*)

virtue power, capacity, strength, force, efficacy, excellence, value, morality, goodness, uprightness, purity, chastity, salubrity. (*weakness, incapacity*)

visible perceptible, apparent, clear, plain, obvious, conspicuous, observable, discernible, palpable, manifest, distinguishable, evident. (*imperceptible*)

visionary fanciful, dreamy, chimerical, baseless, shadowy, imaginary, unreal, fabulous, romantic. (*actual, real, truthful, sound, substantial, palpable*)

vivid bright, brilliant, luminous, resplendent, lustrous, radiant, graphic, clear, lively, animated, stirring, striking, glowing, sunny, bright, scintillant. (*dull, opaque, nonluminous, obscure, rayless, lurid*)

volume size, body, bulk, dimensions, book, work, tome, capacity, magnitude, compass, quantity. (*diminutiveness, tenuity, minuteness, smallness*)

voluntary deliberate, spontaneous, free, intentional, optional, discretional, unconstrained, willing. (*compulsory, coercive, necessitated, involuntary*)

volunteer offer, proffer, tend, originate. (*withhold, refuse, suppress*)

voluptuous sensual, luxurious, self-indulgent, licentious, highly pleasant. (*unsensual, abstinent*)

vulgar popular, general, loose, ordinary, public, vernacular, plebeian, uncultivated, unrefined, low, mean, coarse, underbred. (*strict, scientific, philosophical, restricted, technical, accurate, patrician, select, choice, cultivated, refined, polite, high-bred, stylish, aristocratic*)

wages remuneration, hire, compensation, stipend, salary, allowance. (*gratuity, douceur, premium, bonus, grace*)

wander ramble, range, stroll, rove, expatiate, roam, deviate, stray, depart, err, swerve, straggle, saunter, navigate, circumnavigate, travel. (*rest, stop, perch, bivouac, halt, lie, anchor, alight, settle*)

want deficiency, lack, failure, insufficiency, scantiness, shortness, omission, neglect, nonproduction, absence. (*supply, sufficiency, provision*)

wanton wandering, roving, sportive, playful, frolicsome, loose, unbridled, uncurbed, reckless, unrestrained, irregular, licentious, dissolute, inconsiderate, heedless, gratuitous. (*stationary, unroving, unsportive, unplayful, unfrolicsome, joyless, thoughtful, demure, sedate, discreet, staid, self-controlled*)

warm blood-warm, thermal, genial, irascible, hot, ardent, affectionate, fervid, fiery, glowing, enthusiastic, zealous, eager, excited, interested, animated. (*frigid, cold, tepid, starved, indifferent*)

warmth ardor, glow, fervor, zeal, heat, excitement, intensity, earnestness, cordiality, animation, eagerness, vehemence, geniality, sincerity, passion, irascibility, emotion, life. (*frigidity, frost, congelation, iciness, coldness, calmness, coolness, indifference, torpidity, insensitiveness, apathy, slowness, ungeniality, insincerity, passionlessness, hypocrisy*)

waste ruin, destroy, devastate, impair, consume, squander, dissipate, throw away, diminish, lavish, desolate, pine, decay, attenuate, dwindle, shrivel, wither, wane. (*restore, repair, conserve, preserve, perpetuate, protect, husband, economize, utilize, hoard, treasure, enrich*)

watchful vigilant, expectant, wakeful, heedful, careful, observant, attentive, circumspect, wary, cautious. (*unwatchful, invigilant, unwakeful, slumbrous, drowsy, heedless, careless, inobservant, inattentive, uncircumspect, unwary, incautious, distracted*)

weak feeble, infirm, enfeebled, powerless, debile, fragile, incompact, inadhesive, pliant, frail, soft, tender, milk and water, flabby, flimsy, wishy-washy, destructible, watery, diluted, imbecile, inefficient, spiritless, foolish, injudicious, unsound, undecided, unconfirmed, impressible, wavering, ductile, easy, malleable, unconvincing, inconclusive, vapid, pointless. (*strong, vigorous, robust, muscular, nervous, powerful, sturdy, hard*)

weaken debilitate, enfeeble, enervate, dilute, impair, paralyze, attenuate, sap. (*strengthen, invigorate, empower, corroborate, confirm*)

wealth influence, riches, mammon, lucre, plenty, affluence, abundance, opulence. (*indigence, poverty, scarcity, impecuniosity*)

wear carry, bear, exhibit, sport, consume, don, waste, impair, rub, channel, groove, excavate, hollow, diminish. (*doff, abandon, repair, renovate, renew, increase, swell, augment*)

weary fatigued, tired, exhausted, worn, jaded, debilitated, spent, toilworn, faint. (*fresh, vigorous, recruited, renovated, hearty*)

weave interlace, braid, intertwine, intermix, plait, complicate, intersect. (*unravel, untwist, disunite, disentangle, extricate, simplify, enucleate*)

weight gravity, ponderosity, heaviness, pressure, burden, importance, power, influence, efficacy, consequence, moment, impressiveness. (*lightness, levity, portableness, alleviation, unimportance, insignificance, weakness, inefficacy, unimpressiveness*)

well rightly, thoroughly, properly, hale, sound, healthy, hearty. (*wrongly, imperfectly, improperly*)

white colorless, pure, snowy, umblemished, unspotted, stainless, innocent, clear. (*black, impure*)

whole total, entire, all, well, complete, sound, healthy, perfect, unimpaired, undiminished, integral, undivided, gross. (*partial, imperfect, incomplete, unsound, sick, impaired, diminished, fractional*)

wholesome healthful, salubrious, salutary, salutiferous, beneficial, nutritious, healing. (*unhealthy, unhealthful, insalubrious, insalutary, prejudicial, unwholesome, deleterious, detrimental, morbific*)

wicked evil, bad, godless, sinful, immoral, iniquitous, criminal, unjust, unrighteous, irreligious, profane, ungodly, vicious, atrocious, black, dark, foul, unhallowed, nefarious, naughty, heinous, flagitious, abandoned, corrupt. (*good, virtuous, just, moral, honest, pure*)

wild untamed, undomesticated, uncultivated, uninhabited, desert, savage, uncivilized, unrefined, rude, ferocious, untrained, violent, ferine, loose, disorderly, turbulent, ungoverned, inordinate, disorderly, chimerical, visionary, incoherent, raving, distracted, haggard. (*tame, domesticated, cultivated, coherent, mild, orderly, sane, calm*)

willful purposed, deliberate, designed, intentional, prepense, premeditated, preconcerted, wayward, refractory, stubborn, self-willed, headstrong. (*undesigned, accidental, unintentional, unpremeditated, docile, obedient, amenable, manageable, deferential, considerate, thoughtful*)

wisdom knowledge, erudition, learning, enlightenment, attainment, information, discernment, judgment, sagacity, prudence, light. (*ignorance, illiterateness, sciolism, indiscernment, injudiciousness, folly, imprudence, darkness, empiricism, smattering, inacquaintance*)

wit mind, intellect, sense, reason, understanding, humor, ingenuity, imagination. (*mindlessness, senselessness, irrationality, dullness, stolidity, stupidity, inanity, doltishness, wash, vapidity, platitude*)

withhold retain, keep, inhibit, cohibit, stay, restrain, refuse, stint, forbear, detain. (*grant, afford, furnish, provide, allow, permit, encourage, incite*)

withstand oppose, resist, confront, thwart, face. (*yield, surrender, submit, acquiesce, countenance, support, encourage, aid, abet, back*)

witness attestation, testimony, evidence, corroboration, cognizance, corroborator, eyewitness, spectator, auditor, testifier, voucher, earwitness. (*invalidation, incognizance, refutation, ignorance*)

wonder amazement, astonishment, surprise, admiration, phenomenon, prodigy, portent, miracle, sign, marvel. (*inastonishment, indifference, apathy, unamazement, anticipation, expectation, familiarity, triviality*)

wonderful amazing, astonishing, wondrous, admirable, strange, striking, surprising, awful, prodigious, portentous, marvelous, miraculous, supernatural, unprecedented, startling. (*unamazing, unastonishing, unsurprising, common, everyday, regular, normal, customary, usual, expected, anticipated, calculated, current, natural, unwonderful, unmarvelous*)

word term, expression, message, account, tidings, order, vocable, signal, engagement, promise. (*idea, conception*)

work exertion, effort, toil, labor, employment, performance, production, product, effect, result, composition, achievement, operation, issue, fruit. (*effortlessness, inertia, rest, inoperativeness, unemployment, nonperformance, nonproduction, abortion, miscarriage, frustration, neutralization, fruitlessness*)

worldly terrestrial, mundane, temporal, secular, earthly, carnal. (*heavenly, spiritual*)

worry harass, irritate, tantalize, importune, vex, molest, annoy, tease, torment, disquiet, plague, fret. (*soothe, calm, gratify, please, amuse, quiet*)

worth value, rate, estimate, cost, price, merit, desert, excellent, rate. (*inappreciableness, cheapness, worthlessness, demerit*)

worthless cheap, vile, valueless, useless, base, contemptible, despicable, reprobate, vicious. (*costly, rich, rare, valuable, worthy, useful, honorable, estimable, excellent, noble, precious, admirable, virtuous*)

wrench wrest, twist, distort, strain, extort, wring.

wretched miserable, debased, humiliated, fallen, ruined, pitiable, mean, paltry, worthless, vile, despicable, contemptible, sorrowful, afflicted, melancholy, dejected. (*flourishing, prosperous, happy, unfallen, admirable, noble, honorable, worthy, valuable, enviable, joyous, felicitous, elated*)

wrong unfit, unsuitable, improper, mistaken, incorrect, erroneous, unjust, illegal, inequitable, immoral, injurious, awry. (*fit, suitable, proper, correct, accurate, right, just, legal, equitable, fair, moral. beneficial, straight*)

yearn long, hanker, crave, covet, desire. (*loathe, revolt, recoil, shudder*)

yet besides, nevertheless, notwithstanding, however, still, eventually, ultimately, at last, so far, thus far.

yield furnish, produce, afford, bear, render, relinquish, give in, let go, forgo, accede, acquiesce, resign, surrender, concede, allow, grant, submit, succumb, comply, consent, agree. (*withdraw, withhold, retain, deny, refuse, vindicate, assert, claim, disallow, appropiate, resist, dissent, protest, recalcitrate, struggle, strive*)

yielding conceding, producing, surrendering, supple, pliant, submissive, accommodating, unresisting. (*firm, defiant, stiff, hard, unyielding, resisting, unfruitful*)

yoke couple, conjoin, connect, link, enslave, subjugate. (*dissever, divorce, disconnect, liberate, release, manumit, enfranchise*)

youth youngster, young person, boy, lad, minority, adolescence, juvenility.

youthful juvenile, young, early, fresh, childish, unripe, puerile, callow, immature, beardless. (*aged, senile, mature, decrepit, decayed, venerable, antiquated, superannuated*)

Z

zeal ardor, interest, energy, eagerness, engagedness, heartiness, earnestness, fervor, enthusiasm. (*apathy, indifference, torpor, coldness, carelessness, sluggishness, incordiality*)

zenith height, highest point, pinnacle, acme, summit, culmination, maximum. (*nadir, lowest point, depth, minimum*)

zest flavor, appetizer, gusto, gust, pleasure, enjoyment, relish, sharpener, recommendation, enhancement. (*distaste, disrelish, detriment*)

a HOMONYMS

able strong, skillful. **Abel** a name.
acclamation applause. **acclimation** used to climate.
acts deeds. **ax** or **axe** tool.
ad advertisement. **add** to increase.
adds increases. **adze** or **adz** a tool.
adherence constancy. **adherents** followers.
ail pain, trouble. **ale** a liquor.
air atmosphere. **ere** before. **heir** inheritor.
aisle passage. **isle** island. **I'll** I will.
ale liquor. **ail** pain, trouble.
all everyone. **awl** a tool.
aloud with noise. **allowed** permitted.
altar for worship. **alter** to change.
Ann a name. **an** one.
annalist historian. **analyst** analyzer.
annalize to record. **analyze** to separate.
ant insect. **aunt** relative.
ante before. **anti** opposed to.
arc part of a circle. **ark** chest, boat.
arrant bad. **errant** wandering.
ascent act of rising. **assent** consent.
assistance help, aid. **assistants** helpers.
ate consumed or devoured. **eight** a number.
attendance waiting on. **attendants** those who attend, are in attendance.
aught anything. **ought** should.
augur to predict. **auger** a tool.
aunt relative. **ant** insect.

auricle external ear. **oracle** counsel.
awl a tool. **all** everyone.
axe a tool. **acts** deeds.
axes tools. **axis** turning line.
aye yes. **eye** organ of sight. **I** myself.

b

bacon pork. **baken** baked.
bad wicked. **bade** past tense of the verb TO BID.
bail security. **bale** a bundle.
bait food to allure. **bate** to lessen.
balze cloth. **bays** water, garland, horses.
bald hairless. **bawled** cried aloud.
balks frustrates, refuses to proceed. **box** case, tree.
ball round body, dance. **bawl** to cry aloud.
bare naked. **bear** animal, to carry.
bard poet. **barred** fastened with a bar.
bark cry of dog, rind of tree. **barque** vessel.
baron nobleman. **barren** unfruitful.
baroness baron's wife. **barrenness** sterility.
base mean. **bass** musical term.
bask to lie in warmth. **basque** fitted tunic.
bass musical term. **base** mean.
beach seashore. **beech** a tree.
bear an animal, to carry. **bare** naked.
beat to strike. **beet** vegetable.

beau man of dress. **bow** archery term.
bee insect. **be** to exist.
been past participle of the verb to be. **bin** container.
beer malt liquor. **bier** carriage for the dead.
berry fruit. **bury** to inter.
berth sleeping place. **birth** act of being born.
better superior. **bettor** one who bets.
bier carriage for the dead. **beer** malt liquor.
bight of a rope. **bite** with the teeth.
billed furnished with a bill. **build** to erect.
bin for grain. **been** of the verb TO BE.
birth being born. **berth** sleeping place.
bite to grip with the teeth. **byte** computing unit.
blew did blow. **blue** a color.
boar swine. **bore** to make a hole.
board timber. **bored** pierced, worried.
bold courageous. **bowled** rolled balls.
boll a pod, a ball. **bowl** basin. **bole** trunk of tree.
border outer edge. **boarder** lodger.
bourn a limit, stream. **borne** carried.
borough a town. **burrow** hole for rabbits.
bow in archery. **beau** boyfriend.
bow to salute, part of ship. **bough** branch of tree.
bowl basin. **bole** trunk of tree. **boll** a pod, a ball.
boy male child. **buoy** floating signal.
braid to plait. **brayed** did bray.
brake device for retarding motion. **break** opening, to part.
breach a gap, a break. **breech** part of a gun.

bread food. **bred** brought up.

brewed fermented. **brood** offspring.

brews ferments. **bruise** to crush.

bridal belonging to a wedding. **bridle** a curb.

Briton native of Great Britain. **Britain** another name for the United Kingdom.

broach to utter. **brooch** a jewel.

brows edges. **browse** to feed.

bruit noise, report. **brute** a beast.

build to erect. **billed** furnished with a bill.

buoy floating signal. **boy** male child.

burrow hole for rabbit. **borough** a town.

bury to cover with earth. **berry** a fruit.

but except, yet. **butt** to push with head.

by at, near. **buy** to purchase.

byte computing unit. **bite** to grip with the teeth.

C

cache hole for hiding goods. **cash** money.

Cain man's name. **cane** walking stick.

calendar almanac. **calender** to polish.

calk to stop leaks. **cauk or cawk** mineral.

call to name. **caul** a membrane.

can could, container. **Cannes** French city.

cannon large gun. **canon** a law, a rule.

canvas cloth. **canvass** to solicit, to examine.

capital upper part, principal. **capitol** statehouse.
carat weight. **caret** mark. **carrot** vegetable.
carol song of joy. **Carroll** a name.
carrot vegetable. **carat** weight. **caret** mark.
cash money. **cache** hole for hiding goods.
cask wooden container. **casque** a helmet.
cast to throw, to mold. **caste** rank.
castor a beaver. **caster** frame for bottles, roller.
cause that which produces. **caws** cries of crows.
cede to give up. **seed** germ of plants.
ceiling of a room. **sealing** fastening.
cell small room. **sell** to part for price.
cellar a room under house. **seller** one who sells.
censor critic. **censer** vessel.
cent coin. **sent** caused to go. **scent** odor.
cession yielding. **session** a sitting.
cetaceous whale species. **setaceous** bristly.
chagrin ill-humor. **shagreen** fish skin.
chance accident. **chants** melodies.
champaign open country. **champagne** a wine.
chaste pure. **chased** pursued.
cheap inexpensive. **cheep** a bird's chirp.
chews masticates. **choose** to select.
choir singers. **quire** of paper.
choler anger. **collar** neckwear.
chord musical sound. **cord** string. **cored** taken from center.
chronical a long duration. **chronicle** history.
cite to summon, to quote, to enumerate. **site** situation, sight, view.

clause part of a sentence. **claws** talons.
climb to ascend. **clime** climate.
close shut, near. **clothes** pieces of clothing.
coal fuel. **cole** cabbage.
coaled supplied with coal. **cold** frigid, not hot.
coarse rough. **course** route.
coat garment. **cote** coop.
codling apples. **coddling** parboiling.
coffer money chest. **cougher** one who coughs.
coin money. **quoin** wedge.
collar neckwear. **choler** *anger.*
colonel officer. **kernel** seed in a nut.
color tint. **culler** a chooser.
complacence satisfaction. **complaisance** affability, compliance.
complacent civil. **complaisant** seeking to please.
compliment flattery. **complement** the full number.
confidant one trusted with secrets. **confident** having full belief.
consonance concord. **consonants** letters which are not vowels.
consequence that which follows. **consequents** deduction.
coral from the ocean. **corol** a corolla.
cord string. **chord** musical sound. **cored** taken from center.
cores inner parts. **corps** soldiers.
correspondence interchange of letters. **correspondents** those who correspond.
council assembly. **counsel** advice.
cousin relative. **cozen** to cheat
coward one without courage. **cowered** frightened.
creak harsh noise. **creek** stream.

crewel yarn. **cruel** savage.
crews sailors. **cruise** voyage.
cue hint. **queue** waiting line.
culler a selecter. **color** a tint.
currant fruit. **current** flowing stream.
cygnet a swan. **signet** a seal.
cymbal musical instrument. **symbol** sign.
cypress a tree. **Cyprus** an island.

d

dam wall for stream. **damn** to doom or curse.
dammed confined by banks. **damned** doomed.
Dane a native of Denmark. **deign** condescend.
day time. **dey** a governor.
days plural of day. **daze** to dazzle.
dear beloved, costly. **deer** an animal.
deign to condescend. **Dane** native of Denmark.
demean to criticize. **demesne** land.
dents marks. **dense** close, compact.
dependents subordinates. **dependence** reliance.
depravation corruption. **deprivation** loss.
descent downward. **dissent** disagreement.
descendent falling. **descendant** offspring.
desert to abandon. **dessert** last course of a meal.
dew moisture. **do** to perform. **due** owed.

die to expire, a stamp. **dye** to color.
dire dreadful. **dyer** one who dyes.
discreet prudent. **discrete** separate.
doe female deer. **dough** unbaked bread.
does female deer. **doze** to slumber.
done performed. **dun** a color.
draft bill. **draught** a drink, a potion.
dual two. **duel** combat.
due owed. **dew** moisture. **do** to perform.
dun color, ask for debt. **done** finished.
dye to color. **die** to expire, a stamp.
dyeing staining. **dying** expiring.
dyer one who dyes. **dire** dreadful.

e

earn to gain by labor. **urn** a vase.
eight a number. **ate** consumed or devoured.
ere before. **air** atmosphere. **heir** inheritor.
errant wandering. **arrant** bad.
ewe female sheep. **yew** tree. **you** *pronoun*.
ewes sheep. **yews** trees. **use** employ.
eye organ of sight. **I** myself. **aye** yes.

f

fain pleased. **fane** temple. **feign** pretend.
faint languid. **feint** pretense.
fair beautiful, just. **fare** price, food.
falter to hesitate. **faulter** one who commits a fault.
fane temple. **fain** pleased. **feign** to pretend.
fare price, food. **fair** beautiful, just.
fate destiny. **fete** a festival.
faulter one who commits a fault. **falter** to hesitate.
fawn young deer. **faun** woodland deity.
feat deed. **feet** plural of foot.
feign pretend. **fain** pleased. **fane** temple.
feint pretense. **faint** languid.
feod tenure. **feud** quarrel.
ferrule metallic band. **ferule** wooden pallet.
feted honored. **fated** destined.
fillip jerk of finger. **Philip** man's name.
filter to strain. **philter** love charm.
find to discover. **fined** punished.
fir tree. **fur** animal hair.
fissure a crack. **fisher** fisherman.
fizz hissing noise. **phiz** the face.
flea insect. **flee** to run away.
flew did fly. **flue** chimney. **flu** influenza.
flour ground grain. **flower** a blossom.
flue chimney. **flu** influenza. **flew** did fly.

for because of. **fore** preceding. **four** cardinal number.

fort fortified place. **forte** peculiar talent.

forth forward. **fourth** ordinal number.

foul unclean. **fowl** a bird.

four cardinal number. **for** because of. **fore** preceding.

fourth ordinal number. **forth** forward.

franc French coin. **Frank** a name. **frank** generous.

frays quarrels. **phrase** part of a sentence.

freeze to congeal with cold. **frieze** cloth. **frees** to set at liberty.

fungus spongy excresence. **fungous** as fungus.

fur hairy coat of animals. **fir** a tree.

furs skins of beasts. **furze** a shrub.

g

gage a pledge, a fruit. **gauge** a measure.

gait manner of walking. **gate** a door.

gall bile. **Gaul** a Frenchman.

gamble to wager. **gambol** to skip.

gate a door. **gait** manner of walking.

gauge a measure. **gage** a pledge, a fruit.

Gaul a Frenchman. **gall** bile.

gild to overflow with gold. **guild** a corporation.

gilt gold on surface. **guilt** crime.

glare splendor. **glair** white of an egg.

gneiss rock similar to granite. **nice** fine.

gnu animal. **new** not old. **knew** understood.

gourd a plant. **gored** pierced.
grate iron frame. **great** large.
grater a rough instrument. **greater** larger.
great large. **grate** iron frame.
greater larger. **grater** a rough instrument.
Greece country in Europe. **grease** fat.
grisly frightful. **grizzly** an animal, gray.
groan deep sigh. **grown** increased.
grocer merchant. **grosser** coarser.
grown increased. **groan** deep sigh.
guessed conjectured. **guest** visitor.
guild a corporation. **gild** to overflow with gold.
guilt crime. **gilt** gold on surface.
guise appearance. **guys** ropes.

h

hail ice, to salute. **hale** healthy.
hair of the head. **hare** a rabbit.
hale healthy. **hail** ice, to salute.
hall large room, a passage. **haul** to pull.
hare a rabbit. **hair** of the head.
hart an animal. **heart** seat of life.
haul to pull. **hall** a large room, a passage.
hay dried grass. **hey** an expression.
heal to cure. **heel** part of foot or shoe, the end of a loaf of bread, a scoundrel.

hear to hearken. **here** in this place.

heard did hear. **herd** a drove.

heart seat of life. **hart** an animal.

heel part of foot or shoe, the end of a loaf of bread, a scoundrel. **heal** to cure. **he'll** he will.

heir inheritor. **air** atmosphere. **ere** before.

herd a drove. **heard** did hear.

here in this place. **hear** to hearken.

hew to cut down. **hue** color. **Hugh** man's name.

hey an expression. **hay** dried grass.

hide skin, to conceal. **hied** hastened.

hie to hasten. **high** lofty, tall.

hied hastened. **hide** skin, to conceal.

higher more lofty. **hire** to employ.

him that man. **hymn** sacred song.

hire to employ. **higher** more lofty.

ho cry, stop. **hoe** tool.

hoard to lay up. **horde** tribe.

hoarse rough voice. **horse** animal.

hoe tool. **ho** cry, stop.

hoes tools. **hose** stockings, tubing.

hole cavity. **whole** all, entire.

holm evergreen oak. **home** dwelling.

holy pure sacred. **wholly** completely.

home dwelling. **holm** evergreen oak.

horde tribe. **hoard** to lay up.

horse animal. **hoarse** rough voice.

hose stockings, tubing. **hoes** tools.

hour sixty minutes. **our** belonging to us.
hue color. **hew** to cut down. **Hugh** man's name.
hymn sacred song. **him** that man.

i

idol image. **idle** unemployed. **idyl** poem.
I'll I will. **isle** island. **aisle** passage.
in within. **inn** a tavern.
incidence single happening. **incidents** events.
indict to accuse. **indite** to dictate, write, compose.
indiscreet imprudent. **indiscrete** not separated.
indite to dictate. **indict** to accuse.
inn a tavern. **in** within.
innocence purity. **innocents** harmless things.
instants moments. **instance** example.
intense extreme. **intents** designs.
intention purpose. **intension** energetic use or exercise.
intents designs. **intense** extreme.
invade to infringe. **inveighed** censured.
irruption invasion. **eruption** bursting forth.
Isle island. **I'll** I will. **aisle** passage.

j

jail prison. **gaol** prison.

jam preserves. **jamb** side of door.

k

kernel seed in nut. **colonel** officer.

key for a lock. **quay** wharf.

knag knot in wood. **nag** small horse.

knap protuberance, noise. **nap** short sleep.

knave rogue. **nave** center, hub.

knead work dough. **need** want. **kneed** using a knee to land a blow.

kneel to rest on knee. **neal** to temper.

knew understood. **gnu** animal. **new** not old.

knight title of honor. **night** darkness.

knit unite, weave, frown. **nit** insect's egg.

knot tied. **not** word of refusal.

know understand. **no** not so.

knows understands. **nose** organ of smell.

l

lacks wants, needs. **lax** loose, slack.
lade to load. **laid** placed, produced eggs.
lane a road. **lain** rested.
Latin language. **latten** brass.
lax loose, slack. **lacks** wants, needs.
lea meadow. **lee** shelter place.
leach to filtrate. **leech** a worm.
lead metal. **led** guided.
leaf part of a plant. **lief** willingly.
leak a hole. **leek** a plant.
lean not fat, to rest, to slant. **lien** mortgage.
leased rented. **least** smallest.
led guided. **lead** metal.
lee shelter, place. **lea** meadow.
leech a worm. **leach** to filtrate.
leek a plant. **leak** a hole.
lesson task. **lessen** to diminish.
levee bank, visit. **levy** to collect.
liar falsifier. **lyre** musical instrument.
lie falsehood. **lye** liquid.
lief willingly. **leaf** part of a plant.
lien legal claim. **lean** not fat, to rest, to slant.
lightning electricity. **lightening** unloading.
limb branch. **limn** to draw.
links connecting rings. **lynx** an animal.

lo look, see. **low** not high, mean.
loan to lend. **lone** solitary.
lock hair, fastening. **loch** or **lough** lake.
lone solitary. **loan** to lend.
low not high, mean. **lo** look, see.
lye liquid. **lie** falsehood.
lynx animal. **links** connecting rings.
lyre musical instrument. **liar** falsifier.

m

made created. **maid** unmarried woman.
mail armor, post bag. **male** masculine.
main principal. **mane** hair. **Maine** a state.
maize corn. **maze** intricate.
male masculine. **mail** armor, post bag.
mall hammer, walk. **maul** to beat.
manner method. **manor** landed estate.
mantel chimney piece. **mantle** a cloak.
mark visible line. **marque** a pledge.
marshall officer. **martial** warlike.
marten an animal. **martin** a bird.
martial warlike. **marshall** officer.
maul to beat. **mall** hammer, walk.
mead drink. **meed** reward.
mean low. **mien** aspect.
meat food. **meet** to encounter, a match, suitable.

mead drink. **meed** reward.
meddle interfere. **medal** a token.
meddler one who meddles. **medlar** a tree.
meed reward. **mead** drink.
meet to encounter, a match, suitable. **meat** food.
mettle spirit, courage. **metal** mineral.
mew or **mue** to melt. **mew** fowl enclosure.
mewl to cry. **mule** an animal.
mews cat cries. **muse** deep thought.
mien look, aspect. **mean** low.
might power. **mite** insect.
mince to cut. **mints** coining places.
miner worker in mines. **minor** one underage.
mints coining places. **mince** to cut.
missal religious book. missel bird. missile weapon
mite insect, small. **might** power.
moan lament. **mown** cut down.
moat ditch. **mote** small particle.
mode manner. **mowed** cut down.
morning before noon. **mourning** grief.
mote small particle. **moat** ditch.
mowed cut down. **mode** manner.
mucous slimy. **mucus** a fluid.
mue to molt. **mew** fowl enclosure.
mule an animal. **mewl** to cry.
muscat grape. **musket** gun.
muse deep thought. **mews** cat cries.
mustard plant. **mustered** assembled.

n

nag small horse. **knag** knot in wood.

nap short sleep. **knap** protuberance, noise.

naval nautical. **navel** center of abdomen.

nave center, hub. **knave** rogue.

navel center of abdomen. **naval** nautical.

nay no. **neigh** whinny of a horse.

neal to temper. **kneel** to rest on knee.

need necessity, want. **knead** work dough. **kneed** using a knee to land a blow.

neigh whinny of a horse. **nay** no.

new not old. **gnu** animal. **knew** understood.

nice fine. **kneiss** rock similar to granite.

night darkness. **knight** title of honor.

nit insect's egg. **knit** to unite, to form.

no not so. **know** to understand.

none no one. **nun** female devotee.

nose organ of smell. **knows** understands.

not word of refusal. **knot** a tie.

nun female devotee. **none** no one.

o

oar rowing blade. **o'er** over. **ore** mineral.

ode poem. **owed** under obligation.

o'er over. **oar** paddle. **ore** mineral.
oh denoting pain. **O!** surprise. **owe** indebted.
one single unit. **won** gained.
onerary fit for burdens. **honorary** conferring honor.
oracle counsel. **auricle** external ear.
ordinance a law. **ordnance** military supplies.
ore mineral. **o'er** over. **oar** paddle.
ought should. **aught** anything.
our belonging to us. **hour** sixty minutes.
owe to be indebted. **oh** denoting surprise. **O!** surprise.
owed under obligation. **ode** poem.

p

paced moved slowly. **paste** flour and water mixed.
packed bound in a bundle. **pact** contract.
pail bucket. **pale** whitish.
pain agony. **pane** a square of glass.
pair a couple, two. **pare** to peel. **pear** a fruit.
palace royal home. **Pallas** ancient Greek deity.
palate organ of taste. **pallette** artist's board. **pallet** a bed.
pale whitish. **pail** bucket.
pall covering for the dead. **Paul** man's name.
pare to peel. **pair** a couple, two. **pear** a fruit.
passable tolerable. **passible** with feeling.
paste flour and water mixed. **paced** moved slowly.

patience calmness. **patients** sick persons.

paw foot of an animal. **pa** papa.

paws animals' feet. **pause** stop.

peace quiet. **piece** a part.

peak the top. **pique** grudge. **peek** to peep.

peal loud sound. **peel** to pare.

pealing sounding loudly. **peeling** rinds.

pear a fruit. **pair** a couple, two. **pare** to peel.

pearl a precious substance. **purl** a knitting stitch.

pedal for the feet. **peddle** to sell.

peek to peep. **peak** the top. **pique** grudge.

peer equal. **pier** column, wharf.

pencil writing instrument. **pensile** suspended.

pendant an ornament. **pendent** hanging.

philter love charm. **filter** to strain.

phiz the face. **fizz** hissing noise.

phrase expression. **frays** quarrels.

piece a part. **peace** quiet.

pier a column, wharf. **peer** equal.

pique grudge. **peak** the top. **peek** to peep.

pistil part of a flower. **pistol** firearm.

place situation. **plaice** a fish.

plain clear, simple. **plane** flat surface, tool.

pleas arguments. **please** to delight.

plum a fruit. **plumb** perpendicular, leaden weight.

pole stick. **poll** count.

pore opening. **pour** cause to flow.

poring looking intently. **pouring** raining, flowing.

port harbor. **Porte** Turkish court.

praise commendation. **prays** entreats, petitions. **preys** feeds by violence, plunders.

pray to supplicate. **prey** plunder.

presence being present. **presents** gifts.

pride self-esteem. **pried** moved by a lever.

prier inquirer. **prior** previous.

pries looks into. **prize** reward.

prints impressions. **prince** king's son.

principal chief. **principle** a rule.

prior previous. **prier** inquirer.

prize reward. **pries** looks into.

profit gain. **prophet** a foreteller.

purl a knitting stitch. **pearl** precious substance.

q

quarts measure. **quartz** rock crystal.

quay wharf. **key** lock fastener.

queen king's wife. **quean** worthless woman.

queue pigtail, waiting line. **cue** hint, rod.

r

rabbet a joint. **rabbit** small animal.

radical of first principles. **radicle** a root.
rain water. **reign** rule. **rein** bridle.
raise to lift. **rays** sunbeams. **raze** to demolish.
raised lifted. **razed** demolished.
raiser one who raises. **razor** shaving blade.
rancor spite. **ranker** stronger, more immoderate.
rap to strike. **wrap** to fold.
rapped quick blows. **wrapped** enclosed.
rapping striking. **wrapping** a cover.
rays sunbeams. **raise** to lift. **raze** to demolish.
raze to demolish. **raise** to lift. **rays** sunbeams.
razed demolished. **raised** lifted.
razor shaving blade. **raiser** one who raises.
read to peruse. **reed** a plant.
real true. **reel** winding machine, to stagger.
receipt acknowledgment. **reseat** to sit again.
reck to heed. **wreck** destruction.
red color. **read** perused.
reek to emit vapor. **wreak** to inflict.
reel winding machine, to stagger. **real** true.
reign rule. **rein** bridle. **rain** water.
reseat to seat again. **receipt** acknowledgment.
residence place of abode. **residents** citizens.
rest quiet. **wrest** to twist.
retch to vomit. **wretch** miserable person.
rheum thin, watery matter. **room** space.
Rhodes name of an island. **roads** highways.
rhumb point of a compass. **rum** liquor.

rhyme harmonical sound. **rime** hoar frost.
rigger rope fixer. **rigor** severity.
right correct. **rite** ceremony. **write** to form letters.
rime hoar frost. **rhyme** harmonical sound.
ring circle, sound. **wring** to twist.
road way. **rode** did ride. **rowed** did row.
roads highways. **Rhodes** name of an island.
roan color. **rown** impelled by oars. **Rhone** river.
roe deer. **row** to impel with oars, a line.
roes eggs, deer. **rows** uses oars. **rose** a flower.
role a character in a movie or play. **roll** a list.
Rome city in Italy. **roam** to wander.
rood a measure. **rude** rough.
rote memory of words. **wrote** did write.
rough not smooth. **ruff** plaited collar.
rouse stir up, provoke. **rows** disturbances.
rout rabble, disperse. **route** road.
row to impel with oars, a line. **roe** a deer.
rowed did row. **road** way. **rode** did ride.
rows uses oars. **roes** deer. **rose** a flower.
rude rough. **rood** measure.
ruff collar. **rough** not smooth.
rum liquor. **rhumb** point of a compass.
rung sounded, a step. **wrung** twisted.
rye grain. **wry** crooked.

S

sail canvas of a ship. **sale** reduction in price.
sailer vessel. **sailor** seaman.
sale traffic. **sail** canvas of a ship.
sane sound in mind. **seine** fish net.
saver one who saves. **savor** taste, scent.
scene a view. **seen** viewed.
scent odor. **sent** caused to go. **cent** coin.
scull oar, boat. **skull** bone of the head.
sea ocean. **see** to perceive.
seal stamp, an animal. **seel** to keel over, to close the eyes.
sealing fastening. **ceiling** top of a room.
seam a juncture. **seem** to appear.
seamed joined together. **seemed** appeared.
sear to burn. **seer** prophet.
seas water. **sees** looks. **seize** take hold of.
seed germ of a plant. **cede** to give up.
seen viewed. **scene** a view.
seine a net. **sane** sound in mind.
sell to part for price. **cell** small room.
seller one who sells. **cellar** room.
sense feeling. **scents** odors. **cents** coins.
sent caused to go. **scent** odor. **cent** coin.
serf a slave. **surf** of the sea.
serge a cloth. **surge** a billow.
serrate notched, like a saw. **cerate** salve.

session a sitting. **cession** a yielding.
sew to stitch. **sow** to scatter seed. **so** in this manner.
sewer one who uses a needle. **sower** one who scatters seed.
sewer a drain. **suer** one who entreats.
shear to clip. **sheer** to deviate, pure.
shoe covering for foot. **shoo** begone.
shone did shine. **shown** exhibited.
shoo begone. **shoe** covering for foot.
shoot to let fly, to kill. **chute** a slide.
shown exhibited. **shone** did shine.
side edge, margin. **sighed** did sigh.
sigher one who sighs. **sire** father.
sighs deep breathings. **size** bulk.
sight view. **site** situation. **cite** to summon.
sign token, mark. **sine** geometrical term.
signet a seal. **cygnet** a swan.
single alone. **cingle** a girth.
sit to rest. **cit** a citizen.
skull bone of the head. **scull** oar, boat.
slay to kill. **sleigh** vehicle.
sleeve cover for arm. **sleave** untwisted silk.
slew killed. **slough** bog.
slight neglect, small. **sleight** artful trick.
sloe a berry. **slow** not swift.
soar to rise high. **sore** painful.
soared ascended. **sword** a weapon.
sold did sell. **soled** furnished with soles. **souled** instinct with soul or feeling.

sole part of foot, only. **soul** spirit of man.
some a part. **sum** the whole.
son a male child. **sun** luminous orb.
sow to scatter seed. **sew** to stitch.
sower one who scatters seed. **sewer** one who uses a needle.
staid sober, remained. **stayed** supported.
stair steps. **stare** to gaze.
stake a post, a wager. **steak** meat.
stare to gaze. **stair** steps.
stationary motionless. **stationery** paper, etc.
steel metal. **steal** to thieve.
sticks pieces of wood. **Styx** a legendary river.
stile stairway. **style** manner.
straight not crooked. **strait** narrow pass.
style manner. **stile** stairway.
Styx a legendary river. **sticks** pieces of wood.
subtler more cunning. **sutler** trader.
succor aid. **sucker** a shoot of a plant, a fish.
suer one who entreats. **sewer** a drain.
suite train of followers. **sweet** having a pleasant taste, dear.
sum the whole. **some** a part.
sun luminous orb. **son** a male child.
surcle a twig. **circle** a round figure.
surf dashing waves. **serf** a slave.
surge a billow. **serge** cloth.
sutler trader. **subtler** more cunning.
swap to barter. **swop** a blow.
symbol emblem, representative. **cymbal** musical instrument.

t

tacked changed course of ship. **tact** skill.
tacks small nails. **tax** a tribute.
tale story. **tail** the hinder part.
taper a wax candle. **tapir** an animal.
tare a week, allowance. **tear** to pull to pieces.
taught instructed. **taut** tight.
team two or more horses. **teem** to be full.
tear moisture from eyes. **tier** a rank, a row.
tear to pull to pieces. **tare** weed, allowance.
teas different kinds of tea. **tease** to torment.
tense rigid, form of a verb. **tents** canvas houses.
the adjective. **thee** thyself.
their belonging to them. **there** in that place. **they're** they are.
threw did throw. **through** from end to end.
throne seat of a king. **thrown** hurled.
throw to hurl. **throe** extreme pain.
thrown hurled. **throne** seat of a king.
thyme a plant. **time** duration.
tide stream, current. **tied** fastened.
tier a rank, a row. **tear** moisture from eyes.
timber wood. **timbre** crest, quality.
time duration. **thyme** a plant.
tire part of a wheel, weary. **Tyre** an ancient city. **tier** one who ties.
toad reptile. **toed** having toes. **towed** drawn.
toe part of foot. **tow** hemp, to drag.

told related. **tolled** rang.
ton a weight. **tun** a large cask.
too denoting excess. **to** toward. **two** couple.
tracked followed. **tract** region.
tray shallow vessel. **trey** three of cards.
tun a large cask. **ton** a weight.
two a couple. **to** toward. **too** denoting excess.

u

urn a vase. **earn** to gain by labor.
use to employ. **yews** trees. **ewes** sheep.

v

vain proud, delusive. **vane** weathercock. **vein** blood vessel.
vale valley. **vail** a fee. **veil** to cover.
vane weathercock. **vein** blood vessel. **vain** proud, delusive.
veil a covering for face. **veil** to cover. **vail** a fee.
vein blood vessel. **vane** weathercock. **vain** proud, delusive.
Venus planet. **venous** relating to the veins.
vial a bottle. **viol** violin. **vile** wicked.
vice sin. **vise** a press.

W

wade to walk in water. **weighed** balanced.

wail to moan. **wale** a mark. **whale** a sea animal.

waist part of the body. **waste** destruction.

wait to stay for. **weight** heaviness.

waive to relinquish. **wave** a billow.

wane to decrease. **wain** a wagon.

want desire. **wont** custom, habit.

ware merchandise, see **wear**.

wart hard, excrescence. **wort** beer.

way road, manner. **whey** curdled milk. **weigh** to balance.

weak not strong. **week** seven days.

weal happiness. **wheel** circular body.

wear to impair by use, to have clothes on. **ware** merchandise. **where** location.

weather condition of air. **whether** if.

weigh to balance. **way** road. **whey** of milk.

weighed balanced. **wade** walk in water.

weight heaviness. **wait** to stay for.

wen a tumor. **when** at what time.

what that which. **wot** to know.

wheel circular body. **wheal** a pustule.

whey thin part of milk. **way** road, manner. **weigh** to balance.

which a question word. **witch** a woman who does magic.

Whig name of a political party. **wig** false hair.

whole all, entire. **hole** a cavity.

wholly completely. **holy** sacred, pure.

wig false hair. **Whig** name of a political party.

won gained. **one** single, unit.

wont custom, habit. **want** desire.

wood substance of trees. **would** was willing.

wort beer, herb. **wart** hard excrescence.

wrap to fold. **rap** to strike.

wrapped covered. **rapped** struck with quick blows.

wrapping a cover. **rapping** striking.

wreak to inflict. **reek** to emit vapor.

wrest to twist. **rest** quiet.

wretch miserable person. **retch** to vomit.

wring to twist. **ring** a circle, a sound.

write to form letters. **wright** workman. **right** correct.

wrote did write. **rote** a memory of words.

wrung twisted. **rung** sounded.

wry crooked. **rye** a grain.

yew a tree. **you** person spoken to. **ewe** a sheep.

yews trees. **use** employ. **ewes** sheep.

yolk yellow of egg. **yoke** collar for oxen.

your belonging to you. **you're** you are.

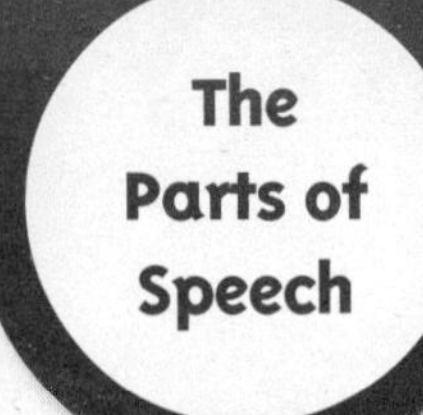

The Parts of Speech

All the words in English can be divided into eight groups called the parts of speech.

Nouns

Persons	Places	Things	Ideas
grandmother	farm	pencil	freedom
Margaret	continent	window	happiness
teacher	city	banana	bravery
kitten	house	telephone	childhood

Uses of Nouns

Subject: who or what performs the action of the verb	*The **dog** bit the man.*
Direct Object: who or what receives the action of the verb	*The dog bit the **man**.*
Indirect Object: shows *to* or *for* whom	*She baked the **girl** a cake and gave the **boy** a cookie.*
Object of a Preposition: comes after a preposition	*They went to a **restaurant** after the **movies**.*
Possession: shows ownership	*The **kid's** sneakers were new.*
Noun of Direct Address: the person spoken to	***David**, please help me fix my computer.*
Predicate Noun: comes after the verb of being, means the same thing as the subject	*My mother is the **mayor** of this town.*
Appositive: follows a noun, gives information about it	*Jen, my **neighbor**, has two cats.*

Verbs

A verb shows action (doing) or being.

Tense: tells time. Verbs have six tenses.

Present	*Karen **writes** a poem.*
Past	*Karen **wrote** a poem.*
Future	*Karen **will write** a poem.*
Present Perfect	*Karen **has written** a poem.*
Past Perfect	*Karen **had written** a poem.*
Future Perfect	*Karen **will have written** a poem.*

The verb **to be** (of being) is ***am, are, is, was, were, be, being, been***

Adjectives

An adjective describes a noun or pronoun and answers these questions:

What kind of?	*It was a **beautiful** day.*
How many? How much?	*I'd like **three** apples and **some** grapes, please.*
Which one? Which ones?	***That** tie is mine; **those** socks are yours.*

Adverbs

An adverb describes a verb, adjective, or other adverb and answers four questions:

How?	*The cat howled **loudly**.*
When?	*The cat howled **today**.*
Where?	*The cat howled **there**.*
To what extent (by how much)?	*The cat howled **extremely** loudly.*

Prepositions

A preposition shows the relationship of one noun to another.

*The mouse is **in** the house.*
*The cow is **near** the plow.*
*The fish is **on** the dish.*
*The bug is **under** the rug.*
*The bee is **between** the tree and the sea.*

Pronouns

A pronoun takes the place of a noun.

Subject pronouns	*I, you, he, she, it, we, they*
Object pronouns	*me, you, him, her, it, us, them*
Possessive pronouns	*my, mine, your, yours, his, her, hers, its, our, ours, their, theirs*

***Mary** told **Christopher** to wash **Christopher's** hands. **She** told **him** to wash **his** hands.*

Conjunctions

A conjunction joins words or parts of sentences together. Some common conjunctions are:

and	either/or	when	nor	however	where
so	but	therefore	or	for	nevertheless
if	after	yet	since	although	unless
while	though	because			

*The boy **and** the girl are related, **but** they don't look alike, **so** they must be in disguise, **or** my glasses are foggy.*

Interjections

An interjection is a word that expresses strong feelings or emotions.

***Wow**, it's great!*
***Eek**, a snake!*
***Hey**, don't do that!*
***Gosh**, that's nice.*
***Yippee**, we won!*
***Hurray**, it's raining!*
***Ouch**, that hurts.*
***Well**, that's all, folks.*
***Whoa**, slow down!*
***Ugh**, how disgusting!*

Four Kinds of Sentences

Declarative: states a **fact**
The baseball game is tomorrow.

Interrogative: asks a **question**
How many feet are in a mile?

Imperative: gives an **order**
Please line up in single file.

Exclamatory: expresses **strong feelings**
The animals have escaped from their cages!

Glossary of Grammar Terms

Articles: *a, an, the*
Clause: a group of words with a subject and a verb
Paragraph: a group of sentences written together about the same thing
Phrase: a group of words
Sentence: a group of words with a subject and a verb that makes complete sense